THE MODERN LIBRARY

OF THE WORLD'S BEST BOOKS

SELECTED PAPERS

OF

BERTRAND RUSSELL

The publishers will be pleased to send, upon request, an illustrated folder setting forth the purpose and scope of THE MODERN LIBRARY, *and listing each volume in the series. Every reader of books will find titles he has been looking for, handsomely printed, in unabridged editions, and at an unusually low price.*

THE MODERN LIBRARY

OF THE WORLD'S BEST BOOKS

SELECTED PAPERS

OF

BERTRAND RUSSELL

SELECTED
PAPERS OF
BERTRAND
RUSSELL

SELECTED AND WITH A
SPECIAL INTRODUCTION BY
BERTRAND RUSSELL

THE MODERN LIBRARY · NEW YORK

CONTENTS

ACKNOWLEDGMENTS

Acknowledgments are due to the publishers of the works of Bertrand Russell for their generous permission to reprint papers in this volume.

For making this volume possible, special thanks are due Boni and Liveright, The Century Co., Harcourt, Brace and Company, Harper and Brothers, Henry Holt and Company, The Macmillan Company, The Open Court Publishing Company, and Longmans Green and Company of London.

INTRODUCTION

To write an Introduction to a selection from one's own works is no easy task. If I might be permitted an Irish bull, I should say that it would be much easier if I were dead. Until then, it is impossible to see oneself as a whole, or to distinguish between a phase and a permanent change. However, I will do what I can to narrate the causes which have made my present style of writing different from that of earlier years.

From the age of eleven, when I began the study of Euclid, I had a passionate interest in mathematics, combined with a belief that science must be the source of all human progress. Youthful ambition made me wish to be a benefactor of mankind, the more so as I lived in an atmosphere in which public spirit was taken for granted. I hoped to pass from mathematics to science, and lived a solitary life amid day-dreams such as may have inspired Galileo or Descartes in adolescence. But it turned out that, while not without aptitude for pure mathematics, I was completely destitute of the concrete kinds of skill which are necessary in science. Moreover, within mathematics it was the most abstract parts which I understood best: I had no difficulty with elliptic functions, but could never succeed in mastering optics. Science was therefore closed to me as a career.

At the same time, I found myself increasingly attracted to philosophy, not, as is often the case, by the hope of ethical or theological comfort, but by the wish to discover whether we possess anything that can be called knowledge. At the age of fifteen, I recorded in my diary that no fact seemed indubitable except consciousness. (Now, I no longer make this exception.) Mathematics, I thought, had a better chance of being true than anything else that passed as general knowledge. But when, at the age of eighteen, I read Mill's *Logic*, I was horrified by his credulity: the arguments which he advanced for believing in arithmetic and geometry were such as to confirm my doubts. I therefore decided that, before doing anything else, I would find out whether any grounds were ascertainable for regarding mathematics as true.

This task turned out to be considerable; it occupied me, with a few intervals, until the year 1910. In that year Dr. Whitehead and I completed the MS. of *Principia Mathematica*, which contained all that I could hope to contribute towards the solution of the problem which had begun to trouble me more than twenty years earlier. The main question remained, of course, unanswered; but incidentally we had been led to the invention of a new method in philosophy and a new branch of mathematics.

After the completion of *Principia Mathematica,* I felt that it was no longer necessary to concentrate so narrowly as hitherto upon one kind of work. I cannot remember an age when I was not interested in politics; I was taught English constitutional history almost before I could read. My first book, published in 1896, was a study of German Social Democracy. From 1907 onwards, I took an active part in the campaign for women's suffrage. In 1902 I wrote: "The Free Man's Worship," and two other essays (one on mathematics and one on history) expressing a similar outlook. But it is probable that I should have remained mainly academic and abstract but for the war. I had watched with growing anxiety the policies of all the European Great Powers in the years before 1914, and was quite unable to accept the superficial melodramatic explanations of the catastrophe which were promulgated by all the belligerent governments. The attitude of ordinary men and women during the first months amazed me, particularly the fact that they found a kind of pleasure in the excitement, as well as their readiness to believe all kinds of myths. It became obvious that I had lived in a fool's paradise. Human nature, even among those who had thought themselves civilized, had dark depths that i had not suspected. Civilization, which I had thought secure, showed itself capable of generating destructive forces which threatened a disaster comparable to the fall of Rome. Everything that I had valued was jeopardized, and only an infinitesimal minority seemed to mind.

While the war lasted, abstract pursuits were impossible to me. As much as any soldier who enlisted, I felt the necessity of "doing my bit," but I could not feel that the victory of either side would solve any problem. During 1915, I wrote *Principles of Social Reconstruction* (or *Why Men Fight,* as it is called in America), in the hope that, as men grew weary of fighting, they would become interested in the problem of building a pacific society. It was obvious that this would require changes in the impulses and unconscious desires of ordinary human beings; but modern psychology shows that such changes can be brought about without great difficulty. It was obvious also that nothing could be achieved by writings addressed exclusively to specialists. Thus throughout the years of the war I was endeavoring, however unsuccessfully, to write so as to be read by the general public. When the war was over, I found it impossible to return to a purely academic life, although the opportunity was open to me. The problems which interest me are no longer those with which I was concerned before 1914, and I find it impossible now to shut the world out of my thoughts when I enter my study. I do not pretend that this is an improvement; I merely record it as a fact.

The effect which the war had upon me was intensified by travels after the war was over. Western Europe and America were familiar to me, but I had never come across any non-occidental culture. In 1920 I spent five weeks in Soviet Russia; I had interviews with many leading Bolsheviks, including an hour's conversation with Lenin; I stayed in Leningrad and Moscow, and traveled down the Volga from Nijni-Novgorod to Astrakhan, visiting all the towns and many of the villages on the way. The Bolshevik philosophy appeared to me profoundly unsatisfactory, not because of its communism, but because of the elements which it shares with the philosophy of Western financial magnates. While the problems raised by the spectacle of Russia were still unsolved in my mind, I went to China, where I spent nearly a year. In that country I found a way of life less energetically destructive than that of the West, and possessing a beauty which the West can only extirpate. There appeared no hope that the traditional merits of non-industrial civilizations could survive; the problem was to combine industrialism with a humane way of life, more especially with art and with individual liberty. No Western nation has yet begun to solve this problem; but one may hope that it will be solved first in those countries which have assimilated industrialism most completely, since it can only be solved by a community which uses machines without being enthusiastic about them.

Everything in which the modern world differs from that of the Renaissance, whether for good or evil, is traceable ultimately to the influence of science. The scientific nations are the strongest in war, in commerce, and in prestige. Nothing that goes against science has any chance of lasting success in the modern world. Consequently certain things which we inherit from the Middle Ages are rapidly disappearing. Religion has already been profoundly modified by its reluctant concessions to science, and will doubtless be modified still further. The hereditary principle is rapidly disappearing in politics and will probably disappear in economics. The ideal of contemplation, which the monks took over from the neo-platonists, and modern men of learning from the monks, is being hustled and bustled out of existence by those who urge that everything should be "dynamic." In Asia, the revolutionary effect of science, and its offspring industrialism, is beginning to be even more pronounced than in Europe; for in Europe science grew spontaneously out of the Renaissance, whereas in Asia there was nothing indigenous to prepare the way for it. Throughout the world, therefore, science and industrialism must be accepted as irresistible, and our hopes for mankind must all be within this framework.

At the same time, when I examine my own conception of human excellence, I find that, doubtless owing to early environment, it contains many elements which have hitherto been associated with aristocracy, such as fearlessness, independence of judgment, emancipation from the herd, and leisurely culture. Is it possible to preserve these qualities, and even make them widespread, in an industrial community? And is it possible to dissociate them from the typical aristocratic vices: limitation of sympathy, haughtiness, and cruelty to those outside a charmed circle? These bad qualities could not exist in a community in which the aristocratic virtues were universal. But that could only be achieved through economic security and leisure, which are the two sources of what is good in aristocracies. It has at last become technically possible, through the progress of machinery and the consequent increased productivity of labor, to create a society in which every man and woman has economic security and sufficient leisure—for complete leisure is neither necessary nor desirable. But although the technical possibility exists, there are formidable political and psychological obstacles. It would be necessary to the creation of such a society to secure three conditions: first, a more even distribution of the produce of labor; second, security against large-scale wars; and third, a population which is stationary or very nearly so. Until these conditions are secured, industrialism will continue to be used feverishly, to increase the wealth of the richest individuals, the territory of the greatest empires, and the population of the most populous nations, no one of which is of the slightest benefit to mankind. These three considerations have inspired what I have written and said on political and social questions since the outbreak of the war, and more particularly since my visits to Russia and China.

At bottom, the obstacles to a better utilization of our new power over nature are all psychological, for the political obstacles have psychological sources. It is evident that, in a world where there was leisure and economic security for all, the happiness of all would be greater than that of ninety-nine per cent of the present inhabitants of the planet. Why, then, do the ninety-nine per cent not combine to overcome the resistance of the privileged one per cent? Partly from inertia; partly because they can be swayed by appeals to hatred, fear, and envy. Instead of combining to produce collective happiness, men compete to produce collective misery. Since this competition among subject populations is useful to the holders of power, they encourage it, under the name of "patriotism," in the schools and the Press. Consequently the worst elements in human nature are artificially strengthened, and everything possible is done to prevent the realization that co-operation, not competition, is the road to happiness.

A radical reform of education is, therefore, an essential preliminary to the creation of a better world. Without this preliminary, a happy world, if it could be created, would speedily make itself miserable, because each nation would find the happiness of other nations intolerable. In schools for the sons of the well-to-do, there is a practical compulsion to acquire military training, while everything possible is done to secure an artificial ignorance on matters of sex. That is to say, everything concerned with the creation of life is thought to be abominable, while everything concerned with taking life is exalted as noble. This is the morality of suicide. It springs from the fact that we attach value to power, rather than to fullness of life: we think a man a fine fellow when he can cause others to be miserable rather than when he can achieve happiness for himself. All that is needed is to give men a just conception of what constitutes their own happiness. Traditional moralists have made a mistake in preaching self-sacrifice, for several reasons. In the first place, very few men will follow such preaching. In the second place, it leads to hypocrisy and self-deception: persuade yourself that you desire A, when in fact you desire B, and you will think you are practicing self-sacrifice in renouncing A. In the third place, the few who do genuinely make sacrifices become self-righteous and envious, and feel that those who will not sacrifice voluntarily deserve to be forced into unhappiness. Morality, therefore, should not be based upon self-sacrifice, but upon correct psychology. There is less pleasure to be derived from keeping a beggar hungry than from filling your own stomach. This may not sound a very exalted maxim, but if it were acted upon war and oppression would cease throughout the world; for war and oppression, as a rule, diminish the happiness of victors and oppressors, not only of the vanquished and oppressed. Generally they do so by actual impoverishment; but in any case they produce the fear of revenge.

But although a rational pursuit of personal happiness, if it were common, would suffice to regenerate the world, it is not probable that so reasonable a motive will alone prove sufficiently powerful. Emotions of expansive affection, generosity, and pleasure in creation also have their part to play. There is no one key: politics, economics, psychology, education all act and react, and no one of them can make any great or stable advance without the help of the others. Narrow specialization, therefore, cannot produce a philosophy which shall be of service to our age. It is necessary to embrace all life and all science—Europe, Asia, and America, physics, biology, and psychology. The task is almost superhuman. All that the present author can hope to do is to make some men conscious of the problem, and of the kind of directions in which solutions are to be sought.

BERTRAND RUSSELL.

LONDON,
    March, 1927.

A FREE MAN'S WORSHIP [1]

To Dr. Faustus in his study Mephistopheles told
the history of the Creation, saying:

"The endless praises of the choirs of angels had
begun to grow wearisome; for, after all, did he not
deserve their praise? Had he not given them endless joy? Would it not be more amusing to obtain
undeserved praise, to be worshiped by beings whom
he tortured? He smiled inwardly, and resolved
that the great drama should be performed.

"For countless ages the hot nebula whirled aim-
lessly through space. At length it began to take
shape, the central mass threw off planets, the planets
cooled, boiling seas and burning mountains heaved
and tossed, from black masses of cloud hot sheets
of rain deluged the barely solid crust. And now
the first germ of life grew in the depths of the ocean,
and developed rapidly in the fructifying warmth
into vast forest trees, huge ferns springing from the
damp mold, sea monsters breeding, fighting, devouring, and passing away. And from the monsters,
as the play unfolded itself, Man was born, with
the power of thought, the knowledge of good and

[1] From *Mysticism and Logic.*

1

evil, and the cruel thirst for worship. And Man
saw that all is passing in this mad, monstrous world,
that all is struggling to snatch, at any cost, a few
brief moments of life before Death's inexorable de-
cree. And Man said: 'There is a hidden purpose,
could we but fathom it, and the purpose is good;
for we must reverence something, and in the visible
world there is nothing worthy of reverence.' And
Man stood aside from the struggle, resolving that
God intended harmony to come out of chaos by
human efforts. And when he followed the instincts
which God had transmitted to him from his ancestry of beasts of prey, he called it Sin, and asked
God to forgive him. But he doubted whether he
could be justly forgiven, until he invented a divine
Plan by which God's wrath was to have been appeased. And seeing the present was bad, he made
it yet worse, that thereby the future might be better.
And he gave God thanks for the strength that enabled him to forgo even the joys that were possible.
And God smiled; and when he saw that Man had
become perfect in renunciation and worship, he
sent another sun through the sky, which crashed into
Man's sun; and all returned again to nebula.

" 'Yes,' he murmured, 'it was a good play; I will
have it performed again.' "

Such, in outline, but even more purposeless, more
void of meaning, is the world which Science presents
for our belief. Amid such a world, if anywhere,

our ideals henceforth must find a home. That Man is the product of causes which had no prevision of the end they were achieving; that his origin, his growth, his hopes and fears, his loves and his beliefs, are but the outcome of accidental collocations of atoms; that no fire, no heroism, no intensity of thought and feeling, can preserve an individual life beyond the grave; that all the labors of the ages, all the devotion, all the inspiration, all the noonday brightness of human genius, are destined to extinction in the vast death of the solar system, and that the whole temple of Man's achievement must inevitably be buried beneath the débris of a universe in ruins—all these things, if not quite beyond dispute, are yet so nearly certain, that no philosophy which rejects them can hope to stand. Only within the scaffolding of these truths, only on the firm foundation of unyielding despair, can the soul's habitation henceforth be safely built.

How, in such an alien and inhuman world, can so powerless a creature as Man preserve his aspirations untarnished? A strange mystery it is that Nature, omnipotent but blind, in the revolutions of her secular hurryings through the abysses of space, has brought forth at last a child, subject still to her power, but gifted with sight, with knowledge of good and evil, with the capacity of judging all the works of his unthinking Mother. In spite of Death, the mark and seal of the parental control, Man is yet free, during his brief years, to examine, to criticize, to know, and in imagination to create. To him alone, in the world with which he is acquainted, this freedom belongs; and in this lies his superiority to the resistless forces that control his outward life.

The savage, like ourselves, feels the oppression of his impotence before the powers of Nature; but having in himself nothing that he respects more than Power, he is willing to prostrate himself before his gods, without inquiring whether they are worthy of his worship. Pathetic and very terrible is the long history of cruelty and torture, of degradation and human sacrifice, endured in the hope of placating the jealous gods: surely, the trembling believer thinks, when what is most precious has been freely given, their lust for blood must be appeased, and more will not be required. The religion of Moloch—as such creeds may be generically called—is in essence the cringing submission of the slave, who dare not, even in his heart, allow the thought that his master deserves no adulation. Since the independence of ideals is not yet acknowledged, Power may be freely worshiped, and receive an unlimited respect, despite its wanton infliction of pain.

But gradually, as morality grows bolder, the claim of the ideal world begins to be felt; and worship, if it is not to cease, must be given to gods of another kind than those created by the savage. Some, though they feel the demands of the ideal, will still consciously reject them, still urging that naked Power is worthy of worship. Such is the attitude inculcated in God's answer to Job out of the whirl-wind: the divine power and knowledge are paraded, but of the divine goodness there is no hint. Such also is the attitude of those who, in our own day, base their morality upon the struggle for survival, maintaining that the survivors are necessarily the fittest. But others, not content with an answer so repugnant to the moral sense, will adopt the posi-tion which we have become accustomed to regard as specially religious, maintaining that, in some hid-den manner the world of fact is really harmonious with the world of ideals. Thus Man creates God, all-powerful and all-good, the mystic unity of what is and what should be.

But the world of fact, after all, is not good; and, in submitting our judgment to it, there is an element of slavishness from which our thoughts must be purged. For in all things it is well to exalt the dignity of Man, by freeing him as far as possible from the tyranny of non-human Power. When we have realized that Power is largely bad, that man, with his knowledge of good and evil, is but a helpless atom in a world which has no such knowledge, the choice is again presented to us: Shall we worship Force, or shall we worship Goodness? Shall our God exist and be evil or shall he be recognized as the creation of our own conscience?

The answer to this question is very momentous, and affects profoundly our whole morality. The worship of Force, to which Carlyle and Nietzsche and the creed of Militarism have accustomed us, is the result of failure to maintain our own ideals against a hostile universe: it is itself a prostrate submission to evil, a sacrifice of our best to Moloch. If strength indeed is to be respected, let us respect rather the strength of those who refuse that false "recognition of facts" which fails to recognize that facts are often bad. Let us admit that, in the world we know, there are many things that would be better otherwise, and that the ideals to which we do and must adhere are not realized in the realm of matter. Let us preserve our respect for truth, for beauty, for the ideal of perfection which life does not permit us to attain, though none of these things meet with the approval of the unconscious universe. If Power is bad, as it seems to be, let us reject it from our hearts. In this lies Man's true freedom: in determination to worship only the God created by our own love of the good, to respect only the heaven which inspires the insight of our best moments. In action, in desire, we must submit perpetually to the tyranny of out-side forces; but in thought, in aspiration, we are free, free from our fellow-men, free from the petty planet on which our bodies impotently crawl, free even, while we live, from the tyranny of death. Let us learn, then, that energy of faith which enables to live constantly in the vision of the good; and let us descend, in action, into the world of fact, with that vision always before us.

When first the opposition of fact and ideal grows fully visible, a spirit of fiery revolt, of fierce hatred of the gods, seems necessary to the assertion of freedom. To defy with Promethean constancy a hostile universe, to keep its evil always in view, always actively hated, to refuse no pain that the malice of Power can invent, appears to be the duty of all who will not bow before the inevitable. But indignation is still a bondage, for it compels our thoughts to be occupied with an evil world; and in the fierceness of desire from which rebellion springs there is a kind of self-assertion which it is necessary for the wise to overcome. Indignation is a submission of our thoughts, but not of our desires; the Stoic freedom in which wisdom consists is found in the submission of our desires, but not of our thoughts. From the submission of our desires springs the virtue of resignation; from the freedom of our thoughts springs the whole world of art and philosophy, and the vision of beauty by which, at last, we half re-conquer the reluctant world. But the vision of beauty is possible only to unfettered contemplation, to thoughts not weighted by the load of eager wishes; and thus Freedom comes only to those who no longer ask of life that it shall yield them any of those personal goods that are subject to the mutations of Time.

Although the necessity of renunciation is evidence of the existence of evil, yet Christianity, in preaching it, has shown a wisdom exceeding that of the Promethean philosophy of rebellion. It must be admitted that, of the things we desire, some, though they prove impossible, are yet real goods; others, however, as ardently longed for, do not form part of a fully purified ideal. The belief that what must be renounced is bad, though sometimes false, is far less often false than untamed passion supposes; and the creed of religion, by providing a reason for proving that it is never false, has been the means of purifying our hopes by the discovery of many austere truths.

But there is in resignation a further good element: even real goods, when they are unattainable, ought not to be fretfully desired. To every man comes, sooner or later, the great renunciation. For the young, there is nothing unattainable; a good thing desired with the whole force of a passionate will, and yet impossible, is to them not credible. Yet, by death, by illness, by poverty, or by the voice of duty, we must learn, each one of us, that the world was not made for us, and that, however beautiful may be the things we crave, Fate may nevertheless forbid them. It is the part of courage, when misfortune comes, to bear without repining the ruin of our hopes, to turn away our thoughts from vain regrets. This degree of submission to Power is not only just and right: it is the very gate of wisdom.

But passive renunciation is not the whole of wisdom; for not by renunciation alone can we build a temple for the worship of our own ideals. Haunting foreshadowings of the temple appear in the realm of imagination, in music, in architecture, in the untroubled kingdom of reason, and in the golden sunset magic of lyrics, where beauty shines and glows, remote from the touch of sorrow, remote from the fear of change, remote from the failures and disenchantments of the world of fact. In the contemplation of these things the vision of heaven will shape itself in our hearts, giving at once a touchstone to judge the world about us, and an inspiration by which to fashion to our needs whatever is not incapable of serving as a stone in the sacred temple.

Except for those rare spirits that are born without sin, there is a cavern of darkness to be traversed before that temple can be entered. The gate of the cavern is despair, and its floor is paved with the gravestones of abandoned hopes. There Self must die; there the eagerness, the greed of untamed desire must be slain, for only so can the soul be freed from the empire of Fate. But out of the cavern the Gate of Renunciation leads again to the daylight of wisdom, by whose radiance a new insight, a new joy, a new tenderness, shine forth to gladden the pilgrim's heart.

When, without the bitterness of impotent rebellion, we have learnt both to resign ourselves to the outward rule of Fate and to recognize that the non-human world is unworthy of our worship, it becomes possible at last so to transform and refashion the unconscious universe, so to transmute it in the crucible of imagination, that a new image of shining gold replaces the old idol of clay. In all the multiform facts of the world—in the visual shapes of trees and mountains and clouds, in the events of the life of man, even in the very omnipotence of Death—the insight of creative idealism can find the reflection of a beauty which its own thoughts first made. In this way mind asserts its subtle mastery over the thoughtless forces of Nature. The more evil the material with which it deals, the more thwarting to untrained desire, the greater is its achievement in inducing the reluctant rock to yield up its hidden treasures, the prouder its victory in compelling the opposing forces to swell the pageant of its triumph. Of all the arts, Tragedy is the proudest, the most triumphant; for it builds its shining citadel in the very center of the enemy's country, on the very summit of his highest mountain; from its impregnable watch-towers, his camps and arsenals, his columns and forts, are all revealed; within its walls the free life continues, while the legions of Death and Pain

and Despair, and all the servile captains of tyrant
Fate, afford the burghers of that dauntless city new
spectacles of beauty. Happy those sacred ramparts,
thrice happy the dwellers on that all-seeing eminence.
Honor to those brave warriors who, through countless ages of warfare, have preserved for us the price-
less heritage of liberty, and have kept undefiled by
sacrilegious invaders the home of the unsubdued.

But the beauty of Tragedy does but make visible
a quality which, in more or less obvious shapes, is
present always and everywhere in life. In the
spectacle of Death, in the endurance of intolerable
pain, and in the irrevocableness of a vanished past,
there is a sacredness, an overpowering awe, a feeling
of the vastness, the depth, the inexhaustible mystery
of existence, in which, as by some strange marriage
of pain, the sufferer is bound to the world by
bonds of sorrow. In these moments of insight, we
lose all eagerness of temporary desire, all struggling
and striving for petty ends, all care for the little
trivial things that, to a superficial view, make up the
common life of day by day; we see, surrounding the
narrow raft illumined by the flickering light of
human comradeship, the dark ocean on whose roll-
ing waves we toss for a brief hour; from the great
night without, a chill blast breaks in upon our
refuge; all the loneliness of humanity amid hostile
forces is concentrated upon the individual soul, which
must struggle alone, with what of courage it can

command, against the whole weight of a universe that cares nothing for its hopes and fears. Victory, in this struggle with the powers of darkness, is the true baptism into the glorious company of heroes, the true initiation into the overmastering beauty of human existence. From that awful encounter of the soul with the outer world, renunciation, wisdom, and charity are born; and with their birth a new life begins. To take into the inmost shrine of the soul the irresistible forces whose puppets we seem to be —Death and change, the irrevocableness of the past, and the powerlessness of man before the blind hurry of the universe from vanity to vanity—to feel these things and know them is to conquer them.

This is the reason why the Past has such magical power. The beauty of its motionless and silent pictures is like the enchanted purity of late autumn, when the leaves, though one breath would make them fall, still glow against the sky in golden glory. The Past does not change or strive; like Duncan, after life's fitful fever it sleeps well; what was eager and grasping, what was petty and transitory, has faded away, the things that were beautiful and eternal shine out of it like stars in the night. Its beauty, to a soul not worthy of it, is unendurable; but to a soul which has conquered Fate it is the key of religion.

The life of Man, viewed outwardly, is but a small thing in comparison with the forces of Nature. The

life; proudly defiant of the irresistible forces that
tolerate, for a moment, his knowledge and his condemnation, to sustain alone, a weary but unyielding
Atlas, the world that his own ideals have fashioned
despite the trampling march of unconscious power.

MYSTICISM AND LOGIC [1]

Metaphysics, or the attempt to conceive the world as a whole by means of thought, has been developed, from the first, by the union and conflict of two very different human impulses, the one urging men towards mysticism, the other urging them towards science. Some men have achieved greatness through one of these impulses alone, others through the other alone: in Hume, for example, the scientific impulse reigns quite unchecked, while in Blake a strong hostility to science coexists with profound mystic insight. But the greatest men who have been philosophers have felt the need both of science and of mysticism: the attempt to harmonize the two was what made their life, and what always must, for all its arduous uncertainty, make philosophy, to some minds, a greater thing than either science or religion.

Before attempting an explicit characterization of the scientific and the mystical impulses, I will illustrate them by examples from two philosophers whose greatness lies in the very intimate blending which they achieved. The two philosophers I mean are Heraclitus and Plato.

Heraclitus, as every one knows, was a believer in

[1] From *Mysticism and Logic.*

universal flux: time builds and destroys all things. From the few fragments that remain, it is not easy to discover how he arrived at his opinions, but there are some sayings that strongly suggest scientific observation as the source.

"The things that can be seen, heard, and learned," he says, "are what I prize the most." This is the language of the empiricist, to whom observation is the sole guarantee of truth. "The sun is new every day," is another fragment; and this opinion, in spite of its paradoxical character, is obviously inspired by scientific reflection, and no doubt seemed to him to obviate the difficulty of understanding how the sun can work its way underground from west to east during the night. Actual observation must also have suggested to him his central doctrine, that Fire is the one permanent substance, of which all visible things are passing phases. In combustion we see things change utterly, while their flame and heat rise up into the air and vanish.

"This world, which is the same for all," he says, "no one of gods or men has made; but it was ever, is now, and ever shall be, an ever-living Fire, with measures kindling, and measures going out."

"The transformations of Fire are, first of all, sea; and half of the sea is earth, half whirlwind."

This theory, though no longer one which science can accept, is nevertheless scientific in spirit. Science, too, might have inspired the famous saying to which

Plato alludes: "You cannot step twice into the same rivers; for fresh waters are ever flowing in upon you." But we find also another statement among the extant fragments: "We step and do not step into the same rivers; we are and are not."

The comparison of this statement, which is mystical, with the one quoted by Plato, which is scientific, shows how intimately the two tendencies are blended in the system of Heraclitus. Mysticism is, in essence, little more than a certain intensity and depth of feeling in regard to what is believed about the universe; and this kind of feeling leads Heraclitus, on the basis of his science, to strangely poignant sayings concerning life and the world, such as:

"Time is a child playing draughts, the kingly power is a child's."

It is poetic imagination, not science, which presents Time as despotic lord of the world, with all the irresponsible frivolity of a child. It is mysticism, too, which leads Heraclitus to assert the identity of opposites: "Good and ill are one," he says; and again: "To God all things are fair and good and right, but men hold some things wrong and some right."

Much of mysticism underlies the ethics of Heraclitus. It is true that a scientific determinism alone might have inspired the statement: "Man's character is his fate"; but only a mystic would have said:

"Every beast is driven to the pasture with blows";
and again:

"It is hard to fight with one's heart's desire. Whatever it wishes to get, it purchases at the cost of
soul"; and again:

"Wisdom is one thing. It is to know the thought
by which all things are steered through all things." [1]

Examples might be multiplied, but those that have
been given are enough to show the character of the
man: the facts of science, as they appeared to him,
fed the flame in his soul, and in its light he saw into
the depths of the world by the reflection of his own
dancing swiftly penetrating fire. In such a nature
we see the true union of the mystic and the man
of science—the highest eminence, as I think, that it
is possible to achieve in the world of thought.

In Plato, the same twofold impulse exists, though
the mystic impulse is distinctly the stronger of the
two, and secures ultimate victory whenever the conflict is sharp. His description of the cave is the
classical statement of belief in a knowledge and
reality truer and more real than that of the senses:

"Imagine [2] a number of men living in an underground cavernous chamber, with an entrance open
to the light, extending along the entire length of the

---

[1] All the above quotations are from Burnet's *Early Greek
Philosophy*. (2nd ed., 1908), pp. 146-156.

[2] *Republic,* 514, translated by Davies and Vaughan.

cavern, in which they have been confined, from their childhood, with their legs and necks so shackled that they are obliged to sit still and look straight forwards, because their chains render it impossible for them to turn their heads round: and imagine a bright fire burning some way off, above and behind them, and an elevated roadway passing between the fire and the prisoners, with a low wall built along it, like the screens which conjurors put up in front of their audience, and above which they exhibit their wonders.

I have it, he replied.

Also figure to yourself a number of persons walking behind this wall, and carrying with them statues of men, and images of other animals, wrought in wood and stone and all kinds of materials, together with various other articles, which overtop the wall; and, as you might expect, let some of the passersby be talking, and others silent.

You are describing a strange scene, and strange prisoners.

They resemble us, I replied.

Now consider what would happen if the course of nature brought them a release from their fetters, and a remedy for their foolishness, in the following manner. Let us suppose that one of them has been released, and compelled suddenly to stand up, and turn his neck round and walk with open eyes towards the light; and let us suppose that he goes through all these actions with pain, and that the dazzling splendor renders him incapable of discerning those objects of which he used formerly to see the shadows. What answer should you expect him to make, if some one were to tell him that in those days he was watching foolish phantoms, but that now he is somewhat nearer to reality, and is turned towards things more real, and sees more correctly; above all, if he were to point out to him the several objects that are passing by, and question him, and compel him to answer what they are? Should you not expect him to be puzzled, and to regard his old visions as truer than the objects now forced upon his notice?

Yes, much truer. . . .

Hence, I suppose, habit will be necessary to enable him to perceive objects in that upper world. At first he will be most successful in distinguishing shadows; then he will discern the reflections of men and other things in water, and afterwards the realities; and after this he will raise his eyes to encounter the light of the moon and stars, finding it less difficult to study the heavenly bodies and the heaven itself by night, than the sun and the sun's light by day.

Doubtless.

Last of all, I imagine, he will be able to observe and contemplate the nature of the sun, not as it *appears* in water or on alien ground, but as it *is* in itself in its own territory.

Of course.

His next step will be to draw the conclusion, that the sun is the author of the seasons and the years, and the guardian of all things in the visible world, and in a manner the cause of all those things which he and his companions used to see.

Obviously, this will be his next step. . . .

Now this imaginary case, my dear Glancon, you must apply in all its parts to our former statements, by comparing the region which the eye reveals, to the prison house, and the light of the fire therein to the power of the sun: and if, by the upward ascent and the contemplation of the upper world, you understand the mounting of the soul into the intellectual region, you will hit the tendency of my own surmises, since you desire to be told what they are; though, indeed, God only knows whether they are correct. But, be that as it may, the view which I take of the subject is to the following effect. In the world of knowledge, the essential Form of Good is the limit of our enquiries, and can barely be perceived; but, when perceived, we cannot help concluding that it is in every case the source of all that is bright and beautiful,—in the visible world giving birth to light and its master, and in the intellectual world dispensing, immediately and with full authority, truth and reason;—and that whosoever would act wisely, either in private or in public, must set this Form of Good before his eyes."

But in this passage, as throughout most of Plato's teaching, there is an identification of the good with the truly real, which became embodied in the philosophical tradition, and is still largely operative in our own day. In thus allowing a legislative function to the good, Plato produced a divorce between philosophy and science, from which, in my opinion, both have suffered ever since and are still suffering. The man of science, whatever his hopes may be, must lay them aside while he studies nature; and the philosopher, if he is to achieve truth must do the same. Ethical considerations can only legitimately appear when the truth has been ascertained: they can and should appear as determining our feeling towards the truth, and our manner of ordering our lives in view of the truth, but not as themselves dictating what the truth is to be.

There are passages in Plato—among those which illustrate the scientific side of his mind—where he seems clearly aware of this. The most noteworthy is the one in which Socrates, as a young man, is explaining the theory of ideas to Parmenides.

After Socrates has explained that there is an idea of the good, but not of such things as hair and mud and dirt, Parmenides advises him "not to despise even the meanest things," and this advice shows the genuine scientific temper. It is with this impartial temper that the mystic's apparent insight into a higher reality and a hidden good has to be combined if philosophy is to realize its greatest possibilities. And it is failure in this respect that has made so much of idealistic philosophy thin, lifeless, and insubstantial. It is only in marriage with the world that our ideals can bear fruit: divorced from it, they remain barren. But marriage with the world is not to be achieved by an ideal which shrinks from fact, or demands in advance that the world shall conform to its desires.

Parmenides himself is the source of a peculiarly interesting strain of mysticism which pervades Plato's thought—the mysticism which may be called "logical" because it is embodied in theories on logic. This form of mysticism, which appears, so far as the West is concerned, to have originated with Parmenides, dominates the reasonings of all the great mystical metaphysicians from his day to that of Hegel and his modern disciples. Reality, he says, is uncreated, indestructible, unchanging, indivisible; it is "immovable in the bonds of mighty chains, without beginning and without end; since coming into being and passing away have been driven afar, and true belief has cast them away." The fundamental principle of his inquiry is stated in a sentence which would not be out of place in Hegel: "Thou canst not know what is not—that is impossible—nor utter it; for it is the same thing that can be thought and that can be." And again: "It needs must be that what can be thought and spoken of is; for it is possible for it to be, and it is not possible for what is nothing to be." The impossibility of change follows from this principle; for what is past can be spoken of, and therefore, by the principle, still is.

Mystical philosophy, in all ages and in all parts of the world, is characterized by certain beliefs which are illustrated by the doctrines we have been considering.

There is, first, the belief in insight as against discursive analytic knowledge: the belief in a way of wisdom, sudden, penetrating, coercive, which is contrasted with the slow and fallible study of outward appearance by a science relying wholly upon the senses. All who are capable of absorption in an inward passion must have experienced at times the strange feeling of unreality in common objects, the loss of contact with daily things, in which the solidity of the outer world is lost, and the soul seems, in utter loneliness, to bring forth, out of its own depths, the mad dance of fantastic phantoms which have hitherto appeared as independently real and living. This is the negative side of the mystic's initiation: the doubt concerning common knowledge, preparing the way for the reception of what seems a higher wisdom. Many men to whom this negative experience is familiar do not pass beyond it, but for the mystic it is merely the gateway to an ampler world.

The mystic insight begins with the sense of a

mystery unveiled, of a hidden wisdom now suddenly become certain beyond the possibility of a doubt. The sense of certainty and revelation comes earlier than any definite belief. The definite beliefs at which mystics arrive are the results of reflection upon the inarticulate experience gained in the moment of insight. Often, beliefs which have no real connection with this moment become subsequently attracted into the central nucleus; thus in addition to the convictions which all mystics share, we find, in many of them, other convictions of a more local and temporary character, which no doubt become amalgamated with what was essentially mystical in virtue of their subjective certainty. We may ignore such inessential accretions, and confine ourselves to the beliefs which all mystics share.

The first and most direct outcome of the moment of illumination is belief in the possibility of a way of knowledge which may be called revelation or insight or intuition, as contrasted with sense, reason, and analysis, which are regarded as blind guides leading to the morass of illusion. Closely connected with this belief is the conception of a Reality behind the world of appearance and utterly different from it. This Reality is regarded with an admiration often amounting to worship; it is felt to be always and everywhere close at hand, thinly veiled by the shows of sense, ready, for the receptive mind, to shine in its glory even through the apparent folly and wickedness of Man. The poet, the artist, and the lover are seekers after that glory: the haunting beauty that they pursue is the faint reflection of its sun. But the mystic lives in the full light of the vision: what others dimly seek he knows, with a knowledge beside which all other knowledge is ignorance.

The second characteristic of mysticism is its belief in unity, and its refusal to admit opposition or division anywhere. We found Heraclitus saying "good and ill are one"; and again he says, "the way up and the way down is one and the same." The same attitude appears in the simultaneous assertion of contradictory propositions, such as: "We step and do not step into the same rivers; we are and are not." The assertion of Parmenides, that reality is one and indivisible, comes from the same impulse towards unity. In Plato, this impulse is less prominent, being held in check by his theory of ideas; but it reappears, so far as his logic permits, in the doctrine of the primacy of the Good.

A third mark of almost all mystical metaphysics is the denial of the reality of Time. This is an out-come of the denial of division; if all is one, the distinction of past and future must be illusory. We have seen this doctrine prominent in Parmenides; and among moderns it is fundamental in the systems of Spinoza and Hegel.

The last of the doctrines of mysticism which we have to consider is its belief that all evil is mere appearance, an illusion produced by the divisions and oppositions of the analytic intellect. Mysticism does not maintain that such things as cruelty, for example, are good, but it denies that they are real: they belong to that lower world of phantoms from which we are to be liberated by the insight of the vision. Sometimes—for example in Hegel, and at least verbally in Spinoza—not only evil, but good also, is regarded as illusory, though nevertheless the emotional attitude towards what is held to be Reality is such as would naturally be associated with the belief that Reality is good. What is, in all cases, ethically characteristic of mysticism is absence of indignation or protest, acceptance with joy, disbelief in the ultimate truth of the division into two hostile camps, the good and the bad. This attitude is a direct outcome of the nature of the mystical experience: with its sense of unity is associated a feeling of infinite peace. Indeed it may be suspected that the feeling of peace produces, as feelings do in dreams, the whole system of associated beliefs which make up the body of mystic doctrine. But this is a difficult question, and one on which it cannot be hoped that mankind will reach agreement.

Four questions thus arise in considering the truth or falsehood of mysticism, namely:

I.   Are there two ways of knowing, which may be called respectively reason and intuition? And if so, is either to be preferred to the other?

II. Is all plurality and division illusory?

III. Is time unreal?

IV. What kind of reality belongs to good and evil?

On all four of these questions, while fully developed mysticism seems to me mistaken, I yet believe that, by sufficient restraint, there is an element of wisdom to be learned from the mystical way of feeling, which does not seem to be attainable in any other manner. If this is the truth, mysticism is to be commended as an attitude towards life, not as a creed about the world. The metaphysical creed, I shall maintain, is a mistaken outcome of the emotion, although this emotion, as coloring and informing all other thoughts and feelings, is the inspirer of whatever is best in Man. Even the cautious and patient investigation of truth by science, which seems the very antithesis of the mystic's swift certainty, may be fostered and nourished by that very spirit of reverence in which mysticism lives and moves.

I. REASON AND INTUITION [1]

Of the reality or unreality of the mystic's world I know nothing. I have no wish to deny it, nor even to declare that the insight which reveals it is not a

[1] This section, and also one or two pages in later sections, have been printed in a course of Lowell lectures *On our knowledge of the external world*, published by the Open Court Publishing Company. But I have left them here, as this is the context for which they were originally written.

genuine insight. What I do wish to maintain—and
it is here that the scientific attitude becomes imperative—is that insight, untested and unsupported,
is an insufficient guarantee of truth, in spite of the
fact that much of the most important truth is first
suggested by its means. It is common to speak of
an opposition between instinct and reason; in the
eighteenth century, the opposition was drawn in favor
of reason, but under the influence of Rousseau and
the romantic movement instinct was given the preference, first by those who rebelled against artificial
forms of government and thought, and then, as the
purely rationalistic defense of traditional theology
became increasingly difficult, by all who felt in
science a menace to creeds which they associated
with a spiritual outlook on life and the world. Bergson, under the name of "intuition," has raised instinct to the position of sole arbiter of metaphysical
truth.   But in fact the opposition of instinct and
reason is mainly illusory.   Instinct, intuition, or insight is what first leads to the belief which subsequent reason confirms or confutes; but the confirmation, where it is possible, consists, in the last
analysis, of agreement with other beliefs no less instinctive.   Reason is a harmonizing, controlling force
rather than a creative one.   Even in the most purely
logical realm, it is insight that first arrives at what
is new.

Where instinct and reason do sometimes conflict

is in regard to single beliefs, held instinctively, and held with such determination that no degree of inconsistency with other beliefs leads to their abandonment. Instinct, like all human faculties, is liable to error. Those in whom reason is weak are often unwilling to admit this as regards themselves, though all admit it in regard to others. Where instinct is least liable to error is in practical matters as to which right judgment is a help to survival: friendship and hostility in others, for instance, are often felt with extraordinary discrimination through very careful disguises. But even in such matters a wrong impression may be given by reserve or flattery; and in matters less directly practical, such as philosophy deals with, very strong instinctive beliefs are sometimes wholly mistaken, as we may come to know through their perceived inconsistency with other equally strong beliefs. It is such considerations that necessitate the harmonizing mediation of reason, which tests our beliefs by their mutual compatibility, and examines, in doubtful cases, the possible sources of error on the one side and on the other. In this there is no opposition to instinct as a whole, but only to blind reliance upon some one interesting aspect of instinct to the exclusion of other more commonplace but not less trustworthy aspects. It is such one-sidedness, not instinct itself, that reason aims at correcting.

These more or less trite maxims may be illustrated

by application to Bergson's advocacy of "intuition" as against "intellect." There are, he says, "two profoundly different ways of knowing a thing. The first implies that we move round the object: the second that we enter into it. The first depends on the point of view at which we are placed and on the symbols by which we express ourselves. The second neither depends on a point of view nor relies on any symbol. The first kind of knowledge may be said to stop at the *relative;* the second, in those cases where it is possible, to attain the *absolute*." [1] The second of these, which is intuition, is, he says, "the kind of *intellectual sympathy* by which one places oneself within an object in order to coincide with what is unique in it and therefore inexpressible" (p. 6). In illustration, he mentions self-knowledge: "there is one reality, at least, which we all seize from within, by intuition and not by simple analysis. It is our own personality in its flowing through time—our self which endures" (p. 8). The rest of Bergson's philosophy consists in reporting, through the imperfect medium of words, the knowledge gained by intuition, and the consequent complete condemnation of all the pretended knowledge derived from science and common sense.

This procedure, since it takes sides in a conflict of instinctive beliefs, stands in need of justification by proving the greater trustworthiness of the beliefs

[1] *Introduction to Metaphysics*, p. i.

on one side than of those on the other. Bergson attempts this justification in two ways, first by explaining that intellect is a purely practical faculty to secure biological success, secondly by mentioning remarkable feats of instinct in animals and by pointing out characteristics of the world which, though intuition can apprehend them, are baffling to intellect as he interprets it.

Of Bergson's theory that intellect is a purely practical faculty, developed in the struggle for survival, and not a source of true beliefs, we may say, first, that it is only through intellect that we know of the struggle for survival and of the biological ancestry of man: if the intellect is misleading, the whole of this merely inferred history is presumably untrue If, on the other hand, we agree with him in thinking that evolution took place as Darwin believed, then it is not only intellect, but all our faculties, that have been developed under the stress of practical utility. Intuition is seen at its best where it is directly useful, for example in regard to other people's characters and dispositions. Bergson apparently holds that capacity for this kind of knowledge is less explicable by the struggle for existence than, for example, capacity for pure mathematics. Yet the savage deceived by false friendship is likely to pay for his mistake with his life; whereas even in the most civilized societies men are not put to death for mathematical incompetence. All the most striking of his instances of intuition in animals have a very direct survival value. The fact is, of course, that both intuition and intellect have been developed because they are useful, and that, speaking broadly, they are useful when they give truth and become harmful when they give falsehood. Intellect, in civilized man, like artistic capacity, has occasionally been developed beyond the point where it is useful to the individual; intuition, on the other hand, seems on the whole to diminish as civilization increases It is greater, as a rule, in children than in adults, in the uneducated than in the educated. Probably in dogs it exceeds anything to be found in human beings. But those who see in these facts a recommendation of intuition ought to return to running wild in the woods, dyeing themselves with woad and living on hips and haws.

Let us next examine whether intuition possesses any such infallibility as Bergson claims for it. The best instance of it, according to him, is our acquaintance with ourselves; yet self-knowledge is proverbially rare and difficult. Most men, for example, have in their nature meannesses, vanities, and envies of which they are quite unconscious, though even their best friends can perceive them without any difficulty. It is true that intuition has a convincingness which is lacking to intellect: while it is present, it is almost impossible to doubt its truth. But if it should appear, on examination, to be at least as fallible as intellect, its greater subjective certainty becomes a demerit, making it only the more irresistibly deceptive. Apart from self-knowledge, one of the most notable examples of intuition is the knowledge people believe themselves to possess of those with whom they are in love: the wall between different personalities seems to become transparent, and people think they see into another soul as into their own. Yet deception in such cases is constantly practiced with success; and even where there is no intentional deception, experience gradually proves, as a rule, that the supposed insight was illusory, and that the slower, more groping methods of the intellect are in the long run more reliable.

Bergson maintains that intellect can only deal with things in so far as they resemble what has been experienced in the past, while intuition has the power of apprehending the uniqueness and novelty that always belong to each fresh moment. That there is something unique and new at every moment, is certainly true; it is also true that this cannot be fully expressed by means of intellectual concepts. Only direct acquaintance can give knowledge of what is unique and new. But direct acquaintance of this kind is given fully in sensation, and does not require, so far as I can see, any special faculty of intuition for its apprehension. It is neither intellect nor intuition, but sensation, that supplies new data; but when the data are new in any remarkable manner, intellect is much more capable of dealing with them than intuition would be. The hen with a brooding of ducklings no doubt has intuition which seems to place her inside them, and not merely to know them analytically; but when the ducklings take to the water, the whole apparent intuition is seen to be illusory, and the hen is left helpless on the shore. Intuition, in fact, is an aspect and development of instinct, and, like all instinct, is admirable in those customary surroundings which have molded the habits of the animal in question, but totally incompetent as soon as the surroundings are changed in a way which demands some non-habitual mode of action.

The theoretical understanding of the world, which is the aim of philosophy, is not a matter of great practical importance to animals, or to savages, or even to most civilized men. It is hardly to be supposed, therefore, that the rapid, rough and ready methods of instinct or intuition will find in this field a favorable ground for their application. It is the older kinds of activity, which bring out our kinship with remote generations of animal and semi-human ancestors, that show intuition at its best. In such matters as self-preservation and love, intuition will act sometimes (though not always) with a swiftness and precision which are astonishing to the critical intellect. But philosophy is not one of the pursuits which illustrate our affinity with the past: it is a highly refined, highly civilized pursuit, demanding, for its success, a certain liberation from the life of instinct, and even, at times. a certain aloofness from all mundane hopes and fears.   It is not in philosophy, therefore, that we can hope to see intuition at its best.   On the contrary, since the true objects of philosophy, and the habit of thought demanded for their apprehension, are strange, unusual, and remote, it is here, more almost than anywhere else, that intellect proves superior to intuition, and that quick unanalyzed convictions are least deserving of uncritical acceptance.

In advocating the scientific restraint and balance, as against the self-assertion of a confident reliance upon intuition, we are only urging, in the sphere of knowledge, that largeness of contemplation, that impersonal disinterestedness, and that freedom from practical preoccupations which have been inculcated by all the great religions of the world.   Thus our conclusion, however it may conflict with the explicit beliefs of many mystics, is, in essence, not contrary to the spirit which inspires those beliefs, but rather the outcome of this very spirit as applied in the realm of thought.

II. UNITY AND PLURALITY

One of the most convincing aspects of the mystic illumination is the apparent revelation of the oneness of all things, giving rise to pantheism in religion and to monism in philosophy. An elaborate logic, beginning with Parmenides, and culminating in Hegel and his followers, has been gradually developed, to prove that the universe is one indivisible Whole, and that what seem to be its parts, if considered as substantial and self-existing, are mere illusion. The conception of a Reality quite other than the world of appearance, a reality one, indivisible, and unchanging, was introduced into Western philosophy by Parmenides, not, nominally at least, for mystical or religious reasons, but on the basis of a logical argument as to the impossibility of not-being, and most subsequent metaphysical systems are the outcome of this fundamental idea.

The logic used in defense of mysticism seems to be faulty as logic, and open to technical criticisms, which I have explained elsewhere. I shall not here repeat these criticisms, since they are lengthy and difficult, but shall instead attempt an analysis of the state of mind from which mystical logic has arisen.

Belief in a reality quite different from what appears to the senses arises with irresistible force in certain moods, which are the source of most mysticism, and of most metaphysics. While such a mood is dominant, the need of logic is not felt, and accordingly the more thorough-going mystics do not employ logic, but appeal directly to the immediate deliverance of their insight. But such fully developed mysticism is rare in the West. When the intensity of emotional conviction subsides, a man who is in the habit of reasoning will search for logical grounds in favor of the belief which he finds in himself. But since the belief already exists, he will be very hospitable to any ground that suggests itself. The paradoxes apparently proved by his logic are really the paradoxes of mysticism, and are the goal which he feels his logic must reach if it is to be in accordance with insight. The resulting logic has rendered most philosophers incapable of giving any account of the world of science and daily life. If they had been anxious to give such an account, they would probably have discovered the errors of their logic; but most of them were less anxious to understand the world of science and daily life than to convict it of unreality in the interests of a supersensible "real" world.

It is in this way that logic has been pursued by those of the great philosophers who were mystics. But since they usually took for granted the supposed insight of the mystic emotion, their logical doctrines were presented with a certain dryness, and were believed by their disciples to be quite independent of the sudden illumination from which they sprang. Nevertheless their origin clung to them, and they remained—to borrow a useful word from Mr. Santayana—"malicious" in regard to the world of science and common sense. It is only so that

we can account for the complacency with which
philosophers have accepted the inconsistency of their
doctrines with all the common and scientific facts
which seem best established and most worthy of
belief.

The logic of mysticism shows, as is natural, the
defects which are inherent in anything malicious.
The impulse to logic, not felt while the mystic mood
is dominant, reasserts itself as the mood fades, but
with a desire to retain the vanishing insight, or at
least to prove that it *was* insight, and that what
seems to contradict it is illusion. The logic which
thus arises is not quite disinterested or candid, and
is inspired by a certain hatred of the daily world
to which it is to be applied. Such an attitude
naturally does not tend to the best results. Every
one knows that to read an author simply in order
to refute him is not the way to understand him; and
to read the book of Nature with a conviction that
it is all illusion is just as unlikely to lead to understanding. If our logic is to find the common world
intelligible, it must not be hostile, but must be inspired by a genuine acceptance such as is not usually
to be found among metaphysicians.

III. TIME

The unreality of time is a cardinal doctrine of
many metaphysical systems, often nominally based,
as already by Parmenides, upon logical arguments.

but originally derived, at any rate in the founders of new systems, from the certainty which is born in the moment of mystic insight. As a Persian Sufi poet says:

> *Past and future are what veil God from our sight.*
> *Burn up both of them with fire! How long*
> *Wilt thou be partitioned by these segments as a reed?*

The belief that what is ultimately real must be immutable is a very common one: it gave rise to the metaphysical notion of substance, and finds, even now, a wholly illegitimate satisfaction in such scientific doctrines as the conservation of energy and mass.

It is difficult to disentangle the truth and the error in this view. The arguments for the contention that time is unreal and that the world of sense is illusory must, I think, be regarded as fallacious. Nevertheless there is some sense—easier to feel than to state —in which time is an unimportant and superficial characteristic of reality. Past and future must be acknowledged to be as real as the present, and a certain emancipation from slavery to time is essential to philosophic thought. The importance of time is rather practical than theoretical, rather in

[1] Whinfield's translation of the *Masnavi* (Trübner, 1887), p. 34.

relation to our desires than in relation to truth. A truer image of the world, I think, is obtained by picturing things as entering into the stream of time from an eternal world outside, than from a view which regards time as the devouring tyrant of all that is. Both in thought and in feeling, even though time be real, to realize the unimportance of time is the gate of wisdom.

That this is the case may be seen at once by asking ourselves why our feelings towards the past are so different from our feelings towards the future. The reason for this difference is wholly practical: our wishes can affect the future but not the past, the future is to some extent subject to our power, while the past is unalterably fixed. But every future will some day be past: if we see the past truly now, it must, when it was still future, have been just what we now see it to be, and what is now future must be just what we shall see it to be when it has become past. The felt difference of quality between past and future, therefore, is not an intrinsic difference, but only a difference in relation to us: to impartial contemplation, it ceases to exist. And impartiality of contemplation is, in the intellectual sphere, that very same virtue of disinterestedness which, in the sphere of action, appears as justice and unselfishness. Whoever wishes to see the world truly, to rise in thought above the tyranny of practical desires, must learn to overcome the difference of attitude towards past and future, and to survey the whole stream of time in one comprehensive vision.

The kind of way in which, as it seems to me, time ought not to enter into our theoretic philosophical thought, may be illustrated by the philosophy which has become associated with the idea of evolution, and which is exemplified by Nietzsche, pragmatism, and Bergson. This philosophy, on the basis of the development which has led from the lowest forms of life up to man, sees in *progress* the fundamental law of the universe, and thus admits the difference between *earlier* and *later* into the very citadel of its contemplative outlook. With its past and future history of the world, conjectural as it is, I do not wish to quarrel. But I think that, in the intoxication of a quick success, much that is required for a true understanding of the universe has been forgotten. Something of Hellenism, something, too, of Oriental resignation, must be combined with its hurrying Western self-assertion before it can emerge from the ardor of youth into the mature wisdom of manhood. In spite of its appeals to science, the true scientific philosophy, I think, is something more arduous and more aloof, appealing to less mundane hopes, and requiring a severer discipline for its successful practice.

Darwin's *Origin of Species* persuaded the world that the difference between different species of animals and plants is not the fixed immutable difference that it appears to be. The doctrine of natural kinds, which had rendered classification easy and definite, which was enshrined in the Aristotelian tradition, and protected by its supposed necessity for orthodox dogma, was suddenly swept away forever out of the biological world. The difference between man and the lower animals, which to our human conceit appears enormous, was shown to be a gradual achievement, involving intermediate beings who could not with certainty be placed either within or without the human family. The sun and the planets had already been shown by Laplace to be very probably derived from a primitive more or less undifferentiated nebula. Thus the old fixed landmarks became wavering and indistinct, and all sharp outlines were blurred. Things and species lost their boundaries, and none could say where they began or where they ended.

But if human conceit was staggered for a moment by its kinship with the ape, it soon found a way to reassert itself, and that way is the "philosophy" of evolution. A process which led from the amœba to Man appeared to the philosophers to be obviously a progress—though whether the amœba would agree with this opinion is not known. Hence the cycle of changes which science had shown to be the probable history of the past was welcomed as revealing a law of development towards good in the universe—an evolution or unfolding of an idea slowly embodying itself in the actual.   But such a view, though it might satisfy Spencer and those whom we may call Hegelian evolutionists, could not be accepted as adequate by the more whole-hearted votaries of change.   An ideal to which the world continuously approaches is, to these minds, too dead and static to be inspiring. Not only the aspiration, but the ideal too, must change and develop with the course of evolution: there must be no fixed goal, but a continual fashioning of fresh needs by the impulse which is life and which alone gives unity to the process.

Life, in this philosophy, is a continuous stream, in which all divisions are artificial and unreal.   Separate things, beginnings and endings, are mere convenient fictions: there is only smooth unbroken transition.   The beliefs of to-day may count as true to-day, if they carry us along the stream; but to-morrow they will be false, and must be replaced by new beliefs to meet the new situation.   All our thinking consists of convenient fictions, imaginary congealings of the stream: reality flows on in spite of all our fictions, and though it can be lived, it cannot be conceived in thought.   Somehow, without explicit statement, the assurance is slipped in that the future, though we cannot foresee it, will be better than the past or the present: the reader is like the child which expects a sweet because it has been told to open its mouth and shut its eyes.   Logic, mathematics, physics disappear in this philosophy, because they are too "static"; what is real is no impulse and movement towards a goal which, like the rainbow, recedes as we advance, and makes every place different when it reaches it from what it appeared to be at a distance.

I do not propose to enter upon a technical examination of this philosophy. I wish only to maintain that the motives and interests which inspire it are so exclusively practical, and the problems with which it deals are so special, that it can hardly be regarded as touching any of the questions that, to my mind, constitute genuine philosophy.

The predominant interest of evolutionism is in the question of human destiny, or at least of the destiny of Life. It is more interested in morality and happiness than in knowledge for its own sake. It must be admitted that the same may be said of many other philosophies, and that a desire for the kind of knowledge which philosophy can give is very rare. But if philosophy is to attain truth, it is necessary first and foremost that philosophers should acquire the disinterested intellectual curiosity which characterizes the genuine man of science. Knowledge concerning the future—which is the kind of knowledge that must be sought if we are to know about human destiny—is possible within certain narrow limits. It is impossible to say how much the limits may be enlarged with the progress of science. But what is evident is that any proposition about the future belongs by its subject-matter to some particular science, and is to be ascertained, if at all, by the methods of that science. Philosophy is not a short cut to the same kind of results as those of the other sciences: if it is to be a genuine study, it must have a province of its own, and aim at results which the other sciences can neither prove nor disprove.

Evolutionism, in basing itself upon the notion of *progress*, which is change from the worse to the better, allows the notion of time, as it seems to me, to become its tyrant rather than its servant, and thereby loses that impartiality of contemplation which is the source of all that is best in philosophic thought and feeling. Metaphysicians, as we saw, have frequently denied altogether the reality of time. I do not wish to do this; I wish only to preserve the mental outlook which inspired the denial, the attitude which, in thought, regards the past as having the same reality as the present and the same importance as the future. "In so far," says Spinoza,[1] "as the mind conceives a thing according to the dictate of reason, it will be equally affected whether the idea is that of a future, past or present thing." It is this "conceiving according to the dictate of reason" that I find lacking in the philosophy which is based on evolution.

[1] *Ethics*, Bk. IV, Prop. LXII.

IV. GOOD AND EVIL

Mysticism maintains that all evil is illusory, and sometimes maintains the same view as regards good, but more often holds that all Reality is good. Both views are to be found in Heraclitus: "Good and ill are one," he says, but again, "To God all things are fair and good and right, but men hold some things wrong and some right." A similar twofold position is to be found in Spinoza, but he uses the word "perfection" when he means to speak of the good that is not merely human. "By reality and perfection I mean the same thing," he says;[1] but elsewhere we find the definition: "By *good* I shall mean that which we certainly know to be useful to us."[2] Thus perfection belongs to Reality in its own nature, but goodness is relative to ourselves and our needs, and disappears in an impartial survey. Some such distinction, I think, is necessary in order to understand the ethical outlook of mysticism: there is a lower mundane kind of good and evil, which divides the world of appearance into what seem to be conflicting parts; but there is also a higher, mystical kind of good, which belongs to Reality and is not opposed by any correlative kind of evil.

It is difficult to give a logically tenable account of this position without recognizing that good and evil are subjective, that what is good is merely that towards which we have one kind of feeling, and

[1] *Ethics*, Pt. II, Df. VI.   [2] Ib., Pt. IV, Df. I.

what is evil is merely that towards which we have another kind of feeling. In our active life, where we have to exercise choice, and to prefer this to that of two possible acts, it is necessary to have a distinction of good and evil, or at least of better and worse. But this distinction, like everything pertaining to action, belongs to what mysticism regards as the world of illusion, if only because it is essentially concerned with time. In our contemplative life, where action is not called for, it is possible to be impartial, and to overcome the ethical dualism which action requires. So long as we remain *merely* impartial, we may be content to say that both the good and the evil of action are illusions. But if, as we must do if we have the mystic vision, we find the whole world worthy of love and worship, if we see

> *The earth, and every common sight . . .*
> *Apparell'd in celestial light,*

we shall say that there is a higher good than that of action, and that this higher good belongs to the whole world as it is in reality. In this way the two-fold attitude and the apparent vacillation of mysticism are explained and justified.

The possibility of this universal love and joy in all that exists is of supreme importance for the conduct and happiness of life, and gives inestimable value to the mystic emotion, apart from any creeds which may be built upon it. But if we are not to be led into false beliefs, it is necessary to realize exactly *what* the mystic emotion reveals. It reveals a possibility of human nature—a possibility of a nobler, happier, freer life than any that can be otherwise achieved. But it does not reveal anything about the non-human, or about the nature of the universe in general. Good and bad, and even the higher good that mysticism finds everywhere, are the reflections of our own emotions on other things, not part of the substance of things as they are in themselves. And therefore an impartial contemplation, freed from all preoccupation with Self, will not judge things good or bad, although it is very easily combined with that feeling of universal love which leads the mystic to say that the whole world is good.

The philosophy of evolution, through the notion of progress, is bound up with the ethical dualism of the worse and the better, and is thus shut out, not only from the kind of survey which discards good and evil altogether from its view, but also from the mystical belief in the goodness of everything. In this way the distinction of good and evil, like time, becomes a tyrant in this philosophy, and introduces into thought the restless selectiveness of action. Good and evil, like time, are, it would seem, not general or fundamental in the world of thought, but late and highly specialized members of the intellectual hierarchy.

Although, as we saw, mysticism can be interpreted so as to agree with the view that good and evil are not intellectually fundamental, it must be admitted that here we are no longer in verbal agreement with most of the great philosophers and religious teachers of the past. I believe, however, that the elimination of ethical considerations from philosophy is both scientifically necessary and—though this may seem a paradox—an ethical advance. Both these contentions must be briefly defended.

The hope of satisfaction to our more human desires—the hope of demonstrating that the world has this or that desirable ethical characteristic—is not one which, so far as I can see, a scientific philosophy can do anything whatever to satisfy. The difference between a good world and a bad one is a difference in the particular characteristics of the particular things that exist in these words: it is not a sufficiently abstract difference to come within the province of philosophy. Love and hate, for example, are ethical opposites, but to philosophy they are closely analogous attitudes towards objects. The general form and structure of those attitudes towards objects which constitute mental phenomena is a problem for philosophy, but the difference between love and hate is not a difference of form or structure, and therefore belongs rather to the special science of psychology than to philosophy. Thus the ethical interests which have often inspired philosophers must remain in the background: some kind of ethical interest may inspire the whole study, but none must obtrude in the detail or be expected in the special results which are sought.

If this view seems at first sight disappointing, we may remind ourselves that a similiar change has been found necessary in all the other sciences. The physicist or chemist is not now required to prove the ethical importance of his ions or atoms; the biologist is not expected to prove the utility of the plants or animals which he dissects. In pre-scientific ages this was not the case. Astronomy, for example, was studied because men believed in astrology: it was thought that the movements of the planets had the most direct and important bearing upon the lives of human beings. Presumably, when this belief decayed and the disinterested study of astronomy began, many who had found astrology absorbingly interesting decided that astronomy had too little human interest to be worthy of study. Physics, as it appears in Plato's *Timæus* for example, is full of ethical notions: it is an essential part of its purpose to show that the earth is worthy of admiration. The modern physicist, on the contrary, though he has no wish to deny that the earth is admirable, is not concerned, as physicist, with its ethical attributes: he is merely concerned to find out facts, not to consider whether they are good or bad. In psychology, the scientific attitude is even more recent and more difficult than in the physical sciences: it is natural to consider that human nature is either good or bad, and to suppose that the difference between good and bad, so all-important in practice, must be important in theory also. It is only during the last century that an ethically neutral psychology has grown up; and here too, ethical neutrality has been essential to scientific success.

In philosophy, hitherto, ethical neutrality has been seldom sought and hardly ever achieved. Men have remembered their wishes, and have judged philosophies in relation to their wishes. Driven from the particular sciences, the belief that the notions of good and evil must afford a key to the understanding of the world has sought a refuge in philosophy. But even from this last refuge, if philosophy is not to remain a set of pleasing dreams, this belief must be driven forth. It is a commonplace that happiness is not best achieved by those who seek it directly; and it would seem that the same is true of the good. In thought, at any rate, those who forget good and evil and seek only to know the facts are more likely to achieve good than those who view the world through the distorting medium of their own desires.

We are thus brought back to our seeming paradox, that a philosophy which does not seek to impose upon the world its own conceptions of good and evil is not only more likely to achieve truth, but is also the outcome of a higher ethical standpoint than one which, like evolutionism and most traditional systems, is perpetually appraising the universe and seeking to find in it an embodiment of present ideals. In religion, and in every deeply serious view of the world and of human destiny, there is an element of submission, a realization of the limits of human power, which is somewhat lacking in the modern world, with its quick material successes and its insolent belief in the boundless possibilities of progress. "He that loveth his life shall lose it"; and there is danger lest, through a too confident love of life, life itself should lose much of what gives it its highest worth. The submission which religion inculcates in action is essentially the same in spirit as that which science teaches in thought; and the ethical neutrality by which its victories have been achieved is the outcome of that submission.

The good which it concerns us to remember is the good which it lies in our power to create—the good in our own lives and in our attitude towards the world. Insistence on belief in an external realization of the good is a form of self-assertion, which while it cannot secure the external good which it desires, can seriously impair the inward good which lies within our power, and destroy that reverence towards fact which constitutes both what is valuable in humility and what is fruitful in the scientific temper.

Human beings cannot, of course, wholly transcend human nature; something subjective, if only the interest that determines the direction of our attention, must remain in all our thought. But scientific philosophy comes nearer to objectivity than any other human pursuit, and gives us, therefore, the closest constant and the most intimate relation with the outer world that it is possible to achieve. To the primitive mind, everything is either friendly or hostile; but experience has shown that friendliness and hostility are not the conceptions by which the world is to be understood. Scientific philosophy thus represents, though as yet only in a nascent condition, a higher form of thought than any pre-scientific belief or imagination, and, like every approach to self-transcendence, it brings with it a rich reward in increase of scope and breadth and comprehension. Evolutionism, in spite of its appeals to particular scientific facts, fails to be a truly scientific philosophy because of its slavery to time, its ethical preoccupations, and its predominant interest in our mundane concerns and destiny. A truly scientific philosophy will be more humble, more piecemeal, more arduous, offering less glitter of outward mirage to flatter fallacious hopes, but more indifferent to fate, and more capable of accepting the world without the tyrannous imposition of our human and temporary demands.

THE STATE [1]

Under the influence of socialism, most liberal thought in recent years had been in favor of increasing the power of the State, but more or less hostile to the power of private property. On the other hand, syndicalism has been hostile both to the State and to private property. I believe that syndicalism is more nearly right than socialism in this respect, that both private property and the State, which are the two most powerful institutions of the modern world, have become harmful to life through excess of power, and that both are hastening the loss of vitality from which the civilized world increasingly suffers. The two institutions are closely connected, but for the present I wish to consider only the State. I shall try to show how great, how unnecessary, how harmful, many of its powers are, and how enormously they might be diminished without loss of what is useful in its activity. But I shall admit that in certain directions its functions ought to be extended rather than curtailed.

Some of the functions of the State, such as the Post Office and elementary education, might be per-

[1] From *Why Men Fight*.

formed by private agencies, and are only undertaken by the State from motives of convenience. But other matters, such as the law, the police, the Army, and the Navy, belong more essentially to the State: so long as there is a State at all it is difficult to imagine these matters in private hands. The distinction between socialism and individualism turns on the non-essential functions of the State, which the socialist wishes to extend and the individualist to restrict. It is the essential functions, which are admitted by individualists and socialists alike, that I wish to criticize, since the others do not appear to me in themselves objectionable.

The essence of the State is that it is the repository of the collective force of its citizens. This force takes two forms, one internal and one external. The internal form is the law and the police; the external form is the power of waging war, as embodied in the Army and Navy. The State is constituted by the combination of all the inhabitants in a certain area using their united force in accordance with the commands of a Government. In a civilized State force is only employed against its own citizens in accordance with rules previously laid down, which constitute the criminal law. But the employment of force against foreigners is not regulated by any code of rules, and proceeds, with few exceptions, according to some real or fancied national interest. There can be no doubt that force employed according to law is less pernicious than force employed capriciously. If international law could acquire sufficient hold on men's allegiance to regulate the relations of States, a very great advance on our present condition would have been made. The primitive anarchy which precedes law is worse than law. But I believe there is a possibility of a stage to some extent above law, where the advantages now secured by the law are secured without loss of freedom, and without the disadvantages which the law and the police render inevitable. Probably some repository of force in the background will remain necessary, but the actual employment of force may become very rare, and the degree of force required very small. The anarchy which precedes law gives freedom only to the strong; the condition to be aimed at will give freedom as nearly as possible to every one. It will do this, not by preventing altogether the existence of organized force, but by limiting the occasions for its employment to the greatest possible extent.

The power of the State is only limited internally by the fear of rebellion and externally by the fear of defeat in war. Subject to these restrictions, it is absolute. In practice, it can seize men's property through taxation, determine the law of marriage and inheritance, punish the expression of opinions which it dislikes, put men to death for wishing the region they inhabit to belong to a different State, and order

all able-bodied males to risk their lives in battle
whenever it considers war desirable. On many matters disagreement with the purposes and opinions of
the State is criminal. Probably the freest States in
the world, before the war, were America and England; yet in America no immigrant may land until
he has professed disbelief in anarchism and polygamy, while in England men were sent to prison in
recent years for expressing disagreement with the
Christian religion[1] or agreement with the teaching
of Christ.[2] In time of war, all criticism of the external policy of the State is criminal. Certain objects having appeared desirable to the majority or to
the effective holders of power, those who do not
consider these objects desirable are exposed to pains
and penalties not unlike those suffered by heretics in
the past. The extent of the tyranny thus exercised
is concealed by its very success: few men consider
it worth while to incur a persecution which is almost certain to be thorough and effective.

Universal military service is perhaps the extreme
example of the power of the State, and the supreme
illustration of the difference between its attitude to
its own citizens and its attitude to the citizens of
other States. The State punishes, with impartial
rigor, both those who kill their compatriots and

[1] The Blasphemy prosecutions.
[2] The Syndicalist prosecutions. [The punishment of conscien-
tious objectors must now be added, 1916.]

those who refuse to kill foreigners. On the whole, the latter is considered the graver crime. The phenomenon of war is familiar, and men fail to realize its strangeness; to those who stand inside the cycle of instincts which lead to war it all seems natural and reasonable. But to those who stand outside the strangeness of it grows with familiarity. It is amazing that the vast majority of men should tolerate a system which compels them to submit to all the horrors of the battlefield at any moment when their Government commands them to do so. A French artist, indifferent to politics, attentive only to his painting, suddenly finds himself called upon to shoot Germans, who, his friends assure him, are a disgrace to the human race. A German musician, equally unknowing, is called upon to shoot the perfidious Frenchman. Why cannot the two men declare a mutual neutrality? Why not leave war to those who like it and bring it on? Yet if the two men declared a mutual neutrality they would be shot by their compatriots. To avoid this fate they try to shoot each other. If the world loses the artist, not the musician, Germany rejoices; if the world loses the musician, not the artist, France rejoices. No one remembers the loss to civilization, which is equal whichever is killed.

This is the politics of Bedlam. If the artist and the musician had been allowed to stand aside from the war, nothing but unmitigated good to mankind would have resulted. The power of the State, which makes this impossible, is a wholly evil thing, quite as evil as the power of the Church which in former days put men to death for unorthodox thought. Yet if, even in time of peace, an international league were founded to consist of Frenchmen and Germans in equal numbers, all pledged not to take part in war, the French State and the German State would persecute it with equal ferocity. Blind obedience, unlimited willingness to kill and die are exacted of the modern citizens of a democracy as much of the Janizaries of medieval sultans or the secret agents of Oriental despots.[1]

The power of the State may be brought to bear, as it often is in England, through public opinion rather than through the laws. By oratory and the influence of the Press, public opinion is largely created by the State, and a tyrannous public opinion is as great an enemy to liberty as tyrannous laws. If the young man who will not fight finds that he is dismissed from his employment, insulted in the streets, cold-shouldered by his friends, and thrown over with scorn by any woman who may formerly have liked him, he will feel the penalty quite as hard to bear as a death sentence.[2] A free community re-

[1] In a democratic country it is the majority who must after all rule, and the minority will be obliged to submit with the best grace possible (*Westminster Gazette* on Conscription, December 29, 1925).

[2] Some very strong remarks on the conduct of the "white

quires not only legal freedom, but a tolerant public opinion, an absence of that instinctive inquisition into our neighbors' affairs which, under the guise of upholding a high moral standard, enables good people to indulge unconsciously a disposition to cruelty and persecution. Thinking ill of others is not in itself a good reason for thinking well of ourselves. But so long as this is not recognized, and so long as the State can manufacture public opinion, except in the rare cases where it is revolutionary, public opinion must be reckoned as a definite part of the power of the State.

feather" women were made by Mr. Reginald Kemp, the Deputy Coroner for West Middlesex, at an inquest at Ealing on Saturday on Richard Charles Roberts, aged thirty-four, a taxicab driver, of Shepherd's Bush, who committed suicide in consequence of worry caused by his rejection from the Army and the taunts of women and other amateur recruiters.

It was stated that he tried to join the Army in October, but was rejected on account of a weak heart. That alone, said his widow, had depressed him, and he had been worried because he thought he would lose his license owing to the state of his heart. He had also been troubled by the dangerous illness of a child.

A soldier relative said that the deceased's life had been made "a perfect misery" by women who taunted him and called him a coward because he did not join the Army. A few days ago two women in Maida Vale insulted him "something shocking."

The Coroner, speaking with some warmth, said the conduct of such women was abominable. It was scandalous that women who knew nothing of individual circumstances should be allowed to go about making unbearable the lives of men who had tried to do their duty. It was a pity they had nothing better to do. Here was a man who perhaps had been driven to death by a pack of silly women. He hoped something would soon be done to put a stop to such conduct (*Daily News,* July 26, 1915).

The power of the State outside its own borders is in the main derived from war or the threat of war. Some power is derived from the ability to persuade its citizens to lend money or not to lend it, but this is unimportant in comparison with the power derived from armies and navies. The external activity of the State—with exceptions so rare as to be negligible —is selfish. Sometimes selfishness is mitigated by the need of retaining the goodwill of other States, but this only modifies the methods employed, not the ends pursued. The ends pursued, apart from mere defense against other States, are, on the one hand, opportunities for successful exploitation of weak or uncivilized countries, on the other hand, power and prestige, which are considered more glorious and less material than money. In pursuit of these objects, no State hesitates to put to death innumerable foreigners whose happiness is not compatible with exploitation or subjection, or to devastate territories into which it is thought necessary to strike terror. Apart from the present war, such acts have been performed within the last twenty years by many minor States and by all the Great Powers[1] except Austria; and in the case of Austria only the opportunity, not the will, was lacking.

Why do men acquiesce in the power of the State?

[1] By England in South Africa, America in the Philippines, France in Morocco, Italy in Tripoli, Germany in Southwest Africa, Russia in Persia and Manchuria, Japan in Manchuria.

There are many reasons, some traditional, some very present and pressing.

The traditional reason for obedience to the State is personal loyalty to the sovereign. European States grew up under the feudal system, and were originally the several territories owned by feudal chiefs. But this source of obedience has decayed, and probably now counts for little except in Japan, and to a lesser extent in Russia.

Tribal feeling, which always underlay loyalty to the sovereign, has remained as strong as it ever was, and is now the chief support for the power of the State. Almost every man finds it essential to his happiness to feel himself a member of a group, animated by common friendships and enmities and banded together for defense and attack. But such groups are of two kinds: there are those which are essentially enlargements of the family, and there are those which are based upon a conscious common purpose. Nations belong to the first kind, Churches to the second. At times when men are profoundly swayed by creeds national divisions tend to break down, as they did in the wars of religion after the Reformation. At such times a common creed is a stronger bond than a common nationality. To a much slighter extent, the same thing has occurred in the modern world with the rise of socialism. Men who disbelieve in private property, and feel the capitalist the real enemy, have a bond which transcends national divisions. It has not been found strong enough to resist the passions aroused by the present war, but it has made them less bitter among socialists than among others, and has kept alive the hope of a European community to be reconstructed when the war is over. In the main, however, the universal disbelief in creeds has left tribal feeling triumphant, and has made nationalism stronger than at any previous period of the world's history. A few sincere Christians, a few sincere socialists, have found in their creed a force capable of resisting the assaults of national passion, but they have been too few to influence the course of events or even to cause serious anxiety to the Governments.

It is chiefly tribal feeling that generates the unity of a national State, but it is not only tribal feeling that generates its strength. Its strength results principally from two fears, neither of which is unreasonable: the fear of crime and anarchy within, and the fear of aggression from without.

The internal orderliness of a civilized community is a great achievement, chiefly brought about by the increased authority of the State. It would be inconvenient if peaceable citizens were constantly in imminent risk of being robbed and murdered. Civilized life would become almost impossible if adventurous people could organize private armies for purposes of plunder. These conditions existed in the Middle Ages, and have not passed away without a great struggle. It is thought by many—especially by the rich, who derive the greatest advantage from law and order—that any diminution in the power of the State might bring back a condition of universal anarchy. They regard strikes as portents of dissolution. They are terrified by such organizations as the *Confédération Générale du Travail* and the International Workers of the World. They remember the French Revolution, and feel a not unnatural desire to keep their heads on their shoulders. They dread particularly any political theory which seems to excuse private crimes, such as sabotage and political assassination. Against these dangers they see no protection except the maintenance of the authority of the State, and the belief that all resistance to the State is wicked.

Fear of the danger within is enhanced by fear of the danger without. Every State is exposed at all times to the risk of foreign invasion. No means has hitherto been devised for minimizing this risk except the increase of armaments. But the armaments which are nominally intended to repel invasion may also be used to invade. And so the means adopted to diminish the external fear have the effect of increasing it, and of enormously enhancing the destructiveness of war when it does break out. In this way a reign of terror becomes universal, and the

State acquires everywhere something of the character of the *Comité du Salut Public*.

The tribal feeling out of which the State develops is natural, and the fear by which the State is strengthened is reasonable under present circumstances. And in addition to these two, there is a third source of strength in a national State, namely, patriotism in its religious aspect.

Patriotism is a very complex feeling, built up out of primitive instincts and highly intellectual convictions. There is love of home and family and friends, making us peculiarly anxious to preserve our own country from invasion. There is the mild instinctive liking for compatriots as against foreigners. There is pride, which is bound up with the success of the community to which we feel that we belong. There is a belief, suggested by pride but reinforced by history, that one's own nation represents a great tradition and stands for ideals that are important to the human race. But besides all these, there is another element, at once nobler and more open to attack, an element of worship, of willing sacrifice, of joyful merging of the individual life in the life of the nation. This religious element in patriotism is essential to the strength of the State, since it enlists the best that is in most men on the side of national sacrifice.

The religious element in patriotism is reinforced by education, especially by a knowledge of the history and literature of one's own country, provided it is not accompanied by much knowledge of the history and literature of other countries. In every civilized country all instruction of the young emphasizes the merits of their own nation and the faults of other nations. It comes to be universally believed that one's own nation, because of its superiority, deserves support in a quarrel, however the quarrel may have originated. This belief is so genuine and deep that it makes men endure patiently, almost gladly, the losses and hardships and sufferings entailed by war. Like all sincerely believed religions, it gives an outlook on life, based upon instinct but sublimating it, causing a devotion to an end greater than any personal end, but containing many personal ends as it were in solution.

Patriotism as a religion is unsatisfactory because of its lack of universality. The good at which it aims is a good for one's own nation only, not for all mankind. The desires which it inspires in an Englishman are not the same as the desires which it inspires in a German. A world full of patriots may be a world full of strife. The more intensely a nation believes in its patriotism, the more fanatically indifferent it will become to the damage suffered by other nations. When once men have learnt to subordinate their own good to the good of a larger whole, there can be no valid reason for stopping short of the human race. It is the admixture of national pride that makes it so easy in practice for men's impulses towards sacrifice to stop short at the frontiers of their own country. It is this admixture that poisons patriotism, and makes it inferior, as a religion, to beliefs which aim at the salvation of all mankind. We cannot avoid having more love for our own country than for other countries, and there is no reason why we should wish to avoid it, any more than we should wish to love all individual men and women equally. But any adequate religion will lead us to temper inequality of affection by love of justice, and to universalize our aims by realizing the common needs of man. This change was effected by Christianity in Judaism, and must be effected in any merely national religion before it can be purged of evil.

In practice, patriotism has many other enemies to contend with. Cosmopolitanism cannot fail to grow as men acquire more knowledge of foreign countries by education and travel. There is also a kind of individualism which is continually increasing, a realization that every man ought to be as nearly free as possible to choose his own ends, not compelled by a geographical accident to pursue ends forced upon him by the community. Socialism, syndicalism, and anti-capitalist movements generally are against patriotism in their tendency, since they make men aware that the present State is largely concerned in defending the privileges of the rich, and that many of the conflicts between States have their origin in the financial interests of a few plutocrats. This kind of opposition is perhaps temporary, a mere incident in the struggle of labor to acquire power. Australia, where labor feels its triumph secure, is full of patriotism and militarism, based upon determination to prevent foreign labor from sharing the benefits of a privileged position. It is not unlikely that England might develop a similar nationalism if it became a socialist State. But it is probable that such nationalism would be purely defensive. Schemes of foreign aggression, entailing great loss of life and wealth in the nation which adopts them, would hardly be initiated except by those whose instincts of dominion have been sharpened through the power derived from private property and the institutions of the capitalist State.

The evil wrought in the modern world by the excessive power of the State is very great, and very little recognized.

The chief harm wrought by the State is promotion of efficiency in war. If all States increase their strength, the balance of power is unchanged, and no one State has a better chance of victory than before. And when the means of offense exist, even though their original purpose may have been defensive, the temptation to use them is likely, sooner or later, to prove overwhelming. In this way the very measures which promoted security within the borders of the

State promote insecurity elsewhere. It is of the essence of the State to suppress violence within and to facilitate it without. The State makes an entirely artificial division of mankind and of our duties toward them: towards one group we are bound by the law, towards the other only by the prudence of highwaymen. The State is rendered evil by its exclusions, and by the fact that, whenever it embarks upon aggressive war, it becomes a combination of men for murder and robbery. The present system is irrational, since external and internal anarchy must be both right or both wrong. It is supported because, so long as others adopt it, it is thought the only road to safety, and because it secures the pleasures of triumph and dominion, which cannot be obtained in a good community. If these pleasures were no longer sought, or no longer possible to obtain, the problem of securing safety from invasion would not be difficult.

Apart from war, the modern great State is harmful from its vastness and the resulting sense of individual helplessness. The citizen who is out of sympathy with the aims of the State, unless he is a man of very rare gifts, cannot hope to persuade the State to adopt purposes which seem to him better. Even in a democracy, all questions except a very few are decided by a small number of officials and eminent men; and even the few questions which are left to the popular vote are decided by a diffused mass-psychology, not by individual initiative. This is especially noticeable in a country like the United States, where, in spite of democracy, most men have a sense of almost complete impotence in regard to all large issues. In so vast a country the popular will is like one of the forces of Nature, and seems nearly as much outside the control of any one man. This state of things leads, not only in America but in all large States, to something of the weariness and discouragement that we associate with the Roman Empire. Modern States, as opposed to the small city States of ancient Greece or medieval Italy, leave little room for initiative, and fail to develop in most men any sense of ability to control their political destinies. The few men who achieve power in such States are men of abnormal ambition and thirst for dominion, combined with skill in cajolery and subtlety in negotiation. All the rest are dwarfed by knowledge of their own impotence.

A curious survival from the old monarchical idea of the State is the belief that there is some peculiar wickedness in a wish to secede on the part of any section of the population. If Ireland or Poland desires independence, it is thought obvious that this desire must be strenuously resisted, and any attempt to secure it is condemned as "high treason." The only instance to the contrary that I can remember is the separation of Norway and Sweden, which was commended but not imitated. In other cases, nothing but defeat in war has induced States to part with territory: although this attitude is taken for granted, it is not one which would be adopted if the State had better ends in view. The reason for its adoption is that the chief end of almost all great States is power, especially power in war. And power in war is often increased by the inclusion of unwilling citizens. If the well-being of the citizens were the end in view, the question whether a certain area should be included, or should form a separate State, would be left freely to the decision of that area. If this principle were adopted, one of the main reasons for war would be obviated, and one of the most tyrannical elements in the State would be removed.

The principal source of the harm done by the State is the fact that power is its chief end. This is not the case in America, because America is safe against aggression; [1] but in all other great nations the chief aim of the State is to possess the greatest possible amount of external force. To this end, the liberty of the citizens is curtailed, and anti-militarist propaganda is severely punished. This attitude is rooted in pride and fear: pride, which refuses to be conciliatory, and fear, which dreads the results of foreign pride conflicting with our own pride. It seems something of a historical accident that these two passions, which by no means exhaust the polit-

[1] This was written in 1915.

ical passions of the ordinary man, should so completely determine the external policy of the State. Without pride, there would be no occasion for fear: fear on the part of one nation is due to the supposed pride of another nation. Pride of dominion, unwillingness to decide disputes otherwise than by force or the threat of force, is a habit of mind greatly encouraged by the possession of power. Those who have long been in the habit of exercising power become autocratic and quarrelsome, incapable of regarding an equal otherwise than as a rival. It is notorious that head masters' conferences are more liable to violent disagreements than most similar bodies: each head master tries to treat the others as he treats his own boys; they resent such treatment, and he resents their resentment. Men who have the habit of authority are peculiarly unfit for friendly negotiation; but the official relations of States are mainly in the hands of men with a great deal of authority in their own country. This is, of course, more particularly the case where there is a monarch who actually governs. It is less true where there is a governing oligarchy, and still less true where there is some approach to real democracy. But it is true to a considerable extent in all countries, because Prime Ministers and Foreign Secretaries are necessarily men in authority. The first step towards remedying this state of things is a genuine interest in foreign affairs on the part of the ordinary citizen, and an insistence that national pride shall not be allowed to jeopardize his other interests. During war, when he is roused, he is willing to sacrifice everything to pride; but in quiet times he will be far more ready than men in authority to realize that foreign affairs, like private concerns, ought to be settled amicably according to principles, not brutally by force or the threat of force.

The effect of personal bias in the men who actually compose the Government may be seen very clearly in labor disputes. French syndicalists affirm that the State is simply a product of capitalism, a part of the weapons which capital employs in its conflict with labor. Even in democratic States there is much to bear out this view. In strikes it is common to order out the soldiers to coerce the strikers; although the employers are much fewer, and much easier to coerce, the soldiers are never employed against them. When labor troubles paralyze the industry of a country, it is the men who are thought to be unpatriotic, not the masters, though clearly the responsibility belongs to both sides. The chief reason for this attitude on the part of Governments is that the men composing them belong, by their success if not by their origin, to the same class as the great employers of labor. Their bias and their associates combine to make them view strikes and lockouts from the standpoint of the rich. In a democracy public opinion and the need of conciliating political supporters partially correct these plutocratic influences, but the correction is always only partial. And the same influences which warp the views of Governments on labor questions also warp their views on foreign affairs, with the added disadvantage that the ordinary citizen has much fewer means of arriving at an independent judgment.

The excessive power of the State, partly through internal oppression, but principally through war and the fear of war, is one of the chief causes of misery in the modern world, and one of the main reasons for the discouragement which prevents men from growing to their full mental stature. Some means of curing this excessive power must be found if men are not to be organized into despair, as they were in the Roman Empire.

The State has one purpose which is on the whole good, namely, the substitution of law for force in the relations of men. But this purpose can only be fully achieved by a world-State, without which international relations cannot be made subject to law. And although law is better than force, law is still not the best way of settling disputes. Law is too static, too much on the side of what is decaying, too little on the side of what is growing. So long as law is in theory supreme, it will have to be tempered, from time to time, by internal revolution and ex-

ternal war. These can only be prevented by per-
petual readiness to alter the law in accordance with
the present balance of forces. If this is not done,
the motives for appealing to force will sooner or
later become irresistible. A world-State or feder-
ation of States, if it is to be successful, will have
to decide questions, not by the legal maxims which
would be applied by the Hague tribunal, but as far
as possible in the same sense in which they would
be decided by war. The function of authority should
be to render the appeal to force unnecessary, not
to give decisions contrary to those which would be
reached by force.

This view may be thought by some to be immoral.
It may be said that the object of civilization should
be to secure justice, not to give the victory to the
strong. But when this antithesis is allowed to pass,
it is forgotten that love of justice may itself set
force in motion. A Legislature which wishes to decide an issue in the same way as it would be decided
if there were an appeal to force will necessarily take
account of justice, provided justice is so flagrantly
on one side that disinterested parties are willing to
take up the quarrel. If a strong man assaults a
weak man in the streets of London, the balance of
force is on the side of the weak man, because, even
if the police did not appear, casual passers-by would
step in to defend him. It is sheer cant to speak of
a contest of might against right, and at the same

time to hope for a victory of the right. If the contest is really between might and right, that *means* that right will be beaten. What is obscurely intended, when this phrase is used, is that the stronger side is only rendered stronger by men's sense of right. But men's sense of right is very subjective, and is only one factor in deciding the preponderance of force. What is desirable in a Legislature is, not that it should decide by its personal sense of right, but that it should decide in a way which is felt to make an appeal to force unnecessary.

Having considered what the State ought not to do, I come now to what it ought to do.

Apart from war and the preservation of internal order, there are certain more positive functions which the State performs, and certain others which it ought to perform.

We may lay down two principles as regards these positive functions.

First: there are matters in which the welfare of the whole community depends upon the practically universal attainment of a certain minimum; in such cases the State has the right to insist upon this minimum being attained.

Secondly: there are ways in which, by insisting upon the maintenance of law, the State, if it does nothing further, renders possible various forms of injustice which would otherwise be prevented by the anger of their victims. Such injustices ought, as far as possible, to be prevented by the State.

The most obvious example of a matter where the general welfare depends upon a universal minimum is sanitation and the prevention of infectious diseases. A single case of plague, if it is neglected, may cause disaster to a whole community. No one can reasonably maintain, on general grounds of liberty, that a man suffering from plague ought to be left free to spread infection far and wide. Exactly similar considerations apply to drainage, notification of fevers, and kindred matters. The interference with liberty remains an evil, but in some cases it is clearly a smaller evil than the spread of disease which liberty would produce. The stamping out of malaria and yellow fever by destroying mosquitoes is perhaps the most striking example of the good which can be done in this way. But when the good is small or doubtful, and the interference with liberty is great, it becomes better to endure a certain amount of preventable disease rather than suffer a scientific tyranny.

Compulsory education comes under the same head as sanitation. The existence of ignorant masses in a population is a danger to the community; when a considerable percentage are illiterate, the whole machinery of government has to take account of the fact. Democracy in its modern form would be quite impossible in a nation where many men can-

not read. But in this case there is not the same
need of absolute universality as in the case of sani-
tary measures. The gypsies, whose mode of life
has been rendered almost impossible by the education authorities, might well have been allowed to
remain a picturesque exception. But apart from
such rather unimportant exceptions, the argument
for compulsory education is irresistible.

What the State does for the care of children at
present is less than what ought to be done, not more.
Children are not capable of looking after their own
interests, and parental responsibility is in many
ways inadequate. It is clear that the State alone
can insist upon the children being provided with the
minimum of knowledge and health which, for the
time being, satisfies the conscience of the community.

The encouragement of scientific research is another matter which comes rightly within the powers
of the State, because the benefits of discoveries ac-
crue to the community, while the investigations are
expensive and never individually certain of achieving
any result. In this matter, Great Britain lags behind all other civilized countries.

The second kind of powers which the State ought
to possess are those that aim at diminishing economic injustice. It is this kind that has been emphasized by socialists. The law creates or facilitates
monopolies, and monopolies are able to exact a toll

from the community. The most glaring example is the private ownership of land. Railways are at present controlled by the State, since rates are fixed by law; and it is clear that if they were uncontrolled, they would acquire a dangerous degree of power.[1] Such considerations, if they stood alone, would justify complete socialism. But I think justice, by itself, is, like law, too static to be made a supreme political principle: it does not, when it has been achieved, contain any seeds of new life or any impetus to development. For this reason, when we wish to remedy an injustice, it is important to consider whether, in so doing, we shall be destroying the incentive to some form of vigorous action which is on the whole useful to the community. No such form of action, so far as I can see, is associated with private ownership of land or of any other source of economic rent; if this is the case, it follows that the State ought to be the primary recipient of rent.

If all these powers are allowed to the State, what becomes of the attempt to rescue individual liberty from its tyranny?

This is part of the general problem which confronts all those who still care for the ideals which inspired liberalism, namely, the problem of combining liberty and personal initiative with organization. Politics and economics are more and more

[1] This would be as true under a syndicalist *régime* as it is at present.

dominated by vast organizations, in face of which the individual is in danger of becoming powerless. The State is the greatest of these organizations, and the most serious menace to liberty. And yet it seems that many of its functions must be extended rather than curtailed.

There is one way by which organization and liberty can be combined, and that is, by securing power for voluntary organizations, consisting of men who have chosen to belong to them because they embody some purpose which all their members consider important, not a purpose imposed by accident or outside force. The State, being geographical, cannot be a wholly voluntary association, but for that very reason there is need of a strong public opinion to restrain it from a tyrannical use of its powers. This public opinion, in most matters, can only be secured by combinations of those who have certain interests or desires in common.

The positive purposes of the State, over and above the preservation of order, ought as far as possible to be carried out, not by the State itself, but by independent organizations, which should be left completely free so long as they satisfied the State that they were not falling below a necessary minimum. This occurs to a certain limited extent at present in regard to elementary education. The universities, also, may be regarded as acting for the State in the matter of higher education and research, except that in their case no minimum of achievement is exacted. In the economic sphere, the State ought to exercise control, but ought to leave initiative to others. There is every reason to multiply opportunities of initiative, and to give the greatest possible share of initiative to each individual, for if this is not done there will be a general sense of impotence and discouragement. There ought to be a constant endeavor to leave the more positive aspects of government in the hands of voluntary organizations, the purpose of the State being merely to exact efficiency and to secure an amicable settlement of disputes, whether within or without its own borders. And with this ought to be combined the greatest possible toleration of exceptions and the least possible insistence upon uniform system.

A good deal may be achieved through local government by trades as well as by areas. This is the most original idea in syndicalism, and it is valuable as a check upon the tyranny which the community may be tempted to exercise over certain classes of its members. All strong organizations which embody a sectional public opinion, such as trade unions, coöperative societies, professions, and universities, are to be welcomed as safeguards of liberty and opportunities for initiative. And there is need of a strong public opinion in favor of liberty itself. The old battles for freedom of thought and freedom of speech, which it was thought had been definitively won, will have to be fought all over again, since most men are only willing to accord freedom to opinions which happen to be popular. Institutions cannot preserve liberty unless men realize that liberty is precious and are willing to exert themselves to keep it alive.

There is a traditional objection to every *imperium in imperio,* but this is only the jealousy of the tyrant. In actual fact, the modern State contains many organizations which it cannot defeat, except perhaps on rare occasions when public opinion is roused against them. Mr. Lloyd George's long fight with the medical profession over the Insurance Act was full of Homeric fluctuations of fortune. The Welsh miners recently routed the whole power of the State, backed by an excited nation. As for the financiers, no Government would dream of a conflict with them. When all other classes are exhorted to patriotism, they are allowed their 4½ per cent. and an increase of interest on their consols. It is well understood on all sides that an appeal to *their* patriotism would show gross ignorance of the world. It is against the traditions of the State to extort their money by threatening to withdraw police protection. This is not due to the difficulty of such a measure, but only to the fact that great wealth wins genuine admiration from us all, and we cannot bear to think of a very rich man being treated with disrespect.

The existence of strong organizations within the

State, such as trade unions, is not undesirable except from the point of view of the official who wishes to wield unlimited power, or of the rival organizations, such as federations of employers, which would prefer a disorganized adversary. In view of the vastness of the State, most men can find little political outlet for initiative except in subordinate organizations formed for specific purposes. Without an outlet for political initiative, men lose their social vigor and their interest in public affairs: they become a prey to corrupt wire-pullers, or to sensation-mongers who have the art of capturing a tired and vagrant attention. The cure for this is to increase rather than diminish the powers of voluntary organizations, to give every man a sphere of political activity small enough for his interest and his capacity, and to confine the functions of the State, as far as possible, to the maintenance of peace among rival interests. The essential merit of the State is that it prevents the internal use of force by private persons. Its essential demerits are, that it promotes the external use of force, and that, by its great size, it makes each individual feel impotent even in a democracy. I shall return in a later lecture to the question of preventing war. The prevention of the sense of individual impotence cannot be achieved by a return to the small City State, which would be as reactionary as a return to the days before machinery. It must be achieved by a method which is in the direction of present tendencies. Such a method would be the increasing devolution of positive political initiative to bodies formed voluntarily for specific purposes, leaving the State rather in the position of a federal authority or a court of arbitration. The State will then confine itself to insisting upon *some* settlement of rival interests: its only principle in deciding what is the right settlement will be an attempt to find the measures most acceptable, on the whole, to all the parties concerned. This is the direction in which democratic States naturally tend, except in so far as they are turned aside by war or the fear of war. So long as war remains a daily imminent danger, the State will remain a Moloch, sacrificing sometimes the life of the individual, and always his unfettered development, to the barren struggle for mastery in the competition with other States. In internal as in external affairs, the worst enemy of freedom is war.

EDUCATION [1]

No political theory is adequate unless it is applicable to children as well as to men and women. Theorists are mostly childless, or, if they have children, they are carefully screened from the disturbances which would be caused by youthful turmoil. Some of them have written books on education, but without, as a rule, having any actual children present to their minds while they wrote. Those educational theorists who have had a knowledge of children, such as the inventors of Kindergarten and the Montessori system,[2] have not always had enough realization of the ultimate goal of education to be able to deal successfully with advanced instruction. I have not the knowledge either of children or of education which would enable me to supply whatever defects there may be in the writings of others. But some questions, concerning education as a political institution, are involved in any hope of social reconstruction, and are not usually considered by writers on educational theory. It is these questions that I wish to discuss.

[1] From *Why Men Fight*.
[2] As regards the education of young children, Madame Montessori's methods seem to be full of wisdom.

The power of education in forming character and opinion is very great and very generally recognized. The genuine beliefs, though not usually the professed precepts, of parents and teachers are almost unconsciously acquired by most children; and even if they depart from these beliefs in later life, something of them remains deeply implanted, ready to emerge in a time of stress or crisis. Education is, as a rule, the strongest force on the side of what exists and against fundamental change: threatened institutions, while they are still powerful, possess themselves of the educational machine, and instill a respect for their own excellence into the malleable minds of the young. Reformers retort by trying to oust their opponents from their position of vantage. The children themselves are not considered by either party; they are merely so much material, to be recruited into one army or the other. If the children themselves were considered, education would not aim at making them belong to this party or that, but at enabling them to choose intelligently between the parties; it would aim at making them able to think, not at making them think what their teachers think. Education as a political weapon could not exist if we respected the rights of children. If we respected the rights of children, we should educate them so as to give them the knowledge and the mental habits required for forming independent opinions; but education as a political institution endeavors to form habits and to circumscribe knowledge in such a way as to make one set of opinions inevitable.

The two principles of *justice* and *liberty*, which cover a very great deal of the social reconstruction required, are not by themselves sufficient where education is concerned. Justice, in the literal sense of equal rights, is obviously not wholly possible as regards children. And as for liberty, it is, to begin with, essentially negative: it condemns all avoidable interference with freedom, without giving a positive principle of construction. But education is essentially constructive, and requires some positive conception of what constitutes a good life. And although liberty is to be respected in education as much as is compatible with instruction, and although a very great deal more liberty than is customary can be allowed without loss to instruction, yet it is clear that some departure from complete liberty is unavoidable if children are to be taught anything, except in the case of unusually intelligent children who are kept isolated from more normal companions. This is one reason for the great responsibility which rests upon teachers: the children must, necessarily, be more or less at the mercy of their elders, and cannot make themselves the guardians of their own interests. Authority in education is to some extent unavoidable, and those who educate have to find a way of exercising authority in accordance with the *spirit* of liberty.

Where authority is unavoidable, what is needed is *reverence*. A man who is to educate really well, and is to make the young grow and develop into their full stature, must be filled through and through with the spirit of reverence. It is reverence towards others that is lacking in those who advocate machine-made cast-iron systems: militarism, capitalism, Fabian scientific organization, and all the other prisons into which reformers and reactionaries try to force the human spirit. In education, with its codes of rules emanating from a Government office, its large classes and fixed curriculum and overworked teachers, its determination to produce a dead level of glib mediocrity, the lack of reverence for the child is all but universal. Reverence requires imagination and vital warmth; it requires most imagination in respect of those who have least actual achievement or power. The child is weak and superficially foolish, the teacher is strong, and in an everyday sense wiser than the child. The teacher without reverence, or the bureaucrat without reverence, easily despises the child for these outward inferiorities. He thinks it is his duty to "mold" the child: in imagination he is the potter with the clay. And so he gives to the child some unnatural shape, which hardens with age, producing strains and spiritual dissatisfactions, out of which grow cruelty and envy, and the belief that others must be compelled to undergo the same distortions.

The man who has reverence will not think it his duty to "mold" the young. He feels in all that lives, but especially in human beings, and most of all in children, something sacred, indefinable, unlimited, something individual and strangely precious, the growing principle of life, an embodied fragment of the dumb striving of the world. In the presence of a child he feels an unaccountable humility—a humility not easily defensible on any rational ground, and yet somehow nearer to wisdom than the easy self-confidence of many parents and teachers. The outward helplessness of the child and the appeal of dependence make him conscious of the responsibility of a trust. His imagination shows him what the child may become, for good or evil, how its impulses may be developed or thwarted, how its hopes must be dimmed and the life in it grow less living, how its trust will be bruised and its quick desires replaced by brooding will. All this gives him a longing to help the child in its own battle; he would equip and strengthen it, not for some outside end proposed by the State or by any other impersonal authority, but for the ends which the child's own spirit is obscurely seeking. The man who feels this can wield the authority of an educator without infringing the principle of liberty.

It is not in a spirit of reverence that education

is conducted by States and Churches and the great institutions that are subservient to them. What is considered in education is hardly ever the boy or girl, the young man or young woman, but almost always, in some form, the maintenance of the existing order. When the individual is considered, it is almost exclusively with a view to worldly success—making money or achieving a good position. To be ordinary, and to acquire the art of getting on, is the ideal which is set before the youthful mind, except by a few rare teachers who have enough energy of belief to break through the system within which they are expected to work. Almost all education has a political motive: it aims at strengthening some group, national or religious or even social, in the competition with other groups. It is this motive, in the main, which determines the subjects taught, the knowledge offered and the knowledge withheld, and also decides what mental habits the pupils are expected to acquire. Hardly anything is done to foster the inward growth of mind and spirit; in fact, those who have had most education are very often atrophied in their mental and spirtual life, devoid of impulses, and possessing only certain mechanical aptitudes which take the place of living thought.

Some of the things which education achieves at present must continue to be achieved by education in any civilized country. All children must continue to be taught how to read and write, and some must continue to acquire the knowledge needed for such professions as medicine or law or engineering. The higher education required for the sciences and the arts is necessary for those to whom it is suited. Except in history and religion and kindred matters, the actual instruction is only inadequate, not positively harmful. The instruction might be given in a more liberal spirit, with more attempt to show its ultimate uses; and of course much of it is traditional and dead. But in the main it is necessary, and would have to form a part of any educational system.

It is in history and religion and other controversial subjects that the actual instruction is positively harmful. These subjects touch the interests by which schools are maintained; and the interests maintain the schools in order that certain views on these subjects may be instilled. History, in every country, is so taught as to magnify that country: children learn to believe that their own country has always been in the right and almost always victorious, that it has produced almost all the great men, and that it is in all respects superior to all other countries. Since these beliefs are flattering, they are easily absorbed, and hardly ever dislodged from instinct by later knowledge.

To take a simple and almost trivial example: the facts about the battle of Waterloo are known in great detail and with minute accuracy; but the facts as taught in elementary schools will be widely different in England, France, and Germany. The ordinary English boy imagines that the Prussians played hardly any part; the ordinary German boy imagines that Wellington was practically defeated when the day was retrieved by Blücher's gallantry. If the facts were taught accurately in both countries, national pride would not be fostered to the same extent, neither nation would feel so certain of victory in the event of war, and the willingness to fight would be diminished. It is this result which has to be prevented. Every State wishes to promote national pride, and is conscious that this cannot be done by unbiased history. The defenseless children are taught by distortions and suppressions and suggestions. The false ideas as to the history of the world which are taught in the various countries are of a kind which encourages strife and serves to keep alive a bigoted nationalism. If good relations between States were desired, one of the first steps ought to be to submit all teaching of history to an international commission, which should produce neutral textbooks free from the patriotic bias which is now demanded everywhere.[1]

---

[1] THE TEACHING OF PATRIOTISM. HIS MAJESTY'S
APPROVAL

THE KING has been graciously pleased to accept a copy of the little book containing suggestions to local education authorities and teachers in Wales as to the teaching of patriotism which has just been issued by the Welsh Department of the Board

Exactly the same thing applies to religion. Elementary schools are practically always in the hands either of some religious body or of a State which has a certain attitude towards religion. A religious body exists through the fact that its members all have certain definite beliefs on subjects as to which the truth is not ascertainable. Schools conducted by religious bodies have to prevent the young, who are often inquiring by nature, from discovering that these definite beliefs are opposed by others which are no more unreasonable, and that many of the men best qualified to judge think that there is no good evidence in favor of any definite belief. When the State is militantly secular, as in France, State schools become as dogmatic as those that are in the hands of the Churches (I understand that the word "God" must not be mentioned in a French elementary school). The result in all these cases is the same: free inquiry is checked, and on the most important matter in the world the child is met with dogma or with stony silence.

It is not only in elementary education that these evils exist. In more advanced education they take

of Education in connection with the observance of the National Anniversary of St. David's Day. His Private Secretary (Lord Stamfordham), in writing to Mr. Alfred T. Davies, the Permanent Secretary of the Welsh Department, says that his Majesty is much pleased with the contents of the book, and trusts that the principles inculcated in it will bear good fruit in the lives and characters of the coming generation.—*Morning Post*, January 20, 1916 subtler forms, and there is more attempt to conceal them, but they are still present. Eton and Oxford set a certain stamp upon a man's mind, just as a Jesuit College does. It can hardly be said that Eton and Oxford have a *conscious* purpose, but they have a purpose which is none the less strong and effective for not being formulated. In almost all who have been through them they produce a worship of "good form," which is as destructive to life and thought as the medieval Church. "Good form" is quite compatible with a superficial open-mindedness, readiness to hear all sides, and a certain urbanity towards opponents. But it is not compatible with fundamental open-mindedness, or with any inward readiness to give weight to the other side. Its essence is the assumption that what is most important is a certain kind of behavior, a behavior which minimizes friction between equals and delicately impresses inferiors with a conviction of their own crudity. As a political weapon for preserving the privileges of the rich in a snobbish democracy it is unsurpassable. As a means of producing an agreeable social *milieu* for those who have money with no strong beliefs or unusual desires it has some merit. In every other respect it is abominable.

The evils of "good form" arise from two sources: its perfect assurance of its own rightness, and its belief that correct manners are more to be desired than intellect, or artistic creation, or vital energy, or any of the other sources of progress in the world. Perfect assurance, by itself, is enough to destroy all mental progress in those who have it. And when it is combined with contempt for the angularities and awkwardnesses that are almost invariably associated with great mental power, it becomes a source of destruction to all who come in contact with it. "Good form" is itself dead and incapable of growth; and by its attitude to those who are without it it spreads its own death to many who might otherwise have life. The harm which it has done to well-to-do Englishmen, and to men whose abilities have led the well-to-do to notice them, is incalculable.

The prevention of free inquiry is unavoidable so long as the purpose of education is to produce belief rather than thought, to compel the young to hold positive opinions on doubtful matters rather than to let them see the doubtfulness and be encouraged to independence of mind. Education ought to foster the wish for truth, not the conviction that some particular creed is the truth. But it is creeds that hold men together in fighting organizations: Churches, States, political parties. It is intensity of belief in a creed that produces efficiency in fighting: victory comes to those who feel the strongest certainty about matters on which doubt is the only rational attitude. To produce this intensity of belief and this efficiency in fighting, the child's nature is warped, and its free outlook is cramped, by cultivating inhibitions as a check to the growth of new ideas. In those whose minds are not very active the result is the omnipotence of prejudice; while the few whose thought cannot be wholly killed become cynical, intellectually hopeless, destructively critical, able to make all that is living seem foolish, unable themselves to supply the creative impulses which they destroy in others.

The success in fighting which is achieved by suppressing freedom of thought is brief and very worthless. In the long run mental vigor is as essential to success as it is to a good life. The conception of education as a form of drill, a means of producing unanimity through slavishness, is very common, and is defended chiefly on the ground that it leads to victory. Those who enjoy parallels from ancient history will point to the victory of Sparta over Athens to enforce their moral. But it is Athens that has had power over men's thoughts and imaginations, not Sparta: any one of us, if we could be born again into some past epoch, would rather be born an Athenian than a Spartan. And in the modern world so much intellect is required in practical affairs that even the external victory is more likely to be won by intelligence than by docility. Education in credulity leads by quick stages to mental decay; it is only by keeping alive the spirit of free inquiry that the indispensable minimum of progress can be achieved.

Certain mental habits are commonly instilled by those who are engaged in educating: obedience and discipline, ruthlessness in the struggle for worldly success, contempt towards opposing groups, and an unquestioning credulity, a passive acceptance of the teacher's wisdom. All these habits are against life. Instead of obedience and discipline, we ought to aim at preserving independence and impulse. Instead of ruthlessness, education should try to develop justice in thought. Instead of contempt, it ought to instill reverence, and the attempt at understanding; towards the opinions of others it ought to produce, not necessarily acquiescence, but only such opposition as is combined with imaginative apprehension and a clear realization of the grounds for opposition. Instead of credulity, the object should be to stimulate constructive doubt, the love of mental adventure, the sense of worlds to conquer by enterprise and boldness in thought. Contentment with the *status quo*, and subordination of the individual pupil to political aims, owing to the indifference to the things of the mind, are the immediate causes of these evils; but beneath these causes there is one more fundamental, the fact that education is treated as a means of acquiring power over the pupil, not as a means of nourishing his own growth. It is in this that lack of reverence shows itself; and it is only by more reverence that a fundamental reform can be effected.

Obedience and discipline are supposed to be indispensable if order is to be kept in a class, and if any instruction is to be given. To some extent this is true; but the extent is much less than it is thought to be by those who regard obedience and discipline as in themselves desirable. Obedience, the yielding of one's will to outside direction, is the counterpart of authority. Both may be necessary in certain cases. Refractory children, lunatics, and criminals may require authority, and may need to be forced to obey. But in so far as this is necessary it is a misfortune: what is to be desired is the free choice of ends with which it is not necessary to interfere. And educational reformers have shown that this is far more possible than our fathers would ever have believed.[1]

What makes obedience seem necessary in schools is the large classes and overworked teachers demanded by a false economy. Those who have no experience of teaching are incapable of imagining the expense of spirit entailed by any really living instruction. They think that teachers can reasonably be expected to work as many hours as bank clerks. Intense fatigue and irritable nerves are the result, and an absolute necessity of performing the day's task mechanically. But the task cannot be

---

[1] What Madame Montessori has achieved in the way of minimizing obedience and discipline with advantage to education is almost miraculous.

performed mechanically except by exacting obedience.

If we took education seriously, and thought it as important to keep alive the minds of children as to secure victory in war, we should conduct education quite differently: we should make sure of achieving the end, even if the expense were a hundredfold greater than it is. To many men and women a small amount of teaching is a delight, and can be done with a fresh zest and life which keeps most pupils interested without any need of discipline. The few who do not become interested might be separated from the rest, and given a different kind of instruction. A teacher ought to have only as much teaching as can be done, on most days, with actual pleasure in the work, and with an awareness of the pupil's mental needs. The result would be a relation of friendliness instead of hostility between teacher and pupil, a realization on the part of most pupils that education serves to develop their own lives and is not merely an outside imposition, interfering with play and demanding many hours of sitting still. All that is necessary to this end is a greater expenditure of money, to secure teachers with more leisure and with a natural love of teaching.

Discipline, as it exists in schools, is very largely an evil. There is a kind of discipline which is necessary to almost all achievement, and which perhaps is not sufficiently valued by those who react against the purely external discipline of traditional methods. The desirable kind of discipline is the kind that comes from within, which consists in the power of pursuing a distant object steadily, forgoing and suffering many things on the way. This involves the subordination of impulse to will, the power of directing action by large creative desires even at moments when they are not vividly alive. Without this, no serious ambition, good or bad, can be realized, no consistent purpose can dominate. This kind of discipline is very necessary, but can only result from strong desires for ends not immediately attainable, and can only be produced by education if education fosters such desires, which it seldom does at present. Such discipline springs from one's own will, not from outside authority. It is not this kind which is sought in most schools, and it is not this kind which seems to me an evil.

Although elementary education encourages the undesirable discipline that consists in passive obedience, and although hardly any existing education encourages the moral discipline of consistent self-direction, there is a certain kind of purely mental discipline which is produced by the traditional higher education. The kind I mean is that which enables a man to concentrate his thoughts at will upon any matter that he has occasion to consider, regardless of preoccupations or boredom or intellectual difficulty. This quality, though it has no important intrinsic

excellence, greatly enhances the efficiency of the mind as an instrument. It is this that enables a lawyer to master the scientific details of a patent case which he forgets as soon as judgment has been given, or a civil servant to deal quickly with many different administrative questions in succession. It is this that enables men to forget private cares during business hours. In a complicated world it is a very necessary faculty for those whose work requires mental concentration.

Success in producing mental discipline is the chief merit of traditional higher education. I doubt whether it can be achieved except by compelling or persuading active attention to a prescribed task. It is for this reason chiefly that I do not believe methods such as Madame Montessori's applicable when the age of childhood has been passed. The essence of her method consists in giving a choice of occupations, any one of which is interesting to most children, and all of which are instructive. The child's attention is wholly spontaneous, as in play; it enjoys acquiring knowledge in this way, and does not acquire any knowledge which it does not desire. I am convinced that this is the best method of education with young children: the actual results make it almost impossible to think otherwise. But it is difficult to see how this method can lead to control of attention by the will. Many things which must be thought about are uninteresting, and even those that are interesting at first often become very weari-some before they have been considered as long as is necessary. The power of giving prolonged attention is very important, and it is hardly to be widely acquired except as a habit induced originally by outside pressure. Some few boys, it is true, have sufficiently strong intellectual desires to be willing to undergo all that is necessary by their own initia-tive and free will; but for all others an external in-ducement is required in order to make them learn any subject thoroughly. There is among educational reformers a certain fear of demanding great efforts, and in the world at large a growing unwillingness to be bored. Both these tendencies have their good sides, but both also have their dangers. The mental discipline which is jeopardized can be preserved by mere advice without external compulsion whenever a boy's intellectual interest and ambition can be sufficiently stimulated. A good teacher ought to be able to do this for any boy who is capable of much mental achievement; and for many of the others the present purely bookish education is probably not the best. In this way, so long as the importance of mental discipline is realized, it can probably be at-tained, whenever it is attainable, by appealing to the pupil's consciousness of his own needs. So long as teachers are not expected to succeed by this method, it is easy for them to slip into a slothful dullness, and blame their pupils when the fault is really their own.

Ruthlessness in the economic struggle will almost unavoidably be taught in schools so long as the economic structure of society remains unchanged. This must be particularly the case in middle-class schools, which depend for their numbers upon the good opinion of parents, and secure the good opinion of parents by advertising the successes of pupils. This is one of many ways in which the competitive organization of the State is harmful. Spontaneous and disinterested desire for knowledge is not at all uncommon in the young, and might be easily aroused in many in whom it remains latent. But it is remorselessly checked by teachers who think only of examinations, diplomas, and degrees. For the abler boys there is no time for thought, no time for the indulgence of intellectual taste, from the moment of first going to school until the moment of leaving the university. From first to last there is nothing but one long drudgery of examination tips and textbook facts. The most intelligent, at the end, are disgusted with learning, longing only to forget it and to escape into a life of action. Yet there, as before, the economic machine holds them prisoners, and all their spontaneous desires are bruised and thwarted.

The examination system, and the fact that instruction is treated mainly as training for a livelihood, leads the young to regard knowledge, from a purely utilitarian point of view, as the road to money, not as the gateway to wisdom. This would not matter so much if it affected only those who have no genuine intellectual interests. But unfortunately it affects most those whose intellectual interests are strongest, since it is upon them that the pressure of examinations falls with most severity. To them most, but to all in some degree, education appears as a means of acquiring superiority over others; it is infected through and through with ruthlessness and glorification of social inequality. Any free, disinterested consideration shows that, whatever inequalities might remain in a Utopia, the actual inequalities are almost all contrary to justice. But our educational system tends to conceal this from all except the failures, since those who succeed are on the way to profit by the inequalities, with every encouragement from the men who have directed their education.

Passive acceptance of the teacher's wisdom is easy to most boys and girls. It involves no effort of independent thought, and seems rational because the teacher knows more than his pupils; it is moreover the way to win the favor of the teacher unless he is a very exceptional man. Yet the habit of passive acceptance is a disastrous one in later life. It causes men to seek a leader, and to accept as a leader whoever is established in that position. It makes the power of Churches, Governments, party caucuses, and all the other organizations by which plain men are misled into supporting old systems which are harmful to the nation and to themselves. It is possible that there would not be much independence of thought even if education did everything to promote it; but there would certainly be more than there is at present. If the object were to make pupils think, rather than to make them accept certain conclusions, education would be conducted quite differently: there would be less rapidity of instruction and more discussion, more occasions when pupils were encouraged to express themselves, more attempt to make education concern itself with matters in which the pupils felt some interest.

Above all, there would be an endeavor to rouse and stimulate the love of mental adventure. The world in which we live is various and astonishing: some of the things that seem plainest grow more and more difficult the more they are considered; other things, which might have been thought quite impossible to discover, have nevertheless been laid bare by genius and industry. The powers of thought, the vast regions which it can master, the much more vast regions which it can only dimly suggest to imagination, give to those whose minds have traveled beyond the daily round an amazing richness of material, an escape from the triviality and wearisomeness of familiar routine, by which the whole of life is filled with interest, and the prison walls of the commonplace are broken down. The same love of adventure which takes men to the South Pole, the same passion for a conclusive trial of strength which leads some men to welcome war, can find in creative thought an outlet which is neither wasteful nor cruel, but increases the dignity of man by incarnating in life some of that shining splendor which the human spirit is bringing down out of the unknown. To give this joy, in a greater or less measure, to all who are capable of it, is the supreme end for which the education of the mind is to be valued.

It will be said that the joy of mental adventure must be rare, that there are few who can appreciate it, and that ordinary education can take no account of so aristocratic a good. I do not believe this. The joy of mental adventure is far commoner in the young than in grown men and women. Among children it is very common, and grows naturally out of the period of make-believe and fancy. It is rare in later life because everything is done to kill it during education. Men fear thought as they fear nothing else on earth—more than ruin, more even than death. Thought is subversive and revolutionary, destructive and terrible; thought is merciless to privilege, established institutions, and comfortable habits; thought is anarchic and lawless, indifferent to authority, careless of the well-tried wisdom of the ages. Thought looks into the pit of hell and is not afraid. It sees man, a feeble speck, surrounded by unfathomable depths of silence; yet it bears itself proudly, as unmoved as if it were lord of the universe. Thought is great and swift and free, the light of the world, and the chief glory of man.

But if thought is to become the possession of many, not the privilege of the few, we must have done with fear. It is fear that holds men back—fear lest their cherished beliefs should prove delusions, fear lest the institutions by which they live should prove harmful, fear lest they themselves should prove less worthy of respect than they have supposed themselves to be. "Should the working man think freely about property? Then what will become of us, the rich? Should young men and young women think freely about sex? Then what will become of morality? Should soldiers think freely about war? Then what will become of military discipline? Away with thought! Back into the shades of prejudice, lest property, morals, and war should be endangered! Better men should be stupid, slothful, and oppressive than that their thoughts should be free. For if their thoughts were free they might not think as we do. And at all costs this disaster must be averted." So the opponents of thought argue in the unconscious depths of their souls. And so they act in their churches, their schools, and their universities.

No institution inspired by fear can further life.

Hope, not fear, is the creative principle in human affairs. All that has made man great has sprung from the attempt to secure what is good, not from the struggle to avert what was thought evil. It is because modern education is so seldom inspired by a great hope that it so seldom achieves a great result. The wish to preserve the past rather than the hope of creating the future dominates the minds of those who control the teaching of the young. Education should not aim at a passive awareness of dead facts, but at an activity directed towards the world that our efforts are to create. It should be inspired, not by a regretful hankering after the extinct beauties of Greece and the Renaissance, but by a shining vision of the society that is to be, of the triumphs that thought will achieve in the time to come, and of the ever-widening horizon of man's survey over the universe. Those who are taught in this spirit will be filled with life and hope and joy, able to bear their part in bringing to mankind a future less somber than the past, with faith in the glory that human effort can create.

SCIENCE AND ART UNDER SOCIALISM [1]

Socialism has been advocated by most of its champions chiefly as a means of increasing the welfare of the wage-earning classes, and more particularly their material welfare. It has seemed, accordingly, to some men whose aims are not material, as if it has nothing to offer toward the general advancement of civilization in the way of art and thought. Some of its advocates, moreover—and among these Marx must be included—have written, no doubt not deliberately, as if with the socialist revolution the millennium would have arrived, and there would be no need of further progress for the human race. I do not know whether our age is more restless than that which preceded it, or whether it has merely become more impregnated with the idea of evolution, but, for whatever reason, we have grown incapable of believing in a state of static perfection. and we demand, of any social system, which is to have our approval, that it shall contain within itself a stimulus and opportunity for progress toward something still better. The doubts thus raised by socialist writers make it necessary to inquire whether socialism would in fact be hostile to art and science, and whether it

[1] From *Proposed Roads to Freedom*.

would be likely to produce a stereotyped society in which progress would become difficult and slow.

It is not enough that men and women should be made comfortable in a material sense. Many members of the well-to-do classes at present, in spite of opportunity, contribute nothing of value to the life of the world, and do not even succeed in securing for themselves any personal happiness worthy to be so called. The multiplication of such individuals would be an achievement of the very minutest value; and if socialism were merely to bestow upon all the kind of life and outlook which is now enjoyed by the more apathetic among the well-to-do, it would offer little that could inspire enthusiasm in any generous spirit.

"The true rôle of collective existence," says M. Naquet,[1] " . . . is to learn, to discover, to know. Eating, drinking, sleeping, living, in a word, is a mere accessory. In this respect, we are not distinguished from the brute. Knowledge is the goal. If I were condemned to choose between a humanity materially happy, glutted after the manner of a flock of sheep in a field, and a humanity existing in misery, but from which emanated, here and there, some eternal truth, it is on the latter that my choice would fall."

This statement puts the alternative in a very extreme form in which it is somewhat unreal. It may

[1] *L'Anarchie et le Collectivisme*, p. 114.

be said in reply that for those who have had the leisure and the opportunity to enjoy "eternal truths" it is easy to exalt their importance at the expense of sufferings which fall on others. This is true; but, if it is taken as disposing of the question, it leaves out of account the importance of thought for progress. Viewing the life of mankind as a whole, in the future as well as in the present, there can be no question that a society in which some men pursue knowledge while others endure great poverty offers more hope of ultimate good than a society in which all are sunk in slothful comfort. It is true that poverty is a great evil, but it is not true that material prosperity is in itself a great good. If it is to have any real value to society, it must be made a means to the advancement of those higher goods that belong to the life of the mind. But the life of the mind does not consist of thought and knowledge alone, nor can it be completely healthy unless it has some instinctive contact, however deeply buried, with the general life of the community. Divorced from the social instinct, thought, like art, tends to become finicky and precious. It is the position of such art and thought as is imbued with the instinctive sense of service to mankind that we wish to consider, for it is this alone that makes up the life of the mind in the sense in which it is a vital part of the life of the community. Will the life of the mind in this sense be helped or hindered by socialism? And will there still be a sufficient spur to progress to prevent a condition of Byzantine immobility?

In considering this question we are, in a certain sense, passing outside the atmosphere of democracy. The general good of the community is realized only in individuals, but it is realized much more fully in some individuals than in others. Some men have a comprehensive and penetrating intellect, enabling them to appreciate and remember what has been thought and known by their predecessors, and to discover new regions in which they enjoy all the high delights of the mental explorer. Others have the power of creating beauty, giving bodily form to impalpable visions out of which joy comes to many. Such men are more fortunate than the mass, and also more important for the collective life. A larger share of the general sum of good is concentrated in them than in the ordinary man and woman; but also their contribution to the general good is greater. They stand out among men and cannot be wholly fitted into the framework of democratic equality. A social system which would render them unproductive would stand condemned, whatever other merits it might have.

The first thing to realize—though it is difficult in a commercial age—is that what is best in creative mental activity cannot be produced by any system of monetary rewards. Opportunity and the stimulus of an invigorating spiritual atmosphere are important, but, if they are present, no financial inducements will be required, while if they are absent, material compensations will be of no avail. Recognition, even if it takes the form of money, can bring a certain pleasure in old age to the man of science who has battled all his life against academic prejudice, or to the artist who has endured years of ridicule for not painting in the manner of his predecessors; but it is not by the remote hope of such pleasures that their work has been inspired. All the most important work springs from an uncalculating impulse, and is best promoted, not by rewards after the event, but by circumstances which keep the impulse alive and afford scope for the activities which it inspires. In the creation of such circumstances our present system is much at fault. Will socialism be better?

I do not think this question can be answered without specifying the kind of socialism that is intended: some forms of socialism would, I believe, be even more destructive in this respect than the present capitalist *régime,* while others would be immeasurably better. Three things which a social system can provide or withhold are helpful to mental creation: first, technical training; second, liberty to follow the creative impulse; third, at least the possibility of ultimate appreciation by some public, whether large or small. We may leave out of our discussion both individual genius and those intangible conditions which make some ages great and others sterile in art and science—not because these are unimportant, but because they are too little understood to be taken account of in economic or political organization. The three conditions we have mentioned seem to cover most of what can be *seen* to be useful or harmful from our present point of view, and it is therefore to them that we shall confine ourselves.

1. *Technical training.*—Technical training at present, whether in science or art, requires one or other of two conditions. Either a boy must be the son of well-to-do parents who can afford to keep him while he acquires his education, or he must show so much ability at an early age as to enable him to subsist on scholarships until he is ready to earn his living. The former condition is, of course, a mere matter of luck, and could not be preserved in its present form under any kind of socialism or communism. This loss is emphasized by defenders of the present system, and no doubt it would be, to some extent, a real loss. But the well-to-do are a small proportion of the population, and presumably on the average no more talented by nature than their less fortunate contemporaries. If the advantages which are enjoyed now by those few among them who are capable of good work in science or art could be extended, even in a slightly attenuated form, to all who are similarly gifted, the result would almost infallibly be a gain, and much ability which is now

wasted would be rendered fruitful. But how is this to be effected?

The system of scholarships obtained by competition, though better than nothing, is objectionable from many points of view. It introduces the competitive spirit into the work of the very young; it makes them regard knowledge from the standpoint of what is useful in examinations rather than in the light of its intrinsic interest or importance; it places a premium upon that sort of ability which is displayed precociously in glib answers to set questions rather than upon the kind that broods on difficulties and remains for a time rather dumb. What is perhaps worse than any of these defects is the tendency to cause overwork in youth, leading to lack of vigor and interest when manhood has been reached. It can hardly be doubted that by this cause, at present, many fine minds have their edge blunted and their keenness destroyed.

State socialism might easily universalize the system of scholarships obtained by competitive examination, and if it did so it is to be feared that it would be very harmful. State socialists at present tend to be enamored of the system, which is exactly of the kind that every bureaucrat loves: orderly, neat, giving a stimulus to industrious habits, and involving no waste of a sort that could be tabulated in statistics or accounts of public expenditure. Such men will argue that free higher education is expensive to the community, and only useful in the case of those who have exceptional abilities; it ought, therefore, they will say, not to be given to all, but only to those who will become more useful members of society through receiving it. Such arguments make a great appeal to what are called "practical" men, and the answers to them are of a sort which it is difficult to render widely convincing. Revolt against the evils of competition is, however, part of the very essence of the socialist's protest against the existing order, and on this ground, if on no other, those who favor socialism may be summoned to look for some better solution.

Much the simplest solution, and the only really effective one, is to make every kind of education free up to the age of twenty-one for all boys and girls who desire it. The majority will be tired of education before that age, and will prefer to begin other work sooner; this will lead to a natural selection of those with strong interests in some pursuit requiring a long training. Among those selected in this way by their own inclinations, probably almost all who have marked abilities of the kind in question will be included. It is true that there will also be many who have very little ability: the desire to become a painter, for example, is by no means confined to those who can paint. But this degree of waste could well be borne by the community; it would be immeasurably less than that now entailed by the support of the idle rich. Any system which aims at avoiding this kind of waste must entail the far more serious waste of rejecting or spoiling some of the best ability in each generation. The system of free education up to any grade for all who desire it is the only system which is consistent with the principles of liberty, and the only one which gives a reasonable hope of affording full scope for talent. This system is equally compatible with all forms of socialism and anarchism. Theoretically, it is compatible with capitalism, but practically it is so opposite in spirit that it would hardly be feasible without a complete economic reconstruction. The fact that socialism would facilitate it must be reckoned a very powerful argument in favor of change, for the waste of talent at present in the poorer classes of society must be stupendous.

2. *Liberty to follow the creative impulse.*—When a man's training has been completed, if he is possessed of really great abilities, he will do his best work if he is completely free to follow his bent, creating what seems good to him, regardless of the judgment of "experts." At present this is only possible for two classes of people: those who have private means, and those who can earn a living by an occupation that does not absorb their whole energies. Under socialism, there will be no one with private means, and if there is to be no loss as regards art and science, the opportunity which now comes by acci-

dent to a few will have to be provided deliberately for a much larger number. The men who have used private means as an opportunity for creative work have been few but important: one might mention Milton, Shelley, Keats, and Darwin as examples. Probably none of these would have produced as good work if they had had to earn their livelihood. If Darwin had been a university teacher, he would of course have been dismissed from his post by the influence of the clerics on account of his scandalous theories.

Nevertheless, the bulk of the creative work of the world is done at present by men who subsist by some other occupation. Science, and research generally, are usually done in their spare time by men who live by teaching. There is no great objection to this in the case of science, provided the number of hours devoted to teaching is not excessive. It is partly because science and teaching are so easily combined that science is vigorous in the present age. In music, a composer who is also a performer enjoys similar advantages, but one who is not a performer must starve, unless he is rich or willing to pander to the public taste. In the fine arts, as a rule, it is not easy in the modern world either to make a living by really good work or to find a subsidiary profession which leaves enough leisure for creation. This is presumably one reason, though by no means the only one, why art is less flourishing than science.

The bureaucratic State socialist will have a simple solution for these difficulties. He will appoint a body consisting of the most eminent celebrities in an art or a science, whose business it shall be to judge the work of young men, and to issue licenses to those whose productions find favor in their eyes. A licensed artist shall be considered to have performed his duty to the community by producing works of art. But of course he will have to prove his industry by never failing to produce in reasonable quantities, and his continued ability by never failing to please his eminent judges—until, in the fullness of time, he becomes a judge himself. In this way, the authorities will insure that the artist shall be competent, regular, and obedient to the best traditions of his art. Those who fail to fulfil these conditions will be compelled by the withdrawal of their license to seek some less dubious mode of earning their living. Such will be the ideal of the State socialist.

In such a world all that makes life tolerable to the lover of beauty would perish. Art springs from a wild and anarchic side of human nature; between the artist and the bureaucrat there must always be a profound mutual antagonism, an age-long battle in which the artist, always outwardly worsted, wins in the end through the gratitude of mankind for the joy that he puts into their lives. If the wild side of human nature is to be permanently subjected to the orderly rules of the benevolent, uncomprehending bureaucrat, the joy of life will perish out of the earth, and the very impulse to live will gradually wither and die. Better a thousandfold the present world with all its horrors than such a dead mummy of a world. Better anarchism, with all its risks, than a State socialism that subjects to rule what must be spontaneous and free if it is to have any value. It is this nightmare that makes artists, and lovers of beauty generally, so often suspicious of socialism. But there is nothing in the essence of socialism to make art impossible: only certain forms of socialism would entail this danger. William Morris was a socialist, and was a socialist very largely because he was an artist. And in this he was not irrational.

It is impossible for art, or any of the higher creative activities, to flourish under any system which requires that the artist shall prove his competence to some body of authorities before he is allowed to follow his impulse. Any really great artist is almost sure to be thought incompetent by those among his seniors who would be generally regarded as best qualified to form an opinion. And the mere fact of having to produce work which will please older men is hostile to a free spirit and to bold innovation. Apart from this difficulty, selection by older men would lead to jealousy and intrigue and back-biting, producing a poisonous atmosphere of underground competition. The only effect of such a plan would be to eliminate the few who now slip through owing to some fortunate accident. It is not by any system, but by freedom alone, that art can flourish.

There are two ways by which the artist could secure freedom under socialism of the right kind. He might undertake regular work outside his art, doing only a few hours' work a day and receiving proportionately less pay than those who do a full day's work. He ought, in that case, to be at liberty to sell his pictures if he could find purchasers. Such a system would have many advantages. It would leave absolutely every man free to become an artist, provided he were willing to suffer a certain economic loss. This would not deter those in whom the impulse was strong and genuine, but would tend to exclude the dilettante. Many young artists at present endure voluntarily much greater poverty than need be entailed by only doing half the usual day's work in a well-organized socialist community; and some degree of hardship is not objectionable, as a test of the strength of the creative impulse, and as an offset to the peculiar joys of the creative life.

The other possibility [1] would be that the necessaries of life should be free, as anarchists desire, to all equally, regardless of whether they work or not. Under this plan, every man could live without work: there would be what might be called a "vagabond's wage," sufficient for existence but not for luxury. The artist who preferred to have his whole time for

[1] See Chapter IV, *Proposed Roads to Freedom.*

art and enjoyment might live on the "vagabond's wage"—traveling on foot when the humor seized him to see foreign countries, enjoying the air and the sun, as free as the birds, and perhaps scarcely less happy. Such men would bring color and diversity into the life of the community; their outlook would be different from that of steady, stay-at-home workers, and would keep alive a much-needed element of light-heartedness which our sober, serious civilization tends to kill. If they became very numerous, they might be too great an economic burden on the workers; but I doubt if there are many with enough capacity for simple enjoyments to choose poverty and freedom in preference to the comparatively light and pleasant work which will be usual in those days.

By either of these methods, freedom can be preserved for the artist in a socialistic commonwealth— far more complete freedom, and far more widespread, than any that now exists except for the possessors of capital.

But there still remain some not altogether easy problems. Take, for example, the publishing of books. There will not, under socialism, be private publishers as at present: under State socialism, presumably the State will be the sole publisher, while under syndicalism or Guild socialism the *Fédération du Livre* will have the whole of the trade in its hands. Under these circumstances, who is to decide what MSS. are to be printed? It is clear that opportunities exist for an Index more rigorous than that of the Inquisition. If the State were the sole publisher, it would doubtless refuse books opposed to State socialism. If the *Fédération du Livre* were the ultimate arbiter, what publicity could be obtained for works criticizing it? And apart from such political difficulties we should have, as regards literature, that very censorship by eminent officials which we agreed to regard as disastrous when we were considering the fine arts in general. The difficulty is serious, and a way of meeting it must be found if literature is to remain free.

Kropotkin, who believes that manual and intellectual work should be combined, holds that authors themselves should be compositors, bookbinders, etc. He even seems to suggest that the whole of the manual work involved in producing books should be done by authors. It may be doubted whether there are enough authors in the world for this to be possible, and in any case I cannot but think that it would be a waste of time for them to leave the work they understand in order to do badly work which others could do far better and more quickly. That, however, does not touch our present point, which is the question how the MSS. to be printed will be selected. In Kropotkin's plan there will presumably be an Authors' Guild, with a Committee of Management, if anarchism allows such things. This Committee of Management will decide which of the books submitted to it are worthy to be printed. Among these will be included those by the Committee and their friends, but not those by their enemies. Authors of rejected MSS. will hardly have the patience to spend their time setting up the works of successful rivals, and there will have to be an elaborate system of log-rolling if any books are to be printed at all. It hardly looks as if this plan would conduce to harmony among literary men, or would lead to the publication of any book of an unconventional tendency. Kropotkin's own books, for example, would hardly have found favor.

The only way of meeting these difficulties, whether under State socialism or Guild socialism or anarchism, seems to be by making it possible for an author to pay for the publication of his book if it is not such as the State or the Guild is willing to print at its own expense. I am aware that this method is contrary to the spirit of socialism, but I do not see what other way there is of securing freedom. The payment might be made by undertaking to engage for an assigned period in some work of recognized utility and to hand over such proportion of the earnings as might be necessary. The work undertaken might of course be, as Kropotkin suggests, the manual part of the production of books, but I see no special reason why it should be. It would have to be an absolute rule that no book should be refused, no matter what the nature of its contents might be, if payment for publication were offered at the standard rate. An author who had admirers would be able to secure their help in payment. An unknown author might, it is true, have to suffer a considerable loss of comfort in order to make his payment, but that would give an automatic means of eliminating those whose writing was not the result of any very profound impulse and would be by no means wholly an evil.

Probably some similar method would be desirable as regards the publishing and performing of new music.

What we have been suggesting will, no doubt, be objected to by orthodox socialists, since they will find something repugnant to their principles in the whole idea of a private person paying to have certain work done. But it is a mistake to be the slave of a system, and every system, if it is applied rigidly, will entail evils which could only be avoided by some concession to the exigencies of special cases. On the whole, a wise form of socialism might afford infinitely better opportunities for the artist and the man of science than are possible in a capitalist community, but only if the form of socialism adopted is one which is fitted for this end by means of provisions such as we have been suggesting.

3. *Possibility of appreciation.*—This condition is one which is not necessary to all who do creative work, but in the sense in which I mean it the great

majority find it very nearly indispensable. I do not mean widespread public recognition, nor that ignorant, half-sincere respect which is commonly accorded to artists who have achieved success. Neither of these serves much purpose. What I mean is rather understanding, and a spontaneous feeling that things of beauty are important. In a thoroughly commercialized society, an artist is respected if he makes money, and because he makes money, but there is no genuine respect for the works of art by which his money has been made. A millionaire whose fortune has been made in button-hooks or chewing-gum is regarded with awe, but none of this feeling is bestowed on the articles from which his wealth is derived. In a society which measures all things by money the same tends to be true of the artist. If he has become rich he is respected, though of course less than the millionaire, but his pictures or books or music are regarded as the chewing-gum or the button-hooks are regarded, merely as a means to money. In such an atmosphere it is very difficult for the artist to preserve his creative impulse pure: either he is contaminated by his surroundings, or he becomes embittered through lack of appreciation for the object of his endeavor.

It is not appreciation of the artist that is necessary so much as appreciation of the art. It is difficult for an artist to live in an environment in which everything is judged by its utility, rather than by its intrinsic quality. The whole side of life of which art is the flower requires something which may be called disinterestedness, a capacity for direct enjoyment without thought of to-morrow's problems and difficulties. When people are amused by a joke they do not need to be persuaded that it will serve some important purpose. The same kind of direct pleasure is involved in any genuine appreciation of art. The struggle for life, the serious work of a trade or profession, is apt to make people too solemn for jokes and too preoccupied for art. The easing of the struggle, the diminution in the hours of work, and the lightening of the burden of existence, which would result from a better economic system, could hardly fail to increase the joy of life and the vital energy available for sheer delight in the world. And if this were achieved there would inevitably be more spontaneous pleasure in beautiful things, and more enjoyment of the work of artists. But none of these good results are to be expected from the mere removal of poverty: they all require also a diffused sense of freedom, and the absence of that feeling of oppression by a vast machine which now weighs down the individual spirit. I do not think State socialism can give this sense of freedom, but some other forms of socialism, which have absorbed what is true in anarchist teaching, can give it to a degree of which capitalism is wholly incapable.

A general sense of progress and achievement is

an immense stimulus to all forms of creative work. For this reason, a great deal will depend, not only in material ways, upon the question whether methods of production in industry and agriculture become stereotyped or continue to change rapidly as they have done during the last hundred years. Improved methods of production will be much more obviously than now to the interest of the community at large, when what every man receives is his due share of the total produce of labor. But there will probably not be any individuals with the same direct and intense interest in technical improvements as now belongs to the capitalist in manufacture. If the natural conservatism of the workers is not to prove stronger than their interest in increasing production, it will be necessary that, when better methods are introduced by the workers in any industry, part at least of the benefit should be allowed for a time to be retained by them. If this is done, it may be presumed that each Guild will be continually seeking for new processes or inventions, and will value those technical parts of scientific research which are useful for this purpose. With every improvement, the question will arise whether it is to be used to give more leisure or to increase the dividend of commodities. Where there is so much more leisure than there is now, there will be many more people with a knowledge of science or an understanding of art. The artist or scientific investigator will be far less cut off than he is at present from the average citizen, and this will almost inevitably be a stimulus to his creative energy.

I think we may fairly conclude that, from the point of view of all three requisites for art and science, namely, training, freedom, and appreciation, State socialism would largely fail to remove existing evils and would introduce new evils of its own; but Guild socialism, or even syndicalism, if it adopted a liberal policy toward those who preferred to work less than the usual number of hours at recognized occupations, might be immeasurably preferable to anything that is possible under the rule of capitalism. There are dangers, but they will all vanish if the importance of liberty is adequately acknowledged. In this as in nearly everything else, the road to all that is best is the road of freedom.

THE WORLD AS IT COULD BE MADE [1]

In the daily lives of most men and women, fear plays a greater part than hope: they are more filled with the thought of the possessions that others may take from them, than of the joy that they might create in their own lives and in the lives with which they come in contact.

It is not so that life should be lived.

Those whose lives are fruitful to themselves, to their friends, or to the world are inspired by hope and sustained by joy: they see in imagination the things that might be and the way in which they are to be brought into existence. In their private relations they are not preoccupied with anxiety lest they should lose such affection and respect as they receive: they are engaged in giving affection and respect freely, and the reward comes of itself without their seeking. In their work they are not haunted by jealousy of competitors, but concerned with the actual matter that has to be done. In politics, they do not spend time and passion defending unjust privileges of their class or nation, but they aim at making the world as a whole happier, less cruel, less full of conflict between rival greeds, and

[1] From *Proposed Roads to Freedom.*

more full of human beings whose growth has not been dwarfed and stunted by oppression.

A life lived in this spirit—the spirit that aims at creating rather than possessing—has a certain fundamental happiness, of which it cannot be wholly robbed by adverse circumstances. This is the way of life recommended in the Gospels, and by all the great teachers of the world. Those who have found it are freed from the tyranny of fear, since what they value most in their lives is not at the mercy of outside power. If all men could summon up the courage and the vision to live in this way in spite of obstacles and discouragement, there would be no need for the regeneration of the world to begin by political and economic reform: all that is needed in the way of reform would come automatically, without resistance, owing to the moral regeneration of individuals. But the teaching of Christ has been nominally accepted by the world for many centuries, and yet those who follow it are still persecuted as they were before the time of Constantine. Experience has proved that few are able to see through the apparent evils of an outcast's life to the inner joy that comes of faith and creative hope. If the domination of fear is to be overcome, it is not enough, as regards the mass of men, to preach courage and indifference to misfortune: it is necessary to remove the causes of fear, to make a good life no longer an unsuccessful one in a worldly sense, and to diminish the harm that can be inflicted upon those who are not wary in self-defense.

When we consider the evils in the lives we know of, we find that they may be roughly divided into three classes. There are, first, those due to physical nature: among these are death, pain and the difficulty of making the soil yield a subsistence. These we will call "physical evils." Second, we may put those that spring from defects in the character or aptitudes of the sufferer: among these are ignorance, lack of will, and violent passions. These we will call "evils of character." Third come those that depend upon the power of one individual or group over another: these comprise not only obvious tyranny, but all interference with free development, whether by force or by excessive mental influence such as may occur in education. These we will call "evils of power." A social system may be judged by its bearing upon these three kinds of evils.

The distinction between the three kinds cannot be sharply drawn. Purely physical evil is a limit, which we can never be sure of having reached: we cannot abolish death, but we can often postpone it by science, and it may ultimately become possible to secure that the great majority shall live till old age; we cannot wholly prevent pain, but we can diminish it indefinitely by securing a healthy life for all; we cannot make the earth yield its fruits in any abundance without labor, but we can diminish the amount of the labor and improve its conditions until it ceases to be an evil. Evils of character are often the result of physical evil in the shape of illness, and still more often the result of evils of power, since tyranny degrades both those who exercise it and (as a rule) those who suffer it. Evils of power are intensified by evils of character in those who have power, and by fear of the physical evil which is apt to be the lot of those who have no power. For all these reasons, the three sorts of evil are intertwined. Nevertheless, speaking broadly, we may distinguish among our misfortunes those which have their proximate cause in the material world, those which are mainly due to defects in ourselves, and those which spring from our being subject to the control of others.

The main methods of combating these evils are: for physical evils, science; for evils of character, education (in the widest sense) and a free outlet for all impulses that do not involve domination; for evils of power, the reform of the political and economic organization of society in such a way as to reduce to the lowest possible point the interference of one man with the life of another. We will begin with the third of these kinds of evil, because it is evils of power specially that Socialism and Anarchism have sought to remedy. Their protest against inequalities of wealth has rested mainly upon their sense of the evils arising from the power conferred

by wealth.   This point has been well stated by
Mr. G. D. H. Cole:—

What, I want to ask, is the fundamental evil in
our modern Society which we should set out to
abolish?

There are two possible answers to that question,
and I am sure that very many well-meaning people
would make the wrong one.   They would answer
POVERTY, when they ought to answer SLAVERY.
Face to face every day with the shameful contrasts
of riches and destitution, high dividends and low
wages, and painfully conscious of the futility of trying to adjust the balance by means of charity, private
or public, they would answer unhesitatingly that they
stand for the ABOLITION OF POVERTY.

Well and good!   On that issue every Socialist is
with them.   But their answer to my question is none
the less wrong.

Poverty is the symptom: slavery the disease.   The
extremes of riches and destitution follow inevitably
upon the extremes of license and bondage.   The
many are not enslaved because they are poor, they
are poor because they are enslaved.   Yet Socialists
have all too often fixed their eyes upon the material
misery of the poor without realizing that it rests upon
the spiritual degradation of the slave.[1]

I do not think any reasonable person can doubt
that the evils of power in the present system are
vastly greater than is necessary, nor that they might

[1] *Self-Government in Industry,* G. Bell & Sons, 1917, pp. 110-
111.

be immeasurably diminished by a suitable form of socialism. A few fortunate people, it is true, are now enabled to live freely on rent or interest, and they could hardly have more liberty under another system. But the great bulk, not only of the very poor, but of all sections of wage-earners and even of the professional classes, are the slaves of the need for getting money. Almost all are compelled to work so hard that they have little leisure for enjoyment or for pursuits outside their regular occupation. Those who are able to retire in later middle age are bored, because they have not learned how to fill their time when they are at liberty, and such interests as they once had apart from work have dried up. Yet these are the exceptionally fortunate: the majority have to work hard till old age, with the fear of destitution always before them, the richer ones dreading that they will be unable to give their children the education or the medical care that they consider desirable, the poorer ones often not far removed from starvation. And almost all who work have no voice in the direction of their work; throughout the hours of labor they are mere machines carrying out the will of a master. Work is usually done under disagreeable conditions, involving pain and physical hardship. The only motive to work is wages: the very idea that work might be a joy, like the work of the artist, is usually scouted as utterly Utopian.

But by far the greater part of these evils are wholly unnecessary. If the civilized portion of mankind could be induced to desire their own happiness more than another's pain, if they could be induced to work constructively for improvements which they would share with all the world rather than destructively to prevent other classes or nations from stealing a march on them, the whole system by which the world's work is done might be reformed root and branch within a generation.

From the point of view of liberty, what system would be the best? In what direction should we wish the forces of progress to move?

From this point of view, neglecting for the moment all other considerations, I have no doubt that the best system would be one not far removed from that advocated by Kropotkin, but rendered more practicable by the adoption of the main principles of Guild socialism. Since every point can be disputed, I will set down without argument the kind of organization of work that would seem best.

Education should be compulsory up to the age of sixteen, or perhaps longer; after that, it should be continued or not at the option of the pupil, but remain free (for those who desire it) up to at least the age of twenty-one. When education is finished no one should be *compelled* to work, and those who choose not to work should receive a bare livelihood, and be left completely free; but probably it would be desirable that there should be a strong public opinion in favor of work, so that only comparatively few should choose idleness. One great advantage of making idleness economically possible is that it would afford a powerful motive for making work not disagreeable; and no community where most work is disagreeable can be said to have found a solution of economic problems. I think it is reasonable to assume that few would choose idleness, in view of the fact that even now at least nine out of ten of those who have (say) £100 a year from investments prefer to increase their income by paid work.

Coming now to that great majority who will not choose idleness, I think we may assume that, with the help of science, and by the elimination of the vast amount of unproductive work involved in internal and international competition, the whole community could be kept in comfort by means of four hours' work a day. It is already being urged by experienced employers that their employees can actually produce as much in a six-hour day as they can when they work eight hours. In a world where there is a much higher level of technical instruction than there is now the same tendency will be accentuated. People will be taught not only, as at present, one trade, or one small portion of a trade, but several trades, so that they can vary their occupation according to the seasons and the fluctuations of demand. Every industry will be self-governing as regards all its internal affairs, and even separate factories will decide for themselves all questions that only concern those who work in them. There will not be a capitalist management, as at present, but management by elected representatives, as in politics. Relations between different groups of producers will be settled by the Guild Congress, matters concerning the community as the inhabitants of a certain area will continue to be decided by Parliament, while all disputes between Parliament and the Guild Congress will be decided by a body composed of representatives of both in equal numbers.

Payment will not be made, as at present, only for work actually required and performed, but for willingness to work. This system is already adopted in much of the better paid work: a man occupies a certain position, and retains it even at times when there happens to be very little to do. The dread of unemployment and loss of livelihood will no longer haunt men like a nightmare. Whether all who are willing to work will be paid equally, or whether exceptional skill will still command exceptional pay, is a matter which may be left to each Guild to decide for itself. An opera singer who received no more pay than a scene-shifter might choose to be a scene-shifter until the system was changed: if so, higher pay would probably be found necessary. But if it were freely voted by the Guild, it could hardly constitute a grievance.

Whatever might be done toward making work agreeable, it is to be presumed that some trades would always remain unpleasant. Men could be attracted into these by higher pay or shorter hours, instead of being driven into them by destitution. The community would then have a strong economic motive for finding ways of diminishing the disagreeableness of these exceptional trades.

There would still have to be money, or something analogous to it, in any community such as we are imagining. The anarchist plan of a free distribution of the total produce of work in equal shares does not get rid of the need for some standard of exchange value, since one man will choose to take his share in one form and another in another. When the day comes for distributing luxuries, old ladies will not want their quota of cigars, nor young men their just proportion of lap-dog; this will make it necessary to know how many cigars are the equivalent of one lap-dog. Much the simplest way is to pay an income, as at present, and allow relative values to be adjusted according to demand. But if actual coin were paid, a man might hoard it and in time become a capitalist. To prevent this, it would be best to pay notes available only during a certain period, say one year from the date of issue. This would enable a man to save up for his annual holiday, but not to save indefinitely.

There is a very great deal to be said for the

anarchist plan of allowing necessaries, and all commodities that can easily be produced in quantities adequate to any possible demand, to be given away freely to all who ask for them, in any amounts they may require. The question whether this plan should be adopted is, to my mind, a purely technical one: would it be, in fact, possible to adopt it without much waste and consequent diversion of labor to the production of necessaries when it might be more usefully employed otherwise? I have not the means of answering this question, but I think it exceedingly probable that, sooner or later, with the continued improvement in the methods of production, this anarchist plan will become feasible; and when it does, it certainly ought to be adopted.

Women in domestic work, whether married or unmarried, will receive pay as they would if they were in industry. This will secure the complete economic independence of wives, which is difficult to achieve in any other way, since mothers of young children ought not to be expected to work outside the home.

The expense of children will not fall, as at present, on the parents. They will receive, like adults, their share of necessaries, and their education will be free.[1] There is no longer to be the present competition for scholarships among the abler children: they

[1] Some may fear that the result would be an undue increase of population, but such fears I believe to be groundless. See Chapter IV, *Work and Pay*. Also, Chapter VI of *Why Men Fight*.

will not be imbued with the competitive spirit from infancy, or forced to use their brains to an unnatural degree with consequent listlessness and lack of health in later life. Education will be far more diversified than at present; greater care will be taken to adapt it to the needs of different types of young people. There will be more attempts to encourage initiative in young pupils, and less desire to fill their minds with a set of beliefs and mental habits regarded as desirable by the State, chiefly because they help to preserve the *status quo*. For the great majority of children it will probably be found desirable to have much more outdoor education in the country. And for older boys and girls whose interests are not intellectual or artistic, technical education, undertaken in a liberal spirit, is far more useful in promoting mental activity than book-learning which they regard (however falsely) as wholly useless except for purposes of examination. The really useful education is that which follows the direction of the child's own instinctive interests, supplying knowledge for which it is seeking, not dry, detailed information wholly out of relation to its spontaneous desires.

Government and law will still exist in our community, but both will be reduced to a minimum. There will still be acts which will be forbidden—for example, murder. But very nearly the whole of that part of the criminal law which deals with property will have become obsolete, and many of the motives which now produce murders will be no longer operative. Those who nevertheless still do commit crimes will not be blamed or regarded as wicked; they will be regarded as unfortunate, and kept in some kind of mental hospital until it is thought that they are no longer a danger. By education and freedom and the abolition of private capital the number of crimes can be made exceedingly small. By the method of individual curative treatment it will generally be possible to secure that a man's first offense shall also be his last, except in the case of lunatics and the feeble-minded, for whom of course a more prolonged but not less kindly detention may be necessary.

Government may be regarded as consisting of two parts: the one, the decisions of the community or its recognized organs; the other, the enforcing of those decisions upon all who resist them. The first part is not objected to by anarchists. The second part, in an ordinary civilized State, may remain entirely in the background: those who have resisted a new law while it was being debated will, as a rule, submit to it when it is passed, because resistance is generally useless in a settled and orderly community. But the possibility of governmental force remains, and indeed is the very reason for the submission which makes force unnecessary. If, as anarchists desire, there were no use of force by government, the majority could still band themselves together and use force against the minority. The only difference would be that their army or their police force would be *ad hoc*, instead of being permanent and professional. The result of this would be that every one would have to learn how to fight, for fear a well-drilled minority should seize power and establish an old-fashioned oligarchic State. Thus the aim of the anarchists seems hardly likely to be achieved by the methods which they advocate.

The reign of violence in human affairs, whether within a country or in its external relations, can only be prevented, if we have not been mistaken, by an authority able to declare all use of force except by itself illegal, and strong enough to be obviously capable of making all other use of force futile, except when it could secure the support of public opinion as a defense of freedom or a resistance to injustice. Such an authority exists within a country: it is the State. But in international affairs it remains to be created. The difficulties are stupendous, but they must be overcome if the world is to be saved from periodical wars, each more destructive than any of its predecessors. Whether, after this war, a League of Nations will be formed, and will be capable of performing this task, it is as yet impossible to fore-tell. However that may be, some method of pre-venting wars will have to be established before our Utopia becomes possible. When once men *believe* that the world is safe from war, the whole difficulty will be solved: there will then no longer be any serious resistance to the disbanding of national armies and navies, and the substitution for them of a small international force for protection against uncivilized races. And when that stage has been reached, peace will be virtually secure.

The practice of government by majorities, which anarchists criticize, is in fact open to most of the objections which they urge against it. Still more objectionable is the power of the executive in matters vitally affecting the happiness of all, such as peace and war. But neither can be dispensed with suddenly. There are, however, two methods of diminishing the harm done by them: (1) Government by majorities can be made less oppressive by devolution, by placing the decision of questions primarily affecting only a section of the community in the hands of that section, rather than of a Central Chamber. In this way, men are no longer forced to submit to decisions made in a hurry by people mostly ignorant of the matter in hand and not personally interested. Autonomy for internal affairs should be given, not only to areas, but to all groups, such as industries or Churches, which have important common interests not shared by the rest of the community. (2) The great powers vested in the executive of a modern State are chiefly due to the frequent need of rapid decisions, especially as regards foreign affairs. If the danger of war were practically eliminated, more cumbrous but less autocratic methods would be possible, and the Legislature might recover many of the powers which the executive has usurped. By these two methods, the intensity of the interfer- ence with liberty involved in government can be gradually diminished. Some interference, and even some danger of unwarranted and despotic interfer- ence, is of the essence of government, and must re- main so long as government remains. But until men are less prone to violence than they are now, a cer- tain degree of governmental force seems the lesser of two evils. We may hope, however, that if once the danger of war is at an end, men's violent im- pulses will gradually grow less, the more so as, in that case, it will be possible to diminish enormously the individual power which now makes rulers auto- cratic and ready for almost any act of tyranny in order to crush opposition. The development of a world where even governmental force has become unnecessary (except against lunatics) must be grad- ual. But as a gradual process it is perfectly pos- sible; and when it has been completed we may hope to see the principles of anarchism embodied in the management of communal affairs.

How will the economic and political system that we have outlined bear on the evils of character? I believe the effect will be quite extraordinarily beneficent.

The process of leading men's thought and imagi- nation away from the use of force will be greatly accelerated by the abolition of the capitalist system, provided it is not succeeded by a form of State socialism in which officials have enormous power. At present, the capitalist has more control over the lives of others than any man ought to have; his friends have authority in the State; his economic power is the pattern for political power. In a world where all men and women enjoy economic freedom, there will not be the same habit of command, nor, consequently, the same love of despotism; a gentler type of character than that now prevalent will gradually grow up. Men are formed by their circumstances, not born ready-made. The bad effect of the present economic system on character, and the immensely better effect to be expected from communal ownership, are among the strongest reasons for advocating the change.

In the world as we have been imagining it, economic fear and most economic hope will be alike removed out of life. No one will be haunted by the dread of poverty or driven into ruthlessness by the hope of wealth. There will not be the distinction of social classes which now plays such an immense part in life. The unsuccessful professional man will not live in terror lest his children should sink in the scale; the aspiring employee will not be looking forward to the day when he can become a sweater in his turn. Ambitious young men will have to dream other day-dreams than that of business success and wealth wrung out of the ruin of competitors and the degradation of labor. In such a world, most of the nightmares that lurk in the background of men's minds will no longer exist; on the other hand, ambition and the desire to excel will have to take nobler forms than those that are encouraged by a commercial society. All those activities that really confer benefits upon mankind will be open, not only to the fortunate few, but to all who have sufficient ambition and native aptitude. Science, labor-saving inventions, technical progress of all kinds, may be confidently expected to flourish far more than at present, since they will be the road to honor, and honor will have to replace money among those of the young who desire to achieve success. Whether art will flourish in a socialistic community depends upon the form of socialism adopted; if the State, or any public authority (no matter what), insists upon controlling art, and only licensing those whom it regards as proficient, the result will be disaster. But if there is real freedom, allowing every man who so desires to take up an artist's career at the cost of some sacrifice of comfort, it is likely that the atmosphere of hope, and the absence of economic compulsion, will lead to a much smaller waste of talent than is involved in our present system, and to a much less degree of crushing of impulse in the mills of the struggle for life.

When elementary needs have been satisfied, the

serious happiness of most men depends upon two things: their work, and their human relations. In the world that we have been picturing, work will be free, not excessive, full of the interest that belongs to a collective enterprise in which there is rapid progress, with something of the delight of creation even for the humblest unit. And in human relations the gain will be just as great as in work. The only human relations that have value are those that are rooted in mutual freedom, where there is no domination and no slavery, no tie except affection, no economic or conventional necessity to preserve the external show when the inner life is dead. One of the most horrible things about commercialism is the way in which it poisons the relations of men and women. The evils of prostitution are generally recognized, but, great as they are, the effect of economic conditions on marriage seems to me even worse. There is not infrequently, in marriage, a suggestion of purchase, of acquiring a woman on condition of keeping her in a certain standard of material comfort. Often and often, a marriage hardly differs from prostitution except by being harder to escape from. The whole basis of these evils is economic. Economic causes make marriage a matter of bargain and contract, in which affection is quite secondary, and its absence constitutes no recognized reason for liberation. Marriage should be a free, spontaneous meeting of mutual instinct, filled with happiness not unmixed with a feeling akin to awe: it should involve that degree of respect of each for the other that makes even the most trifling interference with liberty an utter impossibility, and a common life enforced by one against the will of the other an unthinkable thing of deep horror. It is not so that marriage is conceived by lawyers who make settlements, or by priests who give the name of "sacrament" to an institution which pretends to find something sanctifiable in the brutal lusts or drunken cruelties of a legal husband. It is not in a spirit of freedom that marriage is conceived by most men and women at present: the law makes it an opportunity for indulgence of the desire to interfere, where each submits to some loss of his or her own liberty, for the pleasure of curtailing the liberty of the other. And the atmosphere of private property makes it more difficult than it otherwise would be for any better ideal to take root.

It is not so that human relations will be conceived when the evil heritage of economic slavery has ceased to mold our instincts. Husbands and wives, parents and children, will be only held together by affection: where that has died, it will be recognized that nothing worth preserving is left. Because affection will be free, men and women will not find in private life an outlet and stimulus to the love of domineering, but all that is creative in their love will have the freer scope. Reverence for whatever makes the soul in those who are loved will be less rare than it is now:

nowadays, many men love their wives in the way in which they love mutton, as something to devour and destroy. But in the love that goes with reverence there is a joy of quite another order than any to be found by mastery, a joy which satisfies the spirit and not only the instincts; and satisfaction of instinct and spirit at once is necessary to a happy life, or indeed to any existence that is to bring out the best impulses of which a man or woman is capable.

In the world which we should wish to see, there will be more joy of life than in the drab tragedy of modern everyday existence. After early youth, as things are, most men are bowed down by forethought, no longer capable of light-hearted gayety, but only of a kind of solemn jollification by the clock at the appropriate hours. The advice to "become as little children" would be good for many people in many respects, but it goes with another precept, "take no thought for the morrow," which is hard to obey in a competitive world. There is often in men of science, even when they are quite old, something of the simplicity of a child: their absorption in abstract thought has held them aloof from the world, and respect for their work has led the world to keep them alive in spite of their innocence. Such men have succeeded in living as all men ought to be able to live; but as things are, the economic struggle makes their way of life impossible for the great majority.

What are we to say, lastly, of the effect of our

projected world upon physical evil? Will there be less illness than there is at present? Will the produce of a given amount of labor be greater? Or will population press upon the limits of subsistence, as Malthus taught in order to refute Godwin's optimism?

I think the answer to all these questions turns, in the end, upon the degree of intellectual vigor to be expected in a community which has done away with the spur of economic competition. Will men in such a world become lazy and apathetic? Will they cease to think? Will those who do think find themselves confronted with an even more impenetrable wall of unreflecting conservatism than that which confronts them at present? These are important questions; for it is ultimately to science that mankind must look for their success in combating physical evils.

If the other conditions that we have postulated can be realized, it seems almost certain that there must be less illness than there is at present. Population will no longer be congested in slums; children will have far more of fresh air and open country; the hours of work will be only such as are wholesome, not excessive and exhausting as they are at present.

As for the progress of science, that depends very largely upon the degree of intellectual liberty existing in the new society. If all science is organized and supervised by the State, it will rapidly become stereotyped and dead. Fundamental advances will not be made, because, until they have been made, they will seem too doubtful to warrant the expenditure of public money upon them. Authority will be in the hands of the old, especially of men who have achieved scientific eminence; such men will be hostile to those among the young who do not flatter them by agreeing with their theories. Under a bureaucratic State socialism it is to be feared that science would soon cease to be progressive and acquire a medieval respect for authority.

But under a freer system, which would enable all kinds of groups to employ as many men of science as they chose, and would allow the "vagabond's wage" to those who desired to pursue some study so new as to be wholly unrecognized, there is every reason to think that science would flourish as it has never done hitherto.[1]   And, if that were the case, I do not believe that any other obstacle would exist to the physical possibility of our system.

The question of the number of hours of work necessary to produce general material comfort is partly technical, partly one of organization. We may assume that there would no longer be unproductive labor spent on armaments, national defense, advertisements, costly luxuries for the very rich, or any of the other futilities incidental to our competitive system. If each industrial guild secured for a term of years the advantages, or part of the ad-

[1] See the discussion of this question under "Science and Art under Socialism."

vantages, of any new invention or methods which it introduced, it is pretty certain that every encouragement would be given to technical progress. The life of a discoverer or inventor is in itself agreeable: those who adopt it, as things are now, are seldom much actuated by economic motives, but rather by the interest of the work together with the hope of honor; and these motives would operate more widely than they do now, since fewer people would be prevented from obeying them by economic necessities. And there is no doubt that intellect would work more keenly and creatively in a world where instinct was less thwarted, where the joy of life was greater, and where consequently there would be more vitality in men than there is at present.

There remains the population question, which, ever since the time of Malthus, has been the last refuge of those to whom the possibility of a better world is disagreeable. But this question is now a very different one from what it was a hundred years ago. The decline of the birth-rate in all civilized countries, which is pretty certain to continue, whatever economic system is adopted, suggests that, especially when the probable effects of the war are taken into account, the population of Western Europe is not likely to increase very much beyond its present level, and that of America is likely only to increase through immigration. Negroes may continue to increase in the tropics, but are not likely to be a serious menace to the white inhabitants of temperate regions. There remains, of course, the Yellow Peril; but by the time that begins to be serious it is quite likely that the birth-rate will also have begun to decline among the races of Asia. If not, there are other means of dealing with this question; and in any case the whole matter is too conjectural to be set up seriously as a bar to our hopes. I conclude that, though no certain forecast is possible, there is not any valid reason for regarding the possible increase of population as a serious obstacle to socialism.

Our discussion has led us to the belief that the communal ownership of land and capital, which constitutes the characteristic doctrine of socialism and anarchist communism, is a necessary step toward the removal of the evils from which the world suffers at present and the creation of such a society as any humane man must wish to see realized. But, though a necessary step, socialism alone is by no means sufficient. There are various forms of socialism: the form in which the State is the employer, and all who work receive wages from it, involves dangers of tyranny and interference with progress which would make it, if possible, even worse than the present *régime*. On the other hand, anarchism, which avoids the dangers of State socialism, has dangers and difficulties of its own, which make it probable that, within any reasonable period of time, it could not last long even if it were established. Nevertheless, it remains an ideal to which we should wish to approach as nearly as possible, and which, in some distant age, we hope may be reached completely. Syndicalism shares many of the defects of anarchism, and, like it, would prove unstable, since the need of a central government would make itself felt almost at once.

The system we have advocated is a form of Guild socialism, leaning more, perhaps, towards anarchism than the official Guildsman would wholly approve. It is in the matters that politicians usually ignore— science and art, human relations, and the joy of life—that anarchism is strongest, and it is chiefly for the sake of these things that we included such more or less anarchist proposals as the "vaga- bond's wage." It is by its effects outside economics and politics, at least as much as by effects inside them, that a social system should be judged. And if socialism ever comes, it is only likely to prove benefi- cent if non-economic goods are valued and con- sciously pursued.

The world that we must seek is a world in which the creative spirit is alive, in which life is an adven- ture full of joy and hope, based rather upon the im- pulse to construct than upon the desire to retain what we possess or to seize what is possessed by others. It must be a world in which affection has free play, in which love is purged of the instinct for domination, in which cruelty and envy have been dis pelled by happiness and the unfettered development of all the instincts that build up life and fill it with mental delights. Such a world is possible; it waits only for men to wish to create it.

Meantime, the world in which we exist has other aims. But it will pass away, burned up in the fire of its own hot passions; and from its ashes will spring a new and younger world, full of fresh hope, with the light of morning in its eyes.

THE AIMS OF EDUCATION [1]

Before considering how to educate, it is well to be clear as to the sort of result which we wish to achieve. Dr. Arnold wanted "humbleness of mind," a quality not possessed by Aristotle's "magnanimous man." Nietzsche's ideal is not that of Christianity. No more is Kant's: for while Christ enjoins love, Kant teaches that no action of which love is the motive can be truly virtuous. And even people who agree as to the ingredients of a good character may differ as to their relative importance. One man will emphasize courage, another learning, another kindliness, and another rectitude. One man, like the elder Brutus, will put duty to the State above family affection; another, like Confucius, will put family affection first. All these divergences will produce differences as to education. We must have some conception of the kind of person we wish to produce, before we can have any definite opinion as to the education which we consider best.

Of course an educator may be foolish, in the sense that he produces results other than those at which he was aiming. Uriah Heep was the outcome of lessons

[1] From *Education and the Good Life*.

in humility at a Charity School, which had had an effect quite different from what was intended. But in the main the ablest educators have been fairly successful. Take as examples the Chinese literati, the modern Japanese, the Jesuits, Dr. Arnold, and the men who direct the policy of the American public schools. All these, in their various ways, have been highly successful. The results aimed at in the different cases were utterly different, but in the main the results were achieved. It may be worth while to spend a few moments on these different systems, before attempting to decide what we should ourselves regard as the aims which education should have in view.

Traditional Chinese education was, in some respects, very similar to that of Athens in its best days. Athenian boys were made to learn Homer by heart from beginning to end; Chinese boys were made to learn the Confucian classics with similar thoroughness. Athenians were taught a kind of reverence for the gods which consisted in outward observances, and placed no barrier in the way of free intellectual speculation. Similarly the Chinese were taught certain rites connected with ancestor-worship, but were by no means obliged to have the beliefs which the rites would seem to imply. An easy and elegant skepticism was the attitude expected of an educated adult: anything might be discussed, but it was a trifle vulgar to reach very positive conclusions. Opinions should be such as could be discussed pleasantly at dinner, not such as men would fight for. Carlyle calls Plato "a lordly Athenian gentleman, very much at his ease in Zion." This characteristic of being "at his ease in Zion" is also found in Chinese sages, and is, as a rule, absent from the sages produced by Christian civilizations, except when, like Goethe, they have deeply imbibed the spirit of Hellenism. The Athenians and the Chinese alike wished to enjoy life, and had a conception of enjoyment which was refined by an exquisite sense of beauty.

There were, however, great differences between the two civilizations, owing to the fact that, broadly speaking, the Greeks were energetic and the Chinese were lazy. The Greeks devoted their energies to art and science and mutual extermination, in all of which they achieved unprecedented success. Politics and patriotism afforded practical outlets for Greek energy: when a politician was ousted, he led a band of exiles to attack his native city. When a Chinese official was disgraced, he retired to the hills and wrote poems on the pleasures of country life. Accordingly the Greek civilization destroyed itself, but the Chinese civilization could only be destroyed from without. These differences, however, seem not wholly attributable to education, since Confucianism in Japan never produced the indolent cultured skepticism which characterized the Chinese literati, except in the Kyoto nobility, who formed a kind of Faubourg Saint Germain.

Chinese education produced stability and art; it failed to produce progress or science. Perhaps this may be taken as what is to be expected of skepticism. Passionate beliefs produce either progress or disaster, not stability. Science, even when it attacks traditional beliefs, has beliefs of its own, and can scarcely flourish in an atmosphere of literary skepticism. In a pugnacious world which has been unified by modern inventions, energy is needed for national self-preservation. And without science, democracy is impossible: the Chinese civilization was confined to the small percentage of educated men, and the Greek civilization was based on slavery. For these reasons, the traditional education of China is not suited to the modern world, and has been abandoned by the Chinese themselves. Cultivated eighteenth century gentlemen, who in some respects resembled Chinese literati, have become impossible for the same reasons.

Modern Japan affords the clearest illustration of a tendency which is prominent among all the Great Powers—the tendency to make national greatness the supreme purpose of education. The aim of Japanese education is to produce citizens who shall be devoted to the State through the training of their passions, and useful to it through the knowledge they have acquired. I cannot sufficiently praise the skill

with which this double purpose has been pursued.
Ever since the advent of Commodore Perry's squad-
ron, the Japanese have been in a situation in which
self-preservation was very difficult; their success affords a justification of their methods, unless we are
to hold that self-preservation itself may be culpable.
But only a desperate situation could have justified
their educational methods, which would have been
culpable in any nation not in imminent peril. The
Shinto religion, which must not be called in question
even by university professors, involves history which
is just as dubious as Genesis; the Dayton trial pales
into insignificance beside the theological tyranny in
Japan. There is an equal ethical tyranny: nationalism, filial piety, Mikado-worship, etc., must
not be called in question, and therefore many
kinds of progress are scarcely possible. The great
danger of a cast-iron system of this sort is that
it may provoke revolution as the sole method
of progress. This danger is real, though not immediate, and is largely caused by the educational system.

We have thus in modern Japan a defect opposite
to that of ancient China. Whereas the Chinese literati were too skeptical and lazy, the products of
Japanese education are likely to be too dogmatic and
energetic. Neither acquiescence in skepticism nor
acquiescence in dogma is what education should produce. What it should produce is a belief that knowl-

edge is attainable in a measure, though with difficulty; that much of what passes for knowledge at any given time is likely to be more or less mistaken, but that the mistakes can be rectified by care and industry. In acting upon our beliefs, we should be very cautious where a small error would mean disaster; nevertheless it is upon our beliefs that we must act. This state of mind is rather difficult: it requires a high degree of intellectual culture without emotional atrophy. But though difficult it is not impossible; it is in fact the scientific temper. Knowledge, like other good things, is difficult, but not impossible; the dogmatist forgets the difficulty, the skeptic denies the possibility. Both are mistaken, and their errors, when widespread, produce social disaster.

The Jesuits, like the modern Japanese, made the mistake of subordinating education to the welfare of an institution—in their case, the Catholic Church. They were not concerned primarily with the good of the particular pupil, but with making him a means to the good of the Church. If we accept their theology, we cannot blame them: to save souls from hell is more important than any merely terrestrial concern, and is only to be achieved by the Catholic Church. But those who do not accept this dogma will judge Jesuit education by its results. These results, it is true, were sometimes quite as undesired as Uriah Heep: Voltaire was a product of Jesuit methods. But on the whole, and for a long time, the intended results were achieved: the counter-reformation, and the collapse of Protestantism in France, must be largely attributed to Jesuit efforts. To achieve these ends, they made art sentimental, thought superficial, and morals loose; in the end, the French Revolution was needed to sweep away the harm that they had done. In education, their crime was that they were not actuated by love of their pupils, but by ulterior ends.

Dr. Arnold's system, which has remained in force in English public schools to the present day, had another defect, namely that it was aristocratic. The aim was to train men for positions of authority and power, whether at home or in distant parts of the empire. An aristocracy, if it is to survive, needs certain virtues; these were to be imparted at school. The product was to be energetic, stoical, physically fit, possessed of certain unalterable beliefs, with high standards of rectitude, and convinced that it had an important mission in the world. To a surprising extent, these results were achieved. Intellect was sacrificed to them, because intellect might produce doubt. Sympathy was sacrificed, because it might interfere with governing "inferior" races or classes. Kindliness was sacrificed for the sake of toughness; imagination, for the sake of firmness. In an unchanging world, the result might have been a permanent aristocracy, possessing the merits and defects of the Spartans. But aristocracy is out of date, and subject populations will no longer obey even the most wise and virtuous rulers. The rulers are driven into brutality, and brutality further encourages revolt. The complexity of the modern world increasingly requires intelligence, and Dr. Arnold sacrificed intelligence to "virtue." The battle of Waterloo may have been won on the playing-fields of Eton, but the British Empire is being lost there. The modern world needs a different type, with more imaginative sympathy, more intellectual suppleness, less belief in bulldog courage and more belief in technical knowledge. The administrator of the future must be the servant of free citizens, not the benevolent ruler of admiring subjects. The aristocratic tradition embedded in British higher education is its bane. Perhaps this tradition can be eliminated gradually; perhaps the older educational institutions will be found incapable of adapting themselves. As to that, I do not venture an opinion.

The American public schools achieve successfully a task never before attempted on a large scale: the task of transforming a heterogeneous selection of mankind into a homogeneous nation. This is done so ably, and is on the whole such a beneficent work, that on the balance great praise is due to those who accomplish it. But America, like Japan, is placed in a peculiar situation, and what the special circumstances justify is not necessarily an ideal to be followed everywhere and always. America has had certain advantages and certain difficulties. Among the advantages were· a higher standard of wealth; freedom from the danger of defeat in war; comparative absence of cramping traditions inherited from the Middle Ages. Immigrants found in America a generally diffused sentiment of democracy and an advanced stage of industrial technique. These, I think, are the two chief reasons why almost all of them came to admire America more than their native countries. But actual immigrants, as a rule, retain a dual patriotism: in European struggles they continue to take passionately the side of the nation to which they originally belonged. Their children, on the contrary, lose all loyalty to the country from which their parents have come, and become merely and simply Americans. The attitude of the parents is attributable to the general merits of America; that of the children is very largely determined by their school education. It is only the contribution of the school that concerns us.

In so far as the school can rely upon the genuine merits of America, there is no need to associate the teaching of American patriotism with the inculcation of false standards. But where the Old World is superior to the New, it becomes necessary to instill a contempt for genuine excellences. The intellectual level in Western Europe and the artistic level in Eastern Europe are, on the whole, higher than in

America. Throughout Western Europe, except in Spain and Portugal, there is less theological superstition than in America. In almost all European countries the individual is less subject to herd domination than in America: his inner freedom is greater even where his political freedom is less. In these respects, the American public schools do harm. The harm is essential to the teaching of an exclusive American patriotism. The harm, as with the Japanese and the Jesuits, comes from regarding the pupils as means to an end, not as ends in themselves. The teacher should love his children better than his State or his Church; otherwise he is not an ideal teacher.

When I say that pupils should be regarded as ends, not as means, I may be met by the retort that, after all, everybody is more important as a means than as an end. What a man is as an end perishes when he dies; what he produces as a means continues to the end of time. We cannot deny this, but we can deny the consequences deduced from it. A man's importance as a means may be for good or for evil; the remote effects of human actions are so uncertain that a wise man will tend to dismiss them from his calculations. Broadly speaking, good men have good effects, and bad men bad effects. This, of course, is not an invariable law of nature. A bad man may murder a tyrant because he has committed crimes which the tyrant intends to punish; the effects of his act may be good, though he and his act are bad. Nevertheless, as a broad general rule, a community of men and women who are intrinsically excellent will have better effects than one composed of people who are ignorant and malevolent. Apart from such considerations, children and young people feel instinctively the difference between those who genuinely wish them well and those who regard them merely as raw material for some scheme. Neither character nor intelligence will develop as well or as freely where the teacher is deficient in love; and love of this kind consists essentially in *feeling* the child as an end. We all have this feeling about ourselves: we desire good things for ourselves without first demanding a proof that some great purpose will be furthered by our obtaining them. Every ordinarily affectionate parent feels the same sort of thing about his or her children. Parents want their children to grow, to be strong and healthy, to do well at school, and so on, in just the same way in which they want things for themselves; no effort of self-denial and no abstract principle of justice is involved in taking trouble about such matters. This parental instinct is not always strictly confined to one's own children. In its diffused form, it must exist in any one who is to be a good teacher of little boys and girls. As the pupils grow older, it grows less important. But only those who possess it can be trusted to draw up schemes of education. Those who regard it as one of the purposes of male education to produce men willing to kill and be killed for frivolous reasons are clearly deficient in diffused parental feeling; yet they control education in all civilized countries except Denmark and China.

But it is not enough that the educator should love the young; it is necessary also that he should have a right conception of human excellence. Cats teach their kittens to catch mice and play with them; militarists do likewise with the human young. The cat loves the kitten, but not the mouse; the militarist may love his own son, but not the sons of his country's enemies. Even those who love all mankind may err through a wrong conception of the good life. I shall try, therefore, before going any further, to give an idea of what I consider excellent in men and women, quite without regard to practicality, or to the educational methods by which it might be brought into being. Such a picture will help us afterwards, when we come to consider the details of education; we shall know the direction in which we wish to move.

We must first make a distinction: some qualities are desirable in a certain proportion of mankind, others are desirable universally. We want artists, but we also want men of science. We want great administrators, but we also want plowmen and millers and bakers. The qualities which produce a man of great eminence in some one direction are often such as might be undesirable if they were universal. Shelley describes the day's work of a poet as follows:

> *He will watch from dawn to gloom*
> *The lake-reflected sun illume*
> *The honey-bees in the ivy bloom,*
> *Nor heed nor see what things they be.*

These habits are praiseworthy in a poet, but not—shall we say—in a postman. We cannot therefore frame our education with a view to giving every one the temperament of a poet. But some characteristics are universally desirable, and it is these alone that I shall consider at this stage.

I make no distinction whatever between male and female excellence. A certain amount of occupational training is desirable for a woman who is to have the care of babies, but that only involves the same sort of difference as there is between a farmer and a miller. It is in no degree fundamental, and does not demand consideration at our present level.

I will take four characteristics which seem to me jointly to form the basis of an ideal character: vitality, courage, sensitiveness, and intelligence. I do not suggest that this list is complete, but I think it carries us a good way. Moreover I firmly believe that, by proper physical, emotional, and intellectual care of the young, these qualities could all be made very common. I shall consider each in turn.

Vitality is rather a physiological than a mental characteristic; it is presumably always present where there is perfect health, but it tends to ebb with advancing years, and gradually dwindles to nothing in old age. In vigorous children it quickly rises to a maximum before they reach school age, and then tends to be diminished by education. Where it exists, there is pleasure in feeling alive, quite apart from any specific pleasant circumstances. It heightens pleasures and diminishes pains. It makes it easy to take an interest in whatever occurs, and thus promotes objectivity, which is an essential of sanity. Human beings are prone to become absorbed in themselves, unable to be interested in what they see and hear or in anything outside their own skins. This is a great misfortune to themselves, since it entails at best boredom and at worst melancholia; it is also a fatal barrier to usefulness, except in very exceptional cases. Vitality promotes interest in the outside world; it also promotes the power of hard work. Moreover it is a safeguard against envy, because it makes one's own existence pleasant. As envy is one of the great sources of human misery, this is a very important merit in vitality. Many bad qualities are of course compatible with vitality— for example, those of a healthy tiger. And many of the best qualities are compatible with its absence: Newton and Locke, for example, had very little. Both these men, however, had irritabilities and envies from which better health would have set them free. Probably the whole of Newton's controversy with Leibniz, which ruined English mathematics for over a hundred years, would have been avoided if Newton had been robust and able to enjoy ordinary pleasures. In spite of its limitations, therefore, I reckon vitality among the qualities which it is important that all men should possess.

Courage—the second quality on our list—has several forms, and all of them are complex. Absence of fear is one thing, and the power of controlling fear is another. And absence of fear, in turn, is one thing when the fear is rational, another when it is irrational. Absence of irrational fear is clearly good; so is the power of controlling fear. But absence of rational fear is a matter as to which debate is possible. However, I shall postpone this question until I have said something about the other forms of courage.

Irrational fear plays an extraordinarily large part in the instinctive emotional life of most people. In its pathological forms, as persecution mania, anxiety complex, or what not, it is treated by alienists. But in milder forms it is common among those who are considered sane. It may be a general feeling that there are dangers about, more correctly termed "anxiety," or a specific dread of things that are not dangerous, such as mice or spiders.[1] It used to be

[1] On fear and anxiety in childhood, see e.g. William Stern, *Psychology of Early Childhood*, Chap. XXXV.

supposed that many fears were instinctive, but this is now questioned by most investigators. There are apparently a few instinctive fears—for instance, of loud noises—but the great majority arise either from experience or from suggestion. Fear of the dark, for example, seems to be entirely due to suggestion. Most vertebrates, there is reason to think, do not feel instinctive fear of their natural enemies, but catch this emotion from their elders. When human beings bring them up by hand, the fears usual among the species are found to be absent. But fear is exceedingly infectious: children catch it from their elders even when their elders are not aware of having shown it. Timidity in mothers or nurses is very quickly imitated by children through suggestion. Hitherto, men have thought it attractive in women to be full of irrational terrors, because it gave men a chance to seem protective without incurring any real danger. But the sons of these men have acquired the terrors from their mothers, and have had to be afterwards trained to regain a courage which they need never have lost if their fathers had not desired to despise their mothers. The harm that has been done by the subjection of women is incalculable; this matter of fear affords only one incidental illustration.

I am not at the moment discussing the methods by which fear and anxiety may be minimized; that is a matter which I shall consider later. There is, however, one question which arises at this stage, namely: can we be content to deal with fear by means of repression, or must we find some more radical cure? Traditionally, aristocracies have been trained not to show fear, while subject nations, classes, and sexes have been encouraged to remain cowardly. The test of courage has been crudely behavioristic: a man must not run away in battle; he must be proficient in "manly" sports; he must retain self-command in fires, shipwrecks, earthquakes, etc. He must not merely do the right thing, but he must avoid turning pale, or trembling, or gasping for breath, or giving any other easily observed sign of fear. All this I regard as of great importance: I should wish to see courage cultivated in all nations, in all classes, and in both sexes. But when the method adopted is repressive, it entails the evils always associated with that practice. Shame and disgrace have always been potent weapons in producing the appearance of courage; but in fact they merely cause a conflict of terrors, in which it is hoped that the dread of public condemnation will be the stronger. "Always speak the truth except when something frightens you" was a maxim taught to me in childhood. I cannot admit the exception. Fear should be overcome not only in action, but in feeling; and not only in conscious feeling, but in the unconscious as well. The purely external victory over fear, which satisfies the aristocratic code, leaves the impulse operative under ground, and produces evil twisted reactions which are not recognized as the offspring of terror. I am not thinking of "shell shock," in which the connection with fear is obvious. I am thinking rather of the whole system of oppression and cruelty by which dominant castes seek to retain their ascendancy. When recently in Shanghai a British officer ordered a number of unarmed Chinese students to be shot in the back without warning, he was obviously actuated by terror just as much as a soldier who runs away in battle. But military aristocracies are not sufficiently intelligent to trace such actions to their psychological source; they regard them rather as showing firmness and a proper spirit.

From the point of view of psychology and physiology, fear and rage are closely analogous emotions: the man who feels rage is not possessed of the highest kind of courage. The cruelty invariably displayed in suppressing negro insurrections, communist rebellions, and other threats to aristocracy, is an offshoot of cowardice, and deserves the same contempt as is bestowed upon the more obvious forms of that vice. I believe that it is possible so to educate ordinary men and women that they shall be able to live without fear. Hitherto, only a few heroes and saints have achieved such a life; but what they have done others could do if they were shown the way.

For the kind of courage which does not consist

in repression, a number of factors must be combined. To begin with the humblest: health and vitality are very helpful, though not indispensable. Practice and skill in dangerous situations are very desirable. But when we come to consider, not courage in this and that respect, but universal courage, something more fundamental is wanted. What is wanted is a combination of self-respect with an impersonal outlook on life. To begin with self-respect: some men live from within, while others are mere mirrors of what is felt and said by their neighbors. The latter can never have true courage: they must have admiration, and are haunted by the fear of losing it. The teaching of "humility," which used to be thought desirable, was the means of producing a perverted form of this same vice. "Humility" suppressed self-respect, but not the desire for the respect of others; it merely made nominal self-abasement the means of acquiring credit. Thus it produced hypocrisy and falsification of instinct. Children were taught unreasoning submission, and proceeded to exact it when they grew up; it was said that only those who have learned to obey know how to command. What I suggest is that no one should learn how to obey, and no one should attempt to command. I do not mean, of course, that there should not be leaders in coöperative enterprises; but their authority should be like that of a captain of a football team, which is suffered voluntarily in order to achieve a common purpose. Our purposes should be our own, not the result of external authority; and our purposes should never be forcibly imposed upon others. This is what I mean when I say no one should command and no one should obey.

There is one thing more required for the highest courage, and that is what I called just now an impersonal outlook on life. The man whose hopes and fears are all centered upon himself can hardly view death with equanimity, since it extinguishes his whole emotional universe. Here, again, we are met by a tradition urging the cheap and easy way of repression: the saint must learn to renounce Self, must mortify the flesh and forgo instinctive joys. This can be done, but its consequences are bad. Having renounced pleasure for himself, the ascetic saint renounces it for others also, which is easier. Envy persists underground, and leads him to the view that suffering is ennobling, and may therefore be legitimately inflicted. Hence arises a complete inversion of values: what is good is thought bad, and what is bad is thought good. The source of all the harm is that the good life has been sought in obedience to a negative imperative, not in broadening and developing natural desires and instincts. There are certain things in human nature which take us beyond Self without effort. The commonest of these is love, more particularly parental love, which in some is so generalized as to embrace the whole human race. Another is knowledge. There is no reason to suppose that Galileo was particularly benevolent, yet he lived for an end which was not defeated by his death. Another is art. But in fact every interest in something outside a man's own body makes his life to that degree impersonal. For this reason, paradoxical as it may seem, a man of wide and vivid interests finds less difficulty in leaving life than is experienced by some miserable hypochondriac whose interests are bounded by his own ailments. Thus the perfection of courage is found in the man of many interests, who *feels* his ego to be but a small part of the world, not through despising himself, but through valuing much that is not himself. This can hardly happen except where instinct is free and intelligence is active. From the union of the two grows a comprehensiveness of outlook unknown both to the voluptuary and to the ascetic; and to such an outlook personal death appears a trivial matter. Such courage is positive and instinctive, not negative and repressive. It is courage in this positive sense that I regard as one of the major ingredients in a perfect character.

Sensitiveness, the third quality in our list, is in a sense a corrective of mere courage. Courageous behavior is easier for a man who fails to apprehend dangers, but such courage may often be foolish. We cannot regard as satisfactory any way of acting which is dependent upon ignorance or forgetfulness:

the fullest possible knowledge and realization are an essential part of what is desirable. The cognitive aspect, however, comes under the head of intelligence; sensitiveness, in the sense in which I am using the term, belongs to the emotions. A purely theoretical definition would be that a person is emotionally sensitive when many stimuli produce emotions in him; but taken thus broadly the quality is not necessarily a good one. If sensitiveness is to be good, the emotional reaction must be in some sense *appropriate:* mere intensity is not what is needed. The quality I have in mind is that of being affected pleasurably or the reverse by many things, and by the right things. What are the right things, I shall try to explain. The first step, which most children take at the age of about five months, is to pass beyond mere pleasures of sensation, such as food and warmth, to the pleasure of social approbation. This pleasure, as soon as it has arisen, develops very rapidly: every child loves praise and hates blame. Usually the wish to be thought well of remains one of the dominant motives throughout life. It is certainly very valuable as a stimulus to pleasant behavior, and as a restraint upon impulses of greed. If we were wiser in our admirations, it might be much more valuable. But so long as the most admired heroes are those who have killed the greatest number of people, love of admiration cannot alone be adequate to the good life.

The next stage in the development of a desirable

form of sensitiveness is sympathy. There is a purely physical sympathy: a very young child will cry because a brother or sister is crying. This, I suppose, affords the basis for the further developments. The two enlargements that are needed are: first, to feel sympathy even when the sufferer is not an object of special affection; secondly, to feel it when the suffering is merely known to be occurring, not sensibly present. The second of these enlargements depends mainly upon intelligence. It may only go so far as sympathy with suffering which is portrayed vividly and touchingly, as in a good novel; it may, on the other hand, go so far as to enable a man to be moved emotionally by statistics. This capacity for abstract sympathy is as rare as it is important. Almost everybody is deeply affected when some one he loves suffers from cancer. Most people are moved when they see the sufferings of unknown patients in hospitals. Yet when they read that the death-rate from cancer is such-and-such, they are as a rule only moved to momentary personal fear lest they or some one dear to them should acquire the disease. The same is true of war: people think it dreadful when their son or brother is mutilated, but they do not think it a million times as dreadful that a million people should be mutilated. A man who is full of kindliness in all personal dealings may derive his income from incitement to war or from the torture of children in "backward" countries. All these familiar phenomena are due to the fact that sympathy is not stirred, in most people, by a merely abstract stimulus. A large proportion of the evils in the modern world would cease if this could be remedied. Science has greatly increased our power of affecting the lives of distant people, without increasing our sympathy for them. Suppose you are a shareholder in a company which manufactures cotton in Shanghai. You may be a busy man, who has merely followed financial advice in making the investment; neither Shanghai nor cotton interests you, but only your dividends. Yet you become part of the force leading to massacres of innocent people, and your dividends would disappear if little children were not forced into unnatural and dangerous toil. You do not mind, because you have never seen the children, and an abstract stimulus cannot move you. This is the fundamental reason why large-scale industrialism is so cruel, and why oppression of subject races is tolerated. An education producing sensitiveness to abstract stimuli would make such things impossible.

Cognitive sensitiveness, which should also be included, is practically the same thing as a habit of observation, and this is more naturally considered in connection with intelligence. Æsthetic sensitiveness raises a number of problems which I do not wish to discuss at this stage. I will therefore pass on to the last of the four qualities we enumerated, namely, intelligence.

One of the great defects of traditional morality has been the low estimate it placed upon intelligence. The Greeks did not err in this respect, but the Church led men to think that nothing matters except virtue, and virtue consists in abstinence from a certain list of actions arbitrarily labeled "sin." So long as this attitude persists, it is impossible to make men realize that intelligence does more good than an artificial conventional "virtue." When I speak of intelligence, I include both actual knowledge and receptivity to knowledge. The two are, in fact, closely connected. Ignorant adults are unteachable; on such matters as hygiene or diet, for example, they are totally incapable of believing what science has to say. The more a man has learnt, the easier it is for him to learn still more—always assuming that he has not been taught in a spirit of dogmatism. Ignorant people have never been compelled to change their mental habits, and have stiffened into an unchangeable attitude. It is not only that they are credulous where they should be skeptical; it is just as much that they are incredulous where they should be receptive. No doubt the word "intelligence" properly signifies rather an aptitude for acquiring knowledge than knowledge already acquired; but I do not think this aptitude is acquired except by exercise, any more than the aptitude of a pianist or an acrobat. It is, of course, possible to impart information in ways that do not train intelligence; it is not only possible, but easy, and frequently done. But I do not believe that it is possible to train intelligence without imparting information, or at any rate causing knowledge to be acquired. And without intelligence our complex modern world cannot subsist; still less can it make progress. I regard the cultivation of intelligence, therefore, as one of the major purposes of education. This might seem a commonplace, but in fact it is not. The desire to instill what are regarded as correct beliefs has made educationists too often indifferent to the training of intelligence. To make this clear, it is necessary to define intelligence a little more closely, so as to discover the mental habits which it requires. For this purpose I shall consider only the aptitude for acquiring knowledge, not the store of actual knowledge which might legitimately be included in the definition of intelligence.

The instinctive foundation of the intellectual life is curiosity, which is found among animals in its elementary forms. Intelligence demands an alert curiosity, but it must be of a certain kind. The sort that leads village neighbors to try to peer through curtains after dark has no very high value. The widespread interest in gossip is inspired, not by a love of knowledge, but by malice: no one gossips about other people's secret virtues, but only about their secret vices. Accordingly most gossip is untrue, but care is taken not to verify it. Our neighbors' sins, like the consolations of religion, are so agreeable that we do not stop to scrutinize the evidence closely. Curiosity properly so called, on the other hand, is inspired by a genuine love of knowledge. You may see this impulse, in a moderately pure form, at work in a cat which has been brought to a strange room, and proceeds to smell every corner and every piece of furniture. You will see it also in children, who are passionately interested when a drawer or cupboard, usually closed, is open for their inspection. Animals, machines, thunderstorms, and all forms of manual work, arouse the curiosity of children, whose thirst for knowledge puts the most intelligent adult to shame. This impulse grows weaker with advancing years, until at last what is unfamiliar inspires only disgust, with no desire for a closer acquaintance. This is the stage at which people announce that the country is going to the dogs, and that "things are not what they were in my young days." The thing which is not the same as it was in that far-off time is the speaker's curiosity. And with the death of curiosity we may reckon that active intelligence, also, has died.

But although curiosity lessens in intensity and in extent after childhood, it may for a long time improve in quality. Curiosity about general propositions shows a higher level of intelligence than curiosity about particular facts; broadly speaking, the higher the order of generality the greater is the intelligence involved. (This rule, however, must not be taken too strictly.) Curiosity dissociated from personal advantage shows a higher development than curiosity connected (say) with a chance of food. The cat that sniffs in a new room is not a wholly disinterested scientific inquirer, but probably also wants to find out whether there are mice about. Perhaps it is not quite correct to say that curiosity is best when it is disinterested, but rather that it is best when the connection with other interests is not direct and obvious, but discoverable only by means of a certain degree of intelligence. This point, however, it is not necessary for us to decide.

If curiosity is to be fruitful, it must be associated with a certain technique for the acquisition of knowledge. There must be habits of observation, belief in the possibility of knowledge, patience, and industry. These things will develop of themselves, given the original fund of curiosity and the proper intellectual education. But since our intellectual life is only a part of our activity, and since curiosity is perpetually coming into conflict with other passions, there is need of certain intellectual virtues, such as open-mindedness. We become impervious to new truth both from habit and from desire: we find it hard to disbelieve what we have emphatically believed for a number of years, and also what min·

isters to self-esteem or any other fundamental passion. Open-mindedness should therefore be one of the qualities that education aims at producing. At present, this is only done to a very limited extent, as is illustrated by the following paragraph from *The Daily Herald*, July 31, 1925:

A special committee, appointed to inquire into the allegations of the subversion of children's minds in Bootle schools by their school teachers, has placed its findings before the Bootle Borough Council. The Committee was of opinion that the allegations were substantiated, but the Council deleted the word "substantiated," and stated that "the allegations gave cause for reasonable inquiry." A recommendation made by the Committee, and adopted by the Council, was that in future appointments of teachers, they shall undertake to train the scholars in habits of reverence towards God and religion, and of respect for the civil and religious institutions of the country.

Thus whatever may happen elsewhere, there is to be no open-mindedness in Bootle. It is hoped that the Borough Council will shortly send a deputation to Dayton, Tennessee, to obtain further light upon the best methods of carrying out their program. But perhaps that is unnecessary. From the wording of the resolution, it would seem as if Bootle needed no instruction in obscurantism.

Courage is essential to intellectual probity, as

well as to physical heroism. The real world is more unknown than we like to think; from the first day of life we practice precarious inductions, and confound our mental habits with laws of external nature. All sorts of intellectual systems—Christianity, Socialism, Patriotism, etc.—are ready, like orphan asylums, to give safety in return for servitude. A free mental life cannot be as warm and comfortable and sociable as a life enveloped in a creed: only a creed can give the feeling of a cozy fireside while the winter storms are raging without.

This brings us to a somewhat difficult question: to what extent should the good life be emancipated from the herd? I hesitate to use the phrase "herd instinct," because there are controversies as to its correctness. But, however interpreted, the phenomena which it describes are familiar. We like to stand well with those whom we feel to be the group with which we wish to coöperate—our family, our neighbors, our colleagues, our political party, or our nation. This is natural, because we cannot obtain any of the pleasures of life without coöperation. Moreover, emotions are infectious, especially when they are felt by many people at once. Very few people can be present at an excited meeting without getting excited: if they are opponents, their opposition becomes excited. And to most people such opposition is only possible if they can derive support from the thought of a different crowd in which they will win approbation. That is why the Communion of Saints has afforded such comfort to the persecuted. Are we to acquiesce in this desire for coöperation with a crowd, or shall our education try to weaken it? There are arguments on both sides, and the right answer must consist in finding a just proportion, not in a whole-hearted decision for either party.

I think myself that the desire to please and to coöperate should be strong and normal, but should be capable of being overcome by other desires on certain important occasions. The desirability of a wish to please has already been considered in connection with sensitiveness. Without it, we should all be boors, and all social groups, from the family upwards, would be impossible. Education of young children would be very difficult if they did not desire the good opinion of their parents. The contagious character of emotions also has its uses, when the contagion is from a wiser person to a more foolish one. But in the case of panic fear and panic rage it is of course the very reverse of useful. Thus the question of emotional receptivity is by no means simple. Even in purely intellectual matters, the issue is not clear. The great discoverers have had to withstand the herd, and incur hostility by their independence. But the average man's opinions are much less foolish than they would be if he thought for himself: in science, at least, his respect for authority is on the whole beneficial.

I think that in the life of a man whose circumstances and talents are not very exceptional there should be a large sphere where what is vaguely termed "herd instinct" dominates, and a small sphere into which it does not penetrate. The small sphere should contain the region of his special competence. We think ill of a man who cannot admire a woman unless everybody else also admires her: we think that, in the choice of a wife, a man should be guided by his own independent feelings, not by a reflection of the feelings of his society. It is no matter if his judgments of people in general agree with those of his neighbors, but when he falls in love he ought to be guided by his own independent feelings. Much the same thing applies in other directions. A farmer should follow his own judgment as to the capacities of the fields which he cultivates himself, though his judgment should be formed after acquiring a knowledge of scientific agriculture. An economist should form an independent judgment on currency questions, but an ordinary mortal had better follow authority. Wherever there is special competence, there should be independence. But a man should not make himself into a kind of hedgehog, all bristles to keep the world at a distance. The bulk of our ordinary activities must be coöperative, and coöperation must have an instinctive basis. Nevertheless, we should all learn to be able to think for ourselves about matters that are particularly well known to us, and we ought all to have acquired the courage to proclaim unpopular opinions when we believe them to be important. The application of these broad principles in special cases may, of course, be difficult. But it will be less difficult than it is at present in a world where men commonly have the virtues we have been considering in this chapter. The persecuted saint, for instance, would not exist in such a world. The good man would have no occasion to bristle and become self-conscious; his goodness would result from following his impulses, and would be combined with instinctive happiness. His neighbors would not hate him, because they would not fear him: the hatred of pioneers is due to the terror they inspire, and this terror would not exist among men who had acquired courage. Only a man dominated by fear would join the Ku Klux Klan or the Fascisti. In a world of brave men, such persecuting organizations could not exist, and the good life would involve far less resistance to instinct than it does at present. The good world can only be created and sustained by fearless men, but the more they succeed in their task the fewer occasions there will be for the exercise of their courage.

A community of men and women possessing vitality, courage, sensitiveness, and intelligence, in the highest degree that education can produce, would be very different from anything that has hitherto existed. Very few people would be unhappy. The main causes of unhappiness at present are: ill-health, poverty, and an unsatisfactory sexlife. All of these would become very rare. Good health could be almost universal, and even old age could be postponed. Poverty, since the industrial revolution, is only due to collective stupidity. Sensitiveness would make people wish to abolish it, intelligence would show them the way, and courage would lead them to adopt it. (A timid person would rather remain miserable than do anything unusual.) Most people's sex-life, at present, is more or less unsatisfactory. This is partly due to bad education, partly to persecution by the authorities and Mrs. Grundy. A generation of women brought up without irrational sex fears would soon make an end of this. Fear has been thought the only way to make women "virtuous," and they have been deliberately taught to be cowards, both physically and mentally. Women in whom love is cramped encourage brutality and hypocrisy in their husbands, and distort the instincts of their children. One generation of fearless women could transform the world, by bringing into it a generation of fearless children, not contorted into unnatural shapes, but straight and candid, generous, affectionate, and free. Their ardor would sweep away the cruelty and pain which we endure because we are lazy, cowardly, hard-hearted and stupid. It is education that gives us these bad qualities, and education that must give us the opposite virtues. Education is the key to the new world

QUESTIONS [1]

A European lately arrived in China, if he is of a receptive and reflective disposition, finds himself confronted with a number of very puzzling questions, for many of which the problems of western Europe will not have prepared him. Russian problems, it is true, have important affinities with those of China, but they have also important differences; moreover they are decidedly less complex. Chinese problems, even if they affected no one outside China, would be of vast importance, since the Chinese are estimated to constitute about a quarter of the human race. In fact, however, all the world will be vitally affected by the development of Chinese affairs, which may well prove a decisive factor, for good or evil, during the next two centuries. This makes it important, to Europe and America almost as much as to Asia, that there should be an intelligent understanding of the questions raised by China, even if, as yet, definite answers are difficult to give.

The questions raised by the present condition of China fall naturally into three groups, economic, political, and cultural. No one of these groups, however, can be considered in isolation, because each

[1] From *The Problem of China.*

194

is intimately bound up with the other two. For my part, I think the cultural questions are the most important, both for China and for mankind; if these could be solved, I would accept, with more or less equanimity, any political or economic system which ministered to that end. Unfortunately, however, cultural questions have little interest for practical men, who regard money and power as the proper ends for nations as for individuals. The helplessness of the artist in a hard-headed business community has long been a commonplace of novelists and moralizers, and has made collectors feel virtuous when they bought up the pictures of painters who had died in penury. China may be regarded as an artist nation, with the virtues and vices to be expected of the artist: virtues chiefly useful to others, and vices chiefly harmful to oneself. Can Chinese virtues be preserved? Or must China, in order to survive, acquire, instead, the vices which make for success and cause misery to others only? And if China does copy the model set by all foreign nations with which she has dealings, what will become of all of us?

China has an ancient civilization which is now undergoing a very rapid process of change. The traditional civilization of China had developed in almost complete independence of Europe, and had merits and demerits quite different from those of the West. It would be futile to attempt to strike a balance;

whether our present culture is better or worse, on the whole, than that which seventeenth-century missionaries found in the Celestial Empire is a question as to which no prudent person would venture to pronounce. But it is easy to point to certain respects in which we are better than old China, and to other respects in which we are worse. If intercourse between Western nations and China is to be fruitful, we must cease to regard ourselves as missionaries of a superior civilization, or, worse still, as men who have a right to exploit, oppress, and swindle the Chinese because they are an "inferior" race. I do not see any reason to believe that the Chinese are inferior to ourselves; and I think most Europeans, who have any intimate knowledge of China, would take the same view.

In comparing an alien culture with one's own, one is forced to ask oneself questions more fundamental than any that usually arise in regard to home affairs. One is forced to ask: What are the things that I ultimately value? What would make me judge one sort of society more desirable than another sort? What sort of ends should I most wish to see realized in the world? Different people will answer these questions differently, and I do not know of any argument by which I could persuade a man who gave an answer different from my own. I must therefore be content merely to state the answer which appeals to me, in the hope that the reader may feel likewise.

The main things which seem to me important on their own account, and not merely as means to other things, are: knowledge, art, instinctive happiness, and relations of friendship or affection. When I speak of knowledge, I do not mean all knowledge; there is much in the way of dry lists of facts that is merely useful, and still more that has no appreciable value of any kind. But the understanding of nature, incomplete as it is which is to be derived from science, I hold to be a thing which is good and delightful on its own account. The same may be said, I think, of some biographies and parts of history. To enlarge on this topic would, however, take me too far from my theme. When I speak of art as one of the things that have value on their own account, I do not mean only the deliberate productions of trained artists, though of course these, at their best, deserve the highest place. I mean also the almost unconscious effort after beauty which one finds among Russian peasants and Chinese coolies, the sort of impulse that creates folk-songs, that existed among ourselves before the time of the Puritans, and survives in cottage gardens. Instinctive happiness, or joy of life, is one of the most important widespread popular goods that we have lost through industrialism and the high pressure at which most of us live; its commonness in China is a strong reason for thinking well of Chinese civilization.

In judging a community, we have to consider, not

only how much of good or evil there is within the community, but also what effects it has in promoting good or evil in other communities, and how far the good things which it enjoys depend upon evils elsewhere. In this respect, also, China is better than we are. Our prosperity, and most of what we endeavor to secure for ourselves, can only be obtained by widespread oppression and exploitation of weaker nations, while the Chinese are not strong enough to injure other countries, and secure whatever they enjoy by means of their own merits and exertions alone.

These general ethical considerations are by no means irrelevant in considering the practical problems of China. Our industrial and commercial civilization has been both the effect and the cause of certain more or less unconscious beliefs as to what is worth while; in China one becomes conscious of these beliefs through the spectacle of a society which challenges them by being built, just as unconsciously, upon a different standard of values. Progress and efficiency, for example, make no appeal to the Chinese, except to those who have come under Western influence. By valuing progress and efficiency, we have secured power and wealth; by ignoring them, the Chinese, until we brought disturbance, secured on the whole a peaceable existence and a life full of enjoyment. It is difficult to compare these opposite achievements unless we have some standard of values in our minds; and, unless it is a more or less conscious standard, we shall undervalue the less familiar civilization, because evils to which we are not accustomed always make a stronger impression than those that we have learned to take as a matter of course.

The culture of China is changing rapidly, and undoubtedly rapid change is needed. The change that has hitherto taken place is traceable ultimately to the military superiority of the West; but in future our economic superiority is likely to be quite as potent. I believe that, if the Chinese are left free to assimilate what they want of our civilization, and to reject what strikes them as bad, they will be able to achieve an organic growth from their own tradition, and to produce a very splendid result, combining our merits with theirs. There are, however, two opposite dangers to be avoided if this is to happen. The first danger is that they may become completely westernized, retaining nothing of what has hitherto distinguished them, adding merely one more to the restless, intelligent, industrious, and militaristic nations which now afflict this unfortunate planet. The second danger is that they may be driven, in the course of resistance to foreign aggression, into an intense anti-foreign conservatism as regards everything except armaments. This has happened in Japan, and it may easily happen in China. The future of Chinese culture is intimately bound up with political and economic questions; and it is through their influence that dangers arise.

China is confronted with two very different groups of foreign powers, on the one hand the white nations, on the other hand Japan. In considering the effect of the white races on the Far East as a whole, modern Japan must count as a Western product; therefore the responsibility for Japan's doings in China rests ultimately with her white teachers. Nevertheless, Japan remains very unlike Europe and America, and has ambitions different from theirs as regards China. We must therefore distinguish three possibilities: (1) China may become enslaved to one or more white nations; (2) China may become enslaved to Japan; (3) China may recover and retain her liberty. Temporarily there is a fourth possibility, namely that a consortium of Japan and the white powers may control China; but I do not believe that, in the long run, the Japanese will be able to coöperate with England and America. In the long run, I believe that Japan must dominate the Far East or go under. If the Japanese had a different character this would not be the case; but the nature of their ambitions makes them exclusive and unneighborly. I shall give the reasons for this view when I come to deal with the relations of China and Japan.

To understand the problem of China, we must first know something of Chinese history and culture before the irruption of the white man, then something of modern Chinese culture and its inherent tendencies; next, it is necessary to deal in outline with the military and diplomatic relations of the Western powers with China, beginning with our war of 1840 and ending with the treaty concluded after the Boxer uprising of 1900. Although the Sino-Japanese War comes in this period, it is possible to separate, more or less, the actions of Japan in that war, and to see what system the white powers would have established if Japan had not existed. Since that time, however, Japan has been the dominant foreign influence in Chinese affairs. It is therefore necessary to understand how the Japanese became what they are: what sort of nation they were before the West destroyed their isolation, and what influence the West has had upon them. Lack of understanding of Japan has made people in England blind to Japan's aims in China, and unable to apprehend the meaning of what Japan has done.

Political considerations alone, however, will not suffice to explain what is going on in relation to China; economic questions are almost more important. China is as yet hardly industrialized, and is certainly the most important undeveloped area left in the world. Whether the resources of China are to be developed by China, by Japan, or by the white races, is a question of enormous importance, affecting not only the whole development of Chinese civilization, but the balance of power in the world, the prospects of peace, the destiny of Russia, and the chances of development toward a better economic system in the advanced nations.

The Washington conference has partly exhibited and partly concealed the conflict for the possession of China between nations all of which have guaranteed China's independence and integrity. Its outcome has made it far more difficult than before to give a hopeful answer as regards Far Eastern problems, and in particular as regards the question: Can China preserve any shadow of independence without a great development of nationalism and militarism? I cannot bring myself to advocate nationalism and militarism, yet it is difficult to know what to say to patriotic Chinese who ask how they can be avoided. So far, I have found only one answer. The Chinese nation is the most patient in the world; it thinks of centuries as other nations think of decades. It is essentially indestructible, and can afford to wait. The "civilized" nations of the world with their blockades, their poison gases, their bombs, submarines and negro armies, will probably destroy each other within the next three hundred years, leaving the stage to those whose pacifism has kept them alive, though poor and powerless. If China can avoid being goaded into war, her oppressors may wear themselves out in the end, and leave the Chinese free to pursue humane ends, instead of war and rapine and destruction which all white nations love. It is perhaps a slender hope for China, and for ourselves it is little better than despair. But unless the great powers learn some moderation and some tolerance, I do not see any better possibility, though I see many that are worse.

Our Western civilization is built upon assumptions which, to a psychologist, are rationalizings of excessive energy. Our industrialism, our militarism, our love of progress, our missionary zeal, our imperialism, our passion for dominating and organizing, all spring from a superflux of the itch for activity. The creed of efficiency for its own sake, without regard for the ends to which it is directed, has become somewhat discredited in Europe since the war, which would have never taken place if the Western nations had been slightly more indolent. But in America this creed is still almost universally accepted; so it is in Japan, and so it is by the Bolsheviks, who have been aiming fundamentally at the Americanization of Russia. Russia, like China, may be described as an artist nation; but unlike China it has been governed, since the time of Peter the Great, by men who wished to introduce all the good and evil of the West. In former days, I might have had no doubt that such men were in the right. Some (though not many) of the Chinese returned students resemble them in the belief that Western push and hustle are the most desirable things on earth. I cannot now take this view. The evils produced in China by indolence seem to me far less disastrous, from the point of view of mankind at large, than those produced throughout the world by the domineering cocksureness of Europe and America. The Great War showed that something is wrong with our civilization; experience of Russia and China has made me believe that those countries can help to show us what it is that is wrong. The Chinese have discovered, and have practiced for many centuries, a way of life which, if it could be adopted by all the world, would make all the world happy. We Europeans have not. Our way of life demands strife, exploitation, restless change, discontent, and destruction. Efficiency directed to destruction can only end in annihilation, and it is to this consummation that our civilization is tending, if it cannot learn some of that wisdom for which it despises the East.

It was on the Volga, in the summer of 1920, that I first realized how profound is the disease in our Western mentality, which the Bolsheviks are attempting to force upon an essentially Asiatic population, just as Japan and the West are doing in China. Our boat traveled on, day after day, through an unknown and mysterious land. Our company were noisy, gay, quarrelsome, full of facile theories, with glib explanations of everything, persuaded that there is nothing they could not understand and no human destiny outside the purview of their system. One of us lay at death's door, fighting a grim battle with weakness and terror and the indifference of the strong, assailed day and night by the sounds of loud-voiced love-making and trivial laughter. And all around us lay a great silence, strong as death, unfathomable as the heavens. It seemed that none had leisure to hear the silence, yet it called to me so insistently that I grew deaf to the harangues of propagandists and the endless information of the well-informed.

One night, very late, our boat stopped in a desolate spot where there were no houses, but only a great sandbank, and beyond it a row of poplars with the rising moon behind them. In silence I went ashore, and found on the sand a strange assemblage of human beings, half-nomads, wandering from some remote region of famine, each family huddled together surrounded by all its belongings, some sleeping, others silently making small fires of twigs. The flickering flames lighted up gnarled, bearded faces of wild men, strong, patient, primitive women, and children as sedate and slow as their parents. Human beings they undoubtedly were, and yet it would have been far easier for me to grow intimate with a dog or a cat or a horse than with one of them. I knew that they would wait there day after day, perhaps for weeks, until a boat came in which they could go to some distant place in which they had heard— falsely perhaps—that the earth was more generous

than in the country they had left. Some would die
by the way, all would suffer hunger and thirst and
the scorching midday sun, but their sufferings would
be dumb. To me they seemed to typify the very
soul of Russia, unexpressive, inactive from despair,
unheeded by the little set of westernizers who make
up all the parties of progress or reaction. Russia is
so vast that the articulate few are lost in it as man
and his planet are lost in interstellar space. It is
possible, I thought, that the theorists may increase
the misery of the many by trying to force them into
actions contrary to their primeval instincts, but I
could not believe that happiness was to be brought to
them by a gospel of industrialism and forced labor.

Nevertheless, when morning came I resumed the
interminable discussions of the materialistic conception of history and the merits of a truly popular
government. Those with whom I discussed had not
seen the sleeping wanderers, and would not have
been interested if they had seen them, since they
were not material for propaganda. But something
of that patient silence had communicated itself to
me, something lonely and unspoken remained in my
heart throughout all the comfortable familiar intellectual talk. And at last I began to feel that all
politics are inspired by a grinning devil, teaching
the energetic and quick-witted to torture submissive
populations for the profit of pocket or power or
theory. As we journeyed on, fed by food extracted

from the peasants, protected by an army recruited from among their sons, I wondered what we had to give them in return. But I found no answer. From time to time I heard their sad songs or the haunting music of the balalaika; but the sound mingled with the great silence of the steppes, and left me with a terrible questioning pain in which Occidental hopefulness grew pale.

It was in this mood that I set out for China to seek a new hope.

CHINESE AND WESTERN CIVILIZATION CONTRASTED [1]

There is at present in China a close contact between our civilization and that which is native to the Celestial Empire. It is still a doubtful question whether this contact will breed a new civilization better than either of its parents, or whether it will merely destroy the native culture and replace it by that of America. Contacts between different civilizations have often in the past proved to be landmarks in human progress. Greece learned from Egypt, Rome from Greece, the Arabs from the Roman Empire, medieval Europe from the Arabs, and Renaissance Europe from the Byzantines. In many of these cases, the pupils proved better than their masters. In the case of China, if we regard the Chinese as the pupils, this may be the case again. In fact, we have quite as much to learn from them as they from us, but there is far less chance of our learning it. If I treat the Chinese as our pupils, rather than vice versa, it is only because I fear we are unteachable.

I propose in this chapter to deal with the purely cultural aspects of the questions raised by the contact of China with the West.

[1] From *The Problem of China.*

With the exception of Spain and America in the sixteenth century, I cannot think of any instance of two civilizations coming into contact after such a long period of separate development as has marked those of China and Europe. Considering this extraordinary separateness, it is surprising that mutual understanding between Europeans and Chinese is not more difficult. In order to make this point clear, it will be worth while to dwell for a moment on the historical origins of the two civilizations.

Western Europe and America have a practically homogeneous mental life, which I should trace to three sources: (1) Greek culture; (2) Jewish religion and ethics; (3) modern industrialism, which itself is an outcome of modern science. We may take Plato, the Old Testament, and Galileo as representing these three elements, which have remained singularly separable down to the present day. From the Greeks we derive literature and the arts, philosophy and pure mathematics; also the more urbane portions of our social outlook. From the Jews we derive fanatical belief, which its friends call "faith"; moral fervor, with the conception of sin; religious intolerance, and some part of our nationalism. From science, as applied in industrialism, we derive power and the sense of power, the belief that we are as gods, and may justly be the arbiters of life and death for unscientific races. We derive also the empirical method, by which almost all real knowledge has been acquired. These three elements, I think, account for most of our mentality.

No one of these three elements has had any appreciable part in the development of China, except that Greece indirectly influenced Chinese painting, sculpture and music. China belongs, in the dawn of its history, to the great river empires, of which Egypt and Babylonia contributed to our origins, by the influence which they had upon the Greeks and Jews. Just as these civilizations were rendered possible by the rich alluvial soil of the Nile, the Euphrates, and the Tigris, so the original civilization of China was rendered possible by the Yellow River. Even in the time of Confucius, the Chinese Empire did not stretch far either to south or north of the Yellow River. But in spite of this similarity in physical and economic circumstances, there was very little in common between the mental outlook of the Chinese and that of the Egyptians and Babylonians. Lao-Tze [1] and Confucius, who both belong to the sixth century B.C., have already the characteristics which we should regard as distinctive of the modern Chinese. People who attribute everything to economic causes would be hard put to it to account for the differences between the ancient Chinese and the ancient Egyptians and Babylonians. For my part,

---

[1] With regard to Lao-Tze, the book which bears his name is of doubtful authenticity and was probably compiled two or three centuries after his death. See Giles, *Civilization in China*.

I have no alternative theory to offer. I do not think science can, at present, account wholly for national character. Climate and economic circumstances account for parts, but not the whole. Probably a great deal depends upon the character of dominant individuals who happen to emerge at a formative period, such as Moses, Mohammed, and Confucius.

The oldest known Chinese sage is Lao-Tze, the founder of Taoism. "Lao-Tze" is not really a proper name, but means merely "the old philosopher." He was (according to tradition) an older contemporary of Confucius, and his philosophy is to my mind far more interesting. He held that every person, every animal, and every thing has a certain way or manner of behaving which is natural to him, or her, or it, and that we ought to conform to this way ourselves and encourage others to conform to it. "Tao" means "way," but used in a more or less mystical sense, as in the text: "I am the Way and the Truth and the Life." I think he fancied that death was due to departing from the "way," and that if we all lived strictly according to nature we should be immortal, like the heavenly bodies. In later times Taoism degenerated into mere magic, and was largely concerned with the search for the elixir of life. But I think the hope of escaping from death was an element in Taoist philosophy from the first.

Lao-Tze's book, or rather the book attributed to him, is very short but his ideas were developed by

his disciple Chaung-Tze, who is more interesting
than his master. The philosophy which both advocated was one of freedom. They thought ill of government, and of all interferences with nature. They
complained of the hurry of modern life, which they
contrasted with the calm existence of those whom
they called "the pure men of old." There is a flavor
of mysticism in the doctrine of the Tao, because in
spite of the multiplicity of living things the Tao is
in some sense one, so that if all live according to it
there will be no strife in the world. But both sages
have already the Chinese characteristics of humor,
restraint, and understatement. Their humor is illustrated by Chaung-Tze's account of Po-Lo, who
"understood the management of horses," and trained
them till five out of every ten died.[1] Their restraint
and understatement are evident when they are compared with Western mystics. Both characteristics
belong to all Chinese literature and art, and to the
conversation of cultivated Chinese in the present
day. All classes in China are fond of laughter, and
never miss a chance of a joke. In the educated
classes, the humor is sly and delicate, so that Europeans often fail to see it, which adds to the enjoyment of the Chinese. Their habit of understatement
is remarkable. I met one day in Peking a middle-
aged man who told me he was academically interested in the theory of politics; being new to the

[1] See Chapter IV, *The Problem of China.*

country, I took his statement at its face value, but I afterward discovered that he had been governor of a province, and had been for many years a very prominent politician. In Chinese poetry there is an apparent absence of passion, which is due to the same practice of understatement. They consider that a wise man should always remain calm, and, though they have their passionate moments (being in fact a very excitable race), they do not wish to perpetuate them in art, because they think ill of them. Our romantic movement, which led people to like vehemence, has, so far as I know, no analogue in their literature. Their old music, some of which is very beautiful, makes so little noise that one can only just hear it. In art they aim at being exquisite, and in life at being reasonable. There is no admiration for the ruthless strong man, or for the unrestrained expression of passion. After the more blatant life of the West, one misses at first all the effects at which they are aiming; but gradually the beauty and dignity of their existence become visible, so that the foreigners who have lived longest in China are those who love the Chinese best.

The Taoists, though they survive as magicians, were entirely ousted from the favor of the educated classes by Confucianism. I must confess that I am unable to appreciate the merits of Confucius. His writings are largely occupied with trivial points of etiquette, and his main concern is to teach people how to behave correctly on various occasions. When one compares him, however, with the traditional religious teachers of some other ages and races, one must admit that he has great merits, even if they are mainly negative. His system, as developed by his followers, is one of pure ethics, without religious dogma; it has not given rise to a powerful priesthood, and it has not led to persecution. It certainly has succeeded in producing a whole nation possessed of exquisite manners and perfect courtesy. Nor is Chinese courtesy merely conventional; it is quite as reliable in situations for which no precedent has been provided. And it is not confined to one class; it exists even in the humblest coolie. It is humiliating to watch the brutal insolence of white men received by the Chinese with a quiet dignity which cannot demean itself to answer rudeness with rudeness. Europeans often regard this as weakness, but it is really strength, the strength by which the Chinese have hitherto conquered all their conquerors.

There is one, and only one, important foreign element in the traditional civilization of China, and that is Buddhism. Buddhism came to China from India in the early centuries of the Christian era, and acquired a definite place in the religion of the country. We, with the intolerant outlook which we have taken over from the Jews, imagine that if a man adopts one religion he cannot adopt another. The dogmas of Christianity and Mohammedanism, in their orthodox forms, are so framed that no man can accept both. But in China this incompatibility does not exist; a man may be both a Buddhist and a Confucian, because nothing in either is incompatible with the other. In Japan, similarly, most people are both Buddhists and Shintoists. Nevertheless, there is a temperamental difference between Buddhism and Confucianism, which will cause any individual to lay stress on one or the other even if he accepts both. Buddhism is a religion in the sense in which we understand the word. It has mystic doctrines and a way of salvation and a future life. It has a message to the world intended to cure the despair which it regards as natural to those who have no religious faith. It assumes an instinctive pessimism only to be cured by some gospel. Confucianism has nothing of all this. It assumes people fundamentally at peace with the world, wanting only instruction as to how to live, not encouragement to live at all. And its ethical instruction is not based upon any metaphysical or religious dogma; it is purely mundane. The result of the coexistence of these two religions in China has been that the more religious and contemplative natures turned to Buddhism, while the active administrative type was content with Confucianism, which was always the official teaching, in which candidates for the civil service were examined. The result is that for many ages the government of China has been in the hands of literary skeptics, whose administration has been lacking in those qualities of energy and destructiveness which Western nations demand of their rulers. In fact, they have conformed very closely to the maxims of Chaung-Tze. The result has been that the population has been happy except where civil war brought misery; that subject nations have been allowed autonomy; and that foreign nations have had no need to fear China, in spite of its immense population and resources.

Comparing the civilization of China with that of Europe, one finds in China most of what was to be found in Greece, but nothing of the other two elements of our civilization, namely, Judaism and science. China is practically destitute of religion, not only in the upper classes, but throughout the population. There is a very definite ethical code, but it is not fierce or persecuting, and does not contain the notion "sin." Except quite recently, through European influence, there has been no science and no industrialism.

What will be the outcome of the contact of this ancient civilization with the West? I am not thinking of the political or economic, but of the effect on the Chinese mental outlook. It is difficult to dissociate the two questions altogether, because of course the cultural contact with the West must be affected by the nature of the political and economic contact.

Nevertheless, I wish to consider the cultural question as far as I can in isolation.

There is, in China, a great eagerness to acquire Western learning, not simply in order to acquire national strength and be able to resist Western aggression, but because a very large number of people consider learning a good thing in itself. It is traditional in China to place a high value on knowledge, but in old days the knowledge sought was only of the classical literature. Nowadays it is generally realized that Western knowledge is more useful. Many students go every year to universities in Europe, and still more to America, to learn science or economics or law or political theory. These men, when they return to China, mostly become teachers or civil servants or journalists or politicians. They are rapidly modernizing the Chinese outlook, especially in the educated classes.

The traditional civilization of China had become unprogressive, and has ceased to produce much of value in the way of art and literature. This was not due, I think, to any decadence in the race, but merely to lack of new material. The influx of Western knowledge provides just the stimulus that was needed. Chinese students are able and extraordinarily keen. Higher education suffers from lack of funds and absence of libraries, but does not suffer from any lack of the finest human material. Although Chinese civilization has hitherto been de-

ficient in science, it never contained anything hostile
to science, and therefore the spread of scientific
knowledge encounters no such obstacles as the
Church put in its way in Europe. I have no doubt
that if the Chinese could get a stable government
and sufficient funds, they would, within the next
thirty years, begin to produce remarkable work in
science. It is quite likely that they might outstrip
us, because they come with fresh zest and with all
the ardor of a renaissance. In fact, the enthusiasm
for learning in Young China reminds one constantly
of the renaissance spirit in fifteenth-century Italy.

It is remarkable, as distinguishing the Chinese
from the Japanese, that the things they wish to learn
from us are not those that bring wealth or military
strength, but rather those that have either an ethical
and social value, or a purely intellectual interest.
They are not by any means uncritical of our civilization. Some of them told me that they were less
critical before 1914, but that the war made them
think there must be imperfection in the Western
manner of life. The habit of looking to the West
for wisdom was, however, very strong, and some
of the younger ones thought that Bolshevism could
give what they were looking for. That hope also
must be suffering disappointment, and before long
they will realize that they must work out their own
salvation by means of a new synthesis. The Japanese adopted our faults and kept their own, but it

is impossible to hope that the Chinese will make the opposite selection, keeping their own merits and adopting ours.

The distinctive merit of our civilization, I should say, is the scientific method; the distinctive merit of the Chinese a just conception of the ends of life. It is these two that one must hope to see gradually uniting.

Lao-Tze describes the operation of Tao as "production without possession, action without self-assertion, development without domination." I think one could derive from these words a conception of the ends of life as reflective Chinese see them and it must be admitted that they are very different from the ends which most white men set before themselves. Possession, self-assertion, domination, are eagerly sought, both nationally and individually. They have been erected into a philosophy by Nietzsche, and Nietzsche's disciples are not confined to Germany.

But, it will be said, you have been comparing Western practice with Chinese theory; if you had compared Western theory with Chinese practice, the balance would have come out quite differently. There is, of course, a great deal of truth in this. Possession, which is one of the three things that Lao-Tze wishes us to forgo, is certainly dear to the heart of the average Chinaman. As a race, they are tenacious of money—not perhaps more so than the

French, but certainly more than the English or the Americans. Their politics are corrupt, and their powerful men make money in disgraceful ways. All this it is impossible to deny.

Nevertheless, as regards the other two evils, self-assertion and domination, I notice a definite superiority to ourselves in Chinese practice. There is much less desire than among the white races to tyrannize over other people. The weakness of China internationally is quite as much due to this virtue as to the vices of corruption and so on which are usually assigned as the sole reason. If any nation in the world could ever be "too proud to fight," that nation would be China. The natural Chinese attitude is one of tolerance and friendliness, showing courtesy and expecting it in return. If the Chinese chose, they could be the most powerful nation in the world. But they only desire freedom, not domination. It is not improbable that other nations may compel them to fight for their freedom, and if so, they may lose their virtue and acquire a taste for empire. But at present, though they have been an imperial race for two thousand years, their love of empire is extraordinarily slight.

Although there have been many wars in China, the natural outlook of the Chinese is very pacifistic. I do not know of any other country where a poet would have chosen, as Po-Chui did in one of the poems translated by Mr. Waley, called by him "The

Old Man with the Broken Arm," to make a hero of a recruit who maimed himself to escape military service. Their pacifism is rooted in their contemplative outlook, and in the fact that they do not desire to change whatever they see. They take a pleasure—as their pictures show—in observing characteristic manifestations of different kinds of life, and they have no wish to reduce everything to a preconceived pattern. They have not the ideal of progress which dominates the Western nations, and affords a rationalization of our active impulses. Progress is, of course, a very modern ideal even with us; it is part of what we owe to science and industrialism. The cultivated conservative Chinese of the present day talk exactly as their earliest sages write. If one points out to them that this shows how little progress there has been, they will say: "Why seek progress when you already enjoy what is excellent?" At first, this point of view seems to a European unduly indolent; but gradually doubts as to one's own wisdom grow up, and one begins to think that much of what we call progress is only restless change, bringing us no nearer to any desirable goal.

It is interesting to contrast what the Chinese have sought in the West with what the West has sought in China. The Chinese in the West seek knowledge, in the hope—which I fear is usually vain—that knowledge may prove a gateway to wisdom. White men have gone to China with three motives: to fight, to make money, and to convert the Chinese to our religion. The last of these motives has the merit of being idealistic, and has inspired many heroic lives. But the soldier, the merchant, and the missionary are alike concerned to stamp our civilization upon the world; they are all three, in a certain sense, pugnacious. The Chinese have no wish to convert us to Confucianism; they say "religions are many, but reason is one," and with that they are content to let us go our way. They are good merchants, but their methods are quite different from those of European merchants in China, who are perpetually seeking concessions, monopolies, railways, and mines, and endeavoring to get their claims supported by gunboats. The Chinese are not, as a rule, good soldiers, because the causes for which they are asked to fight are not worth fighting for, and they know it. But that is only proof of their reasonableness.

I think the tolerance of the Chinese is in excess of anything that Europeans can imagine from their experience at home. We imagine ourselves tolerant, because we are more so than our ancestors. But we still practice political and social persecution, and what is more, we are firmly persuaded that our civilization and our way of life are immeasurably better than any other, so that when we come across a nation like the Chinese, we are convinced that the kindest thing we can do to them is to make them like ourselves. I believe this to be a profound mistake. It seemed to me that the average Chinaman, even if he is miserably poor, is happier than the average Englishman, and is happier because the nation is built upon a more humane and civilized outlook than our own. Restlessness and pugnacity not only cause obvious evils, but fill our lives with discontent, incapacitate us for the enjoyment of beauty, and make us almost incapable of the contemplative virtues. In this respect we have grown rapidly worse during the last hundred years. I do not deny that the Chinese go too far in the other direction; but for that very reason I think contact between East and West is likely to be fruitful to both parties. They may learn from us the indispensable minimum of practical efficiency, and we may learn from them something of that contemplative wisdom which has enabled them to persist while all the other nations of antiquity have perished.

When I went to China, I went to teach; but every day that I stayed I thought less of what I had to teach them and more of what I had to learn from them. Among Europeans who had lived a long time in China, I found this attitude not uncommon; but among those whose stay is short, or who go only to make money, it is sadly rare. It is rare because the Chinese do not excel in the things we really value—military prowess and industrial enterprise. But those who value wisdom or beauty, or even the simple enjoyment of life, will find more of these things in China than in the distracted and turbulent West, and will be happy to live where such things are valued. I wish I could hope that China, in return for our scientific knowledge, may give us something of her large tolerance and contemplative peace of mind.

THE CHINESE CHARACTER [1]

There is a theory among Occidentals that the Chinaman is inscrutable, full of secret thoughts, and impossible for us to understand. It may be that a greater experience of China would have brought me to share this opinion; but I could see nothing to support it during the time when I was working in that country. I talked to the Chinese as I should have talked to English people, and they answered me much as English people would have answered a Chinese whom they considered educated and not wholly unintelligent. I do not believe in the myth of the "subtle Oriental": I am convinced that in a game of mutual deception an Englishman or an American can beat a Chinese nine times out of ten. But, as many comparatively poor Chinese have dealings with rich white men, the game is often played only on one side. Then, no doubt, the white man is deceived and swindled; but not more than a Chinese mandarin would be in London.

One of the most remarkable things about the Chinese is their power of securing the affection of foreigners. Almost all Europeans like China, both those who come only as tourists and those who live

[1] From *The Problem of China.*

225

there for many years. In spite of the Anglo-Japanese alliance, I can recall hardly a single Englishman in the Far East who liked the Japanese as well as the Chinese. Those who have lived long among them tend to acquire their outlook and their standards. New arrivals are struck by obvious evils: the beggars, the terrible poverty, the prevalence of disease, the anarchy and corruption in politics. Every energetic Westerner feels at first a strong desire to reform these evils, and of course they ought to be reformed.

But the Chinese, even those who are the victims of preventable misfortunes, show a vast passive indifference to the excitement of the foreigners; they wait for it to go off, like the effervescence of soda-water. And gradually strange hesitations creep into the mind of the bewildered traveler; after a period of indignation, he begins to doubt all the maxims he has hitherto accepted without question. Is it really wise to be always guarding against future misfortune? Is it prudent to lose all enjoyment of the present through thinking of the disasters that may come at some future date? Should our lives be passed in building a mansion that we shall never have leisure to inhabit?

The Chinese answer these questions in the negative, and therefore have to put up with poverty, disease, and anarchy. But, to compensate for these evils, they have retained, as industrial nations have not, the capacity for civilized enjoyment, for leisure and laughter, for pleasure in sunshine and philosophical discourse. The Chinese, of all classes, are more laughter-loving than any other race with which I am acquainted; they find amusement in everything, and a dispute can always be softened by a joke.

I remember one hot day when a party of us were crossing the hills in chairs—the way was rough and very steep, the work for the coolies very severe. At the highest point of our journey, we stopped for ten minutes to let the men rest. Instantly they all sat in a row, brought out their pipes, and began to laugh among themselves as if they had not a care in the world. In any country that had learned the virtue of forethought, they would have devoted the moments to complaining of the heat, in order to increase their tip. We, being Europeans, spent the time worrying whether the automobile would be waiting for us at the right place. Well-to-do Chinese would have started a discussion as to whether the universe moves in cycles or progresses by a rectilinear motion; or they might have set to work to consider whether the truly virtuous man shows *complete* self-abnegation, or may, on occasion, consider his own interest.

One comes across white men occasionally who suffer under the delusion that China is not a civilized country. Such men have quite forgotten what constitutes civilization. It is true that there are no trams in Peking, and that the electric light is poor. It is true that there are places full of beauty, which Europeans itch to make hideous by digging up coal. It is true that the educated Chinaman is better at writing poetry than at remembering the sort of facts which can be looked up in "Whitaker's Almanack." A European, in recommending a place of residence, will tell you that it has a good train service; the best quality he can conceive in any place is that it should be easy to get away from. But a Chinaman will tell you nothing about the trains; if you ask, he will tell you wrong. What he tells you is that there is a palace built by an ancient emperor, and a retreat in a lake for scholars weary of the world, founded by a famous poet of the Tang dynasty. It is this out- look that strikes the Westerner as barbaric.

The Chinese from the highest to the lowest, have an imperturbable quiet dignity, which is usually not destroyed even by a European education. They are not self-assertive, either individually or nationally; their pride is too profound for self-assertion. They admit China's military weakness in comparison with foreign powers, but they do not consider efficiency in homicide the most important quality in a man or a nation. I think that, at bottom, they almost all believe that China is the greatest nation in the world, and has the finest civilization. A Westerner cannot expect to accept this view, because it is based on traditions utterly different from his own. But gradually one comes to feel that it is, at any rate, not an absurd view; that it is, in fact, the logical outcome of a self-consistent standard of values. The typical Westerner wishes to be the cause of as many changes as possible in his environment; the typical Chinaman wishes to enjoy as much and as delicately as possible. This difference is at the bottom of most of the contrast between China and the English-speaking world.

We in the West make a fetish of "progress," which is the ethical camouflage of the desire to be the cause of changes. If we are asked, for instance, whether machinery has really improved the world, the question strikes us as foolish: it has brought great changes and therefore great "progress." What we believe to be a love of progress is really, in nine cases out of ten, a love of power, an enjoyment of the feeling that by our fiat we can make things different. For the sake of this pleasure, a young American will work so hard that, by the time he has acquired his millions, he has become a victim of dyspepsia, compelled to live on toast and water, and to be a mere spectator of the feasts that he offers to his guests. But he consoles himself with the thought that he can control politics, and provoke or prevent wars as may suit his investments. It is this temperament that makes Western nations "progressive."

There are, of course, ambitious men in China, but they are less common than among ourselves. And

their ambition takes a different form—not a better
form, but one produced by the preference of enjoyment to power. It is a natural result of this preference that avarice is a widespread failing of the
Chinese. Money brings the means of enjoyment;
therefore money is passionately desired. With us,
money is desired chiefly as a means to power; politicians, who can acquire power without much money,
are often content to remain poor. In China the
tuchuns (military governors), who have the real
power, almost always use it for the sole purpose of
amassing a fortune. Their object is to escape to
Japan at a suitable moment, with sufficient plunder
to enable them to enjoy life quietly for the rest of
their days. The fact that in escaping they lose
power does not trouble them in the least. It is, of
course, obvious that such politicians, who spread
devastation only in the provinces committed to their
care, are far less harmful to the world than our own,
who ruin whole continents in order to win an election
campaign.

The corruption and anarchy in Chinese politics do
much less harm than one would be inclined to expect.
But for the predatory desires of the great powers—
especially Japan—the harm would be much less than
is done by our own "efficient" government. Nine-
tenths of the activities of a modern government are
harmful; therefore the worse they are performed,
the better. In China, where the government is lazy,

corrupt, and stupid, there is a degree of individual
liberty which has been wholly lost in the rest of the
world.

The laws are just as bad as elsewhere; occasionally, under foreign pressure, a man is imprisoned for
Bolshevist propaganda, just as he might be in England or America. But this is quite exceptional; as a
rule, in practice, there is very little interference with
free speech and a free press.[1] The individual does
not feel obliged to follow the herd, as he has in
Europe since 1914, and America since 1917. Men
still think for themselves, and are not afraid to announce the conclusions at which they arrive. Individualism has perished in the West, but in China
it survives, for good as well as for evil. Self-respect
and personal dignity are possible for every coolie in
China, to a degree which is, among ourselves, possible only for a few leading financiers.

The business of "saving face," which often strikes
foreigners in China as ludicrous, is only the carrying-
out of respect for personal dignity in the sphere of
social manners. Everybody has "face," even the
humblest beggar; there are humiliations that you
must not inflict upon him, if you are not to outrage
the Chinese ethical code. If you speak to a Chinaman in a way that transgresses the code, he will

[1] This vexes the foreigners, who are attempting to establish a
very severe press censorship in Shanghai. See "The Shanghai
Printed Matter Bye-Law." Hollington K. Tong, "Review of
the Far East," April 15, 1922.

laugh, because your words must be taken as spoken in jest if they are not to constitute an offense.

Once I thought that the students to whom I was lecturing were not as industrious as they might be and I told them so in just the same words that I should have used to English students in the same circumstances. But soon I found I was making a mistake. They all laughed uneasily, which surprised me until I saw the reason. Chinese life, even among the most modernized, is far more polite than anything to which we are accustomed. This, of course, interferes with efficiency, and also (what is more serious) with sincerity and truth in personal relations. If I were Chinese, I should wish to see it mitigated. But, to those who suffer from the brutalities of the West, Chinese urbanity is very restful. Whether on the balance it is better or worse than our frankness, I shall not venture to decide.

The Chinese remind one of the English in their love of compromise and in their habit of bowing to public opinion. Seldom is a conflict pushed to its ultimate brutal issue. The treatment of the Manchu emperor may be taken as a case in point. When a Western country becomes a republic, it is customary to cut off the head of the deposed monarch, or at least to cause him to fly the country. But the Chinese have left the emperor his title, his beautiful palace, his troops of eunuchs, and an income of several million dollars a year. He is a boy of sixteen, living peaceably in the Forbidden City. Once, in the course of a civil war, he was nominally restored to power for a few days; but he was deposed again, without being in any way punished for the use to which he had been put.

Public opinion is a very real force in China, when it can be roused. It was, by all accounts, mainly responsible for the downfall of the An Fu party in the summer of 1920. This party was pro-Japanese and was accepting loans from Japan. Hatred of Japan is the strongest and most widespread of political passions in China, and it was stirred up by the students in fiery orations. The An Fu party had, at first, a great preponderance of military strength; but their soldiers melted away when they came to understand the cause for which they were expected to fight. In the end, the opponents of the An Fu party were able to enter Peking and change the government almost without firing a shot.

The same influence of public opinion was decisive in the teachers' strike, which was on the point of being settled when I left Peking. The government, which is always impecunious, owing to corruption, had left its teachers unpaid for many months. At last they struck to enforce payment, and went on a peaceful deputation to the government, accompanied by many students. There was a clash with the soldiers and police, and many teachers and students were more or less severely wounded. This led to a terrific outcry, because the love of education in China is profound and widespread. The newspapers clamored for revolution. The government had just spent nine million dollars in corrupt payments to three *tuchuns* who had descended upon the capital to extort blackmail. It could not find any colorable pretext for refusing the few hundred thousands required by the teachers, and it capitulated in panic. I do not think there is any Anglo-Saxon country where the interests of teachers would have roused the same degree of public feeling.

Nothing astonishes a European more in the Chinese than their patience. The educated Chinese are well aware of the foreign menace. They realize acutely what the Japanese have done in Manchuria and Shantung. They are aware that the English in Hong-Kong are doing their utmost to bring to naught the Canton attempt to introduce good government in the South. They know that all the great powers, without exception, look with greedy eyes upon the undeveloped resources of their country, especially its coal and iron. They have before them the example of Japan, which, by developing a brutal militarism, a cast-iron discipline, and a new reactionary religion, has succeeded in holding at bay the fierce lusts of "civilized" industrialists. Yet they neither copy Japan nor submit tamely to foreign domination. They think not in decades but in centuries. They have been conquered before, first by the Tartars and then by the Manchus; but in both cases they absorbed their conquerors. Chinese civilization persisted, unchanged; and after a few generations the invaders became more Chinese than their subjects.

Manchuria is a rather empty country, with abundant room for colonization. The Japanese assert that they need colonies for their surplus population, yet the Chinese immigrants into Manchuria exceed the Japanese a hundredfold. Whatever may be the temporary political status of Manchuria, it will remain a part of Chinese civilization, and can be recovered whenever Japan happens to be in difficulties. The Chinese derive such strength from their four hundred millions, the toughness of their national customs, their power of passive resistance, and their unrivaled national cohesiveness—in spite of the civil wars, which merely ruffle the surface—that they can afford to despise military methods, and to wait till the feverish energy of their oppressors shall have exhausted itself in internecine combats.

China is much less a political entity than a civilization—the only one that has survived from ancient times. Since the days of Confucius, the Egyptian, Babylonian, Persian, Macedonian, and Roman empires have perished; but China has persisted through a continuous evolution. There have been foreign influences—first Buddhism, and now Western science. But Buddhism did not turn the Chinese into Indians, and Western science will not turn them into Europeans. I have met men in China who knew as much of Western learning as any professor among ourselves; yet they had not been thrown off their balance, nor lost touch with their own people. What is bad in the West—its brutality, its restlessness, its readiness to oppress the weak, its preoccupation with purely material aims—they see to be bad, and do not wish to adopt. What is good, especially its science, they do wish to adopt.

The old indigenous culture of China has become rather dead; its art and literature are not what they were, and Confucius does not satisfy the spiritual needs of a modern man, even if he is Chinese. The Chinese who have had a European or American education realize that a new element is needed to vitalize native traditions, and they look to our civilization to supply it. But they do not wish to construct a civilization just like ours; and it is precisely in this that the best hope lies. If they are not goaded into militarism, they may produce a genuinely new civilization, better than any that we in the West have been able to create.

So far, I have spoken chiefly of the good sides of the Chinese character; but of course China, like every other nation, has its bad sides also. It is disagreeable to me to speak of these, as I experienced so much courtesy and real kindness from the Chinese that I should prefer to say only nice things about them. But for the sake of China, as well as for the sake of truth, it would be a mistake to conceal what is less admirable. I will only ask the reader to remember that, on the balance, I think the Chinese one of the best nations I have come across, and am prepared to draw up a graver indictment against every one of the great powers. Shortly before I left China, an eminent Chinese writer pressed me to say what I considered the chief defects of the Chinese. With some reluctance, I mentioned three: avarice, cowardice, and callousness. Strange to say, my interlocutor, instead of getting angry, admitted the justice of my criticism, and proceeded to discuss possible remedies. This is a sample of the intellectual integrity which is one of China's greatest virtues.

The callousness of the Chinese is bound to strike every Anglo-Saxon. They have none of that humanitarian impulse which leads us to devote 1 per cent of our energy to mitigating the evils wrought by the other 99 per cent. For instance, we have been forbidding the Austrians to join with Germany, to emigrate, or to obtain the raw materials of industry. Therefore the Viennese have starved, except those whom it has pleased us to keep alive from philanthropy. The Chinese would not have had the energy to starve the Viennese, nor the philanthropy to keep some of them alive. While I was in China, millions were dying of famine; men sold their children into slavery for a few dollars, and killed them if this sum was unobtainable. Much was done by

white men to relieve the famine, but very little by
the Chinese, and that little vitiated by corruption.
It must be said, however, that the efforts of the white
men were more effective in soothing their own con-
sciences than in helping the Chinese.   So long as
the present birth-rate and the present methods of
agriculture persist, famines are bound to occur peri-
odically; and those whom philanthropy keeps alive
through one famine are only too likely to perish in
the next.

Famines in China can be permanently cured only
by better methods of agriculture combined with emi-
gration or birth-control on a large scale.   Educated
Chinese realize this, and it makes them indifferent to
efforts to keep the present victims alive.   A great
deal of Chinese callousness has a similar explanation,
and is due to perception of the vastness of the problems involved.   But there remains a residue which
cannot be so explained.   If a dog is run over by an
automobile and seriously hurt, nine out of ten
passers-by will stop to laugh at the poor brute's
howls.   The spectacle of suffering does not of itself
rouse any sympathetic pain in the average Chinaman; in fact, he seems to find it mildly agreeable.
Their history, and their penal code before the revolution of 1911, show that they are by no means destitute of the impulse of active cruelty; but of this I
did not myself come across any instances.   And it
must be said that active cruelty is practiced by all

the great nations, to an extent concealed from us only by our hypocrisy.

Cowardice is *prima facie* a fault of the Chinese; but I am not sure that they are really lacking in courage. It is true that, in battles between rival *tuchuns,* both sides run away, and victory rests with the side that first discovers the flight of the other. But this proves only that the Chinese soldier is a rational man. No cause of any importance is involved, and the armies consist of mere mercenaries. When there is a serious issue, as, for instance, in the Tai-Ping Rebellion, the Chinese are said to fight well, particularly if they have good officers. Nevertheless, I do not think that, in comparison with the Anglo-Saxons, the French, or the Germans, the Chinese can be considered a courageous people, except in the matter of passive endurance. They will endure torture, and even death, for motives which men of more pugnacious races would find insufficient—for example, to conceal the hiding-place of stolen plunder. In spite of their comparative lack of *active* courage, they have less fear of death than we have, as is shown by their readiness to commit suicide.

Avarice is, I should say, the greatest defect of the Chinese. Life is hard, and money is not easily obtained. For the sake of money, all except a very few foreign-educated Chinese will be guilty of corruption. For the sake of a few pence, almost any coolie will run an imminent risk of death. The difficulty of combating Japan has arisen mainly from the fact that hardly any Chinese politician can resist Japanese bribes. I think this defect is probably due to the fact that, for many ages, an honest living has been hard to get; in which case it will be lessened as economic conditions improve. I doubt if it is any worse now in China than it was in Europe in the eighteenth century. I have not heard of any Chinese general more corrupt than Marlborough or of any politician more corrupt than Cardinal Dubois. It is, therefore, quite likely that changed industrial conditions will make the Chinese as honest as we are —which is not saying much.

I have been speaking of the Chinese as they are in ordinary life, when they appear as men of active and skeptical intelligence, but of somewhat sluggish passions. There is, however, another side to them: they are capable of wild excitement, often of a collective kind. I saw little of this myself, but there can be no doubt of the fact. The Boxer rising was a case in point, and one which particularly affected Europeans. But their history is full of more or less analogous disturbances. It is this element in their character that makes them incalculable, and makes it impossible even to guess at their future. One can imagine a section of them becoming fanatically Bolshevist, or anti-Japanese, or Christian, or devoted to some leader who would ultimately declare himself emperor. I suppose it is this element in their character that makes them, in spite of their habitual caution, the most reckless gamblers in the world. And many emperors have lost their thrones through the force of romantic love, although romantic love is far more despised than it is in the West.

To sum up the Chinese character is not easy. Much of what strikes the foreigner is due merely to the fact that they have preserved an ancient civilization which is not industrial. All this is likely to pass away, under the pressure of the Japanese, and of European and American financiers. Their art is already perishing, and being replaced by crude imitations of second-rate European pictures. Most of the Chinese who have had a European education are quite incapable of seeing any beauty in native painting, and merely observe contemptuously that it does not obey the laws of perspective.

The obvious charm which the tourist finds in China cannot be preserved; it must perish at the touch of industrialism. But perhaps something may be preserved, something of the ethical qualities in which China is supreme, and which the modern world most desperately needs. Among these qualities I place first the pacific temper, which seeks to settle disputes on grounds of justice rather than by force. It remains to be seen whether the West will allow this temper to persist, or will force it to give place, in self-defense, to a frantic militarism like that to which Japan has been driven.

CAUSES OF THE PRESENT CHAOS [1]

I

The movement of human society, viewed throughout the period known to history, is partly cyclic,
partly progressive; it resembles a tune played over
and over again, but each time louder and with a
fuller orchestration than before. In this tune there
are quiet passages and passionate passages; there is
a terrific climax, and then a time of silence until the
tune begins again. Such a climax is exemplified by
the period through which we are now passing or
about to pass. If we think only of the one tune,
it seems to end in nothingness; if we think only of
the cycle, it seems that the whole process is futile.
It is only by fixing our attention upon what is progressive, upon what distinguishes one cycle from the
next, that we become aware of the advance made
from age to age, and of the steady movement under-
lying the back-and-forth eddies of the surface.

The ancient empires of Egypt and Babylonia were
swept away by the Persian empire, the Persian by
the Macedonian, the Macedonian by the Roman, the
Roman by the Teutons and Arabs, the Arabs by the

[1] From *The Prospects of Industrial Civilization,* written in collaboration with Dora Russell.

Teutons. At each stage, a civilization which had reached a certain height and then grown decrepit was destroyed, and a new one built upon its ruins, sometimes only after a considerable period of chaos. Our own civilization appears to be growing decrepit and ready to fall. In all this, we see only the cyclic movement of history: birth, growth, decay, and death, in empires and civilizations as with the beasts of the field.

But when we compare any one of these civilizations with its predecessors, we become aware of a definite advance, particularly in two respects: first, the increase of knowledge; and secondly, the growth in the extent of organizations, more particularly of states. From past progress in these two respects, a definite though perhaps not very immediate hope for the future is seen to be justified.

The increase of knowledge and the growth of states are both sources of evil as well as of good: science has made war more destructive, and large empires have made it more widespread. But although both are capable of doing harm, both are indispensable conditions of vital progress. With regard to knowledge this may perhaps be taken as obvious. With regard to the growth of states the view that it is to be regarded as desirable results from considering the chaos in the world and the only possible ways of amending it. The only ultimate cure for war is the creation of a world-state or superstate, strong enough to decide by law all disputes between nations. And a world-state is only conceivable after the different parts of the world have become so intimately related that no part can be indifferent to what happens in any other part. This stage has now been reached. Until recent times, the Far East had no vital relation to Europe. Until Columbus, America was isolated. Until Peter the Great, Russia had little connection with the Western powers. The late war, by its universality of destruction, demonstrated the solidarity of mankind. And this solidarity has resulted from industrialism and mechanical inventions, both of which are products of science. It is science, ultimately, that makes our age different, for good or evil, from the ages that have gone before. And science, whatever harm it may cause by the way, is capable of bringing mankind ultimately into a far happier condition than any that has been known in the past.

On these broad grounds, optimism as to the ultimate issue of the present chaos seems to be justified. Meanwhile the state of the world is frightful, and is only too likely to become worse in the near future. If we would act wisely in this time of darkness, if we would take our share in making the destruction as small as possible and the new construction as swift and solid as it is capable of being, it is necessary that we should face all that is discouraging in the present and all the dangers of the near future; it is necessary that we should diagnose fearlessly, without regard to party shibboleths or to the desire for the easy consolation of fallacious hopes. It is necessary to apply in our thinking the best science and the most enlightened ideals that our age affords. Above all it is necessary to avoid the discouragement and sense of impotence that are too apt to result from the spectacle of apparently irresistible forces arrayed against the ends which we wish to see realized. For this purpose, it is well to remind ourselves that political forces are not strong except when they rest upon popular support, and that, in the main, only ignorance secures popular support for what is evil. Amid the myths and hysterias of opposing hatreds, it is difficult to cause truth to reach the bulk of the people, or to spread the habit of forming opinions on evidence rather than on passion. Yet it is ultimately upon these things, not upon any political panacea, that the hopes of the world must rest.

Reason and the scientific temper of mind are more necessary to the world than they ever were before, because all the creeds and habits which reposed upon irrational authority have broken down. Taboos, religious beliefs, and social customs are the source of order among uncivilized tribes, in so far as any order exists among them; and they remain the source of order through successive stages of culture, until at last the skeptical intellect shows their absurdity. This happened in Athens at the height of its political and cultural glory, and in the resulting chaos Athens perished. It happened in Italy at the end of the fifteenth century, and Italy became enslaved to the fanatical Spaniards. It is happening now to the whole civilized world: the old bonds of authority have been loosed by the war, men will no longer submit merely because their forefathers did so, a reason is demanded for abstaining from claiming one's rights, and the reasons offered are counterfeit reasons, convincing only to those who have a selfish interest in being convinced. This condition of revolt exists in women toward men, in oppressed nations toward their oppressors, and above all in labor toward capital. It is a state full of danger, as all past history shows, yet also full of hope, if only the revolt of the oppressed can result in victory without too terrible a struggle, and their victory can result in the establishment of a stable social order.

What are the forces which are shaping the world and producing its struggles? What are their relative strengths, and what are the prospects of their warfare? I wish to consider these questions dispassionately, not as one of the fighters, but as a scientific investigator.

There are in the world growing forces and diminishing forces. Among the latter some still remain very potent, but their heyday is passed, and they are doomed (if civilization escapes disaster) to dwindle more and more. Among the growing forces, two stand out preëminent among all others; namely, industrialism and nationalism. Behind both of these, non-political itself, yet controlling all political occurrences, is science.

Industrialism and nationalism both have two forms, one for the holders of power, the other for those who are struggling to emancipate themselves. Capitalism and socialism are the two forms of industrialism; imperialism and the attempt to secure freedom for oppressed nations are the two forms of nationalism. Freedom for oppressed nations is what President Wilson endeavored to make popular under the name of "self-determination." The victors in the war decided that this principle should only apply in favor of those oppressed by the enemies of the Entente; those oppressed by the Entente are held to have no right to national independence. The principle of self-determination has therefore been taken up by the Russians as regards territories held by their enemies, and it has thus come into a practical alliance with socialism. But it belongs to an entirely different order of thoughts and sentiments, and can never have more than an external alliance with principles so essentially international as those of Karl Marx.

We have thus four great political forces in the world: the two forms of industrialism, namely capitalism and socialism; and the two forms of nationalism, namely imperialism and self-determination.

The chaos in the world mainly takes the form of a titanic conflict between these forces; capitalism and imperialism on one side; socialism and self-determination on the other.

2

The bitterness of political and military conflict has concealed from the world and from the combatants themselves how much there is in common between the two forms of industrialism, and also between the two forms of nationalism. It is necessary to understand these affinities of rival forces if we are not to go astray in our attempts to analyze the present situation.

First of all, let us be clear as to what we mean by Industrialism.

Industrialism is essentially production (including distribution) by methods requiring much fixed capital,[1] i.e., much expenditure of labor in producing implements for the production of commodities which satisfy our needs and desires. It is an extension of the habit of using tools. The man who first thought of plowing the soil before sowing took the first step toward industrialism: a plow is something which does not in itself satisfy any of our needs or desires, but diminishes the amount of labor required for satis-

[1] Capital is not money but means of production. Money can buy capital, and is normally so employed when it is invested, but capital consists, not of money, but of such things as machinery, railways, ships, etc.

fying our hunger. Industrialism is the extension of this practice of making tools, until the tools grow into modern machinery, which requires for its production and use the coöperation of large numbers of workers. As an example of industrial methods of production, we may take railways. A railway requires a very great amount of labor for its construction, yet when constructed it does not, of itself, enable us to gratify any of our wishes. We cannot eat it, or clothe ourselves with it, or sleep on it (without imminent risk of death). A railway cannot advantageously be consumed, like a loaf of bread; it can only be used, i.e., employed as a means of providing loaves of bread, and other consumable commodities, with less labor than would otherwise be necessary. While the railway is being built, and until it is actually used, those who construct it cannot be kept alive by their own labor, which produces none of the necessaries of life, but must be supported out of the surplus of necessaries produced by other people. Consequently every increase of industrial capital involves a momentary diminution in the satisfaction of wants; a community which is becoming industrialized is constantly forgoing the present satisfaction of wants for the sake of greater satisfaction in the future.

It is obvious that industrialism demands certain qualities in a community which is to practice it successfully. First, there must be a possibility of obtaining large organizations of workers devoted to a common task; a railway, for example, cannot be built by one man or one family. Next, there must be, in those who can direct the labor of the community, a willingness to forgo present gratifications for the sake of greater wealth later. Thirdly, there must be a sufficiently orderly and stable government to render it highly probable that those who make this postponement will be able to reap their reward; otherwise everybody will adopt the maxim, "Let us eat and drink, for to-morrow we die." Fourthly, there must be a large number of skilled workers, because many of the processes of industrial production are difficult. Lastly, there must be a body of scientific knowledge, to make and utilize mechanical inventions. This last condition is the most essential of all: its absence in former times is the reason why industrialism is a recent growth.

It seems almost inevitable that, when a country is in the early stages of industrialism, the economic organization should be oligarchic, and the bulk of the population should be very poor unless it is possible to borrow extensively from more advanced countries. To take first the question of poverty: when a country has not yet become industrial its methods of production are not highly efficient, and do not, in general, produce any very great surplus above what is needed for subsistence. The first effect of a movement toward the development of industry in such a country is to take a number of workers away from work which is immediately productive, and to cause them instead to build railways or construct machines or export their produce to other countries where machines can be bought or such things as steel rails manufactured. The result is that, at first, there is a diminution in the amount of consumable commodities to be distributed. As there was already not much to spare (owing to the country having been hitherto unindustrial), the result of a diminution is apt to be serious poverty for the ordinary worker. The only way to avoid this is to industrialize very slowly, or to borrow heavily from economically more advanced countries. The latter is the expedient usually adopted when the relations with advanced countries are friendly. But when, as in Soviet Russia, borrowing is impossible owing to hostility, there remains only the alternative of great poverty or very slow industrialization.

It is even more inevitable that the economic organization of industry should be oligarchic in a country which is in the early stages of industrial development. In Great Britain, which is the oldest of the industrial countries, there is a powerful movement for self-government in industry, a movement which deserves the fullest sympathy. This is the form of socialism which has most vitality and force among British trade-unionists. But in Russia, though a similar movement existed in 1917 and 1918, it has now been completely suppressed by the authorities, who have restored one-man rule in factories and the undemocratic control of all industry from above. This difference has caused a certain wholly unnecessary division of opinion: Russian communists and their adherents in the West consider Russian experience conclusive against self-government in industry, at any rate for the present, while those who adhere to ideas more akin to syndicalism find themselves impelled, in this respect, to criticize what the Bolsheviks have done. For my part, I consider the difference between English and Russian socialism as regards self-government a necessary result of the different stages of industrial development in the two countries, and I think this would have been evident to all if the habit of thinking in terms of political battle-cries had not obscured what should have been obvious facts. Self-government in industry seems to me plainly impossible in a country as undeveloped as Russia, but nevertheless perfectly possible in England. I will try to make it clear why this must be the case.

To begin with, as we have already seen, the industrializing of an undeveloped country, when it cannot be effected by borrowing, involves considerable hardship for the average working-man, over and above what he suffered before the growth of industry began. If the average working-man has economic control, he will resent this increased hardship, and will not be reconciled to it by the promise of ultimate benefit to his children or grandchildren. In the early days of the industrial revolution in England, gangs of working-men broke up the machinery of the mills, because machinery produced the same output with less labor, and therefore threw men out of work. If working-men had had control of methods of production in those days, the industrial revolution could never have taken place.

But it is not only the temporary increase of poverty that makes self-government in nascent industry impossible. It is also—and this is the most important reason—because when industry is new men have not the habit of coöperation in large groups of producers. Non-industrial production is an individual affair, or an affair of a family or a small group of handicraftsmen. There do not exist the customs which would facilitate voluntary combination of hundreds or thousands of workmen. An organization of a new kind is very rarely created voluntarily. It is possible by means of power to compel a number of people to work together for a common end imposed from above, not chosen by themselves; and when they have the habit of such work and the experience of its usefulness they can carry it on without external compulsion. This has been the case in politics: only where kings have first produced a strongly knit state has democracy subsequently proved successful. I do not except the United States from this rule, because the political habits of the Fathers of the Constitution were those that had been formed in England in the seventeenth century. And I do not believe that an international world-state will ever prove effective except through the domination of one state or of some close alliance of states. When once the necessary organization exists and habits of working within it have been formed, self-government becomes possible and freedom can be gradually achieved. So it is in industry: whether nominally capitalistic or communistic, nascent industry must be more or less despotic, the despot being in one case a capitalist, in the other a state official. All the experience of the Bolsheviks bears out this view, and I have no doubt that it will prove equally true in India, China, and other undeveloped countries.

It follows from these considerations that the practical difference between capitalism and socialism is not so great as politicians on both sides suppose. Certain features will appear in the early stages of industrialism under either system; and under either system certain other features will appear in its later stages. Russian industry under the Bolsheviks reminds one of English industry a hundred years ago: long hours, a sweated wage, prohibition of strikes, absolute submission of the workers to the captains of industry, are all features which the two have in common, and must have in common, since both are attempts to develop industry without the help of foreign capital.

It follows also that the good things at which socialism aims can only be achieved where industry is highly developed and has sunk deep into the habits of the nation. In England or America, socialism, if it could be achieved without prolonged war and industrial dislocation, could bring a very considerable degree of material well-being to the whole population, by exacting only four or five hours of daily labor from every adult citizen. And it would not need to be a centralized bureaucratic system, because the workers, from long practice, have come to understand the industries in which they are employed and would be thoroughly competent to manage them themselves. A gradual approach to these benefits is possible without a catastrophic abolition of the capitalist system, and therefore without the very grave dangers to industrialism and the whole fabric of civilization which are involved in a universal class war. But these benefits cannot be secured in a country as yet almost unindustrial, however much it may be nominally communistic, because in such a country the total produce of labor is not very much more than is needed for subsistence, and there are not, in the general body of the population, the habits, the skill, or the knowledge required for a democratic control of the processes of industrial production.

If these considerations are valid, it follows that

the political disputes which center round the class conflict, important as they are, cannot prevent the still greater importance of the development of machinery, skill, and industrial habits, which will determine certain broad features in the economic life of a nation whatever may be its system of distribution, and will make two backward countries, one socialistic and the other capitalistic, resemble each other more, in many ways, than either will resemble an industrially advanced country.

3

Next to industrialism, the most potent force that molds the modern world is nationalism. Like industrialism, nationalism has two forms, one for the holders of power and the other for those who are struggling to emancipate themselves. Nationalism in the holders of power is called imperialism; in oppressed nations it is called the principle of self-determination. As in the case of industrialism, the two forms have much more in common than they are thought to have by those engaged in the conflict between them.

But let us first be clear as to what we mean by nationalism.

Nationalism is a development of herd-instinct: it is the habit of taking as one's herd the nation to which one belongs. As to what constitutes a nation, the only thing that can be said definitely is that a nation is a group which is defined geographically. One may feel allegiance to various kinds of groups: races, religions, professions, artists, men of science, etc., etc. When a group to which men feel allegiance is geographical, it may be called a nation, and the allegiance which is felt may be called nationalism. Thus "nations" and "nationalism" have to be defined together: they are both constituted by herd-instinct directed to a geographical group. It is a characteristic of the present age that this form of herd-instinct has acquired a very marked predominance over every other. In the past, in many periods, a man's herd consisted rather of his coreligionists than of his compatriots. Marx, who regarded the history of the world as mainly a struggle between classes, the feudal aristocracy giving place to the bourgeoisie and the bourgeoisie to the proletariat, expected a man's herd-instinct to be directed rather to his class than to his nation. Hence his followers have been astonished by the patriotism of working-men and cynical about the apparent patriotism of the capitalist class. "Proletariat of all countries, unite," is the Marxian exhortation to the wage-earner to transfer his herd-instinct from his country to his class. Hitherto this exhortation has been very unsuccessful, as the late war showed; but we cannot be sure that it will remain so.

Rivalry is part of the instinctive apparatus of human nature, and as civilization advances there is a tendency for the rival groups to grow larger and larger, from families to tribes, from tribes to small nations, and from small nations to the great nations of the present day. The essence of nationalism is the sense of rivalry between one's own nation and others. This brings with it a whole train of loyalties and friendly sentiments toward compatriots, with a correlative train of hatreds and pugnacities toward the members of rival nations. A person afflicted with nationalism believes that his own country is the most civilized and humane country in the world, while its enemies are guilty of every imaginable atrocity and vileness. Since they are so vile and atrocious, while we are so civilized and humane, there is no degree of vileness and atrocity which we may not legitimately practice toward them. This is the creed of nationalism.

It is obvious that this creed is, by its very nature, founded in falsehood and leading to strife, brutality, and destruction. The beliefs of a nationalist are different in every country. The Germans considered their Kultur so superior as to be worth spreading at the cost of a European war; the English, on the contrary, consider their own so preferable to every other as to be worth propagating by the bayonet and the lash.[1] The English and the Germans did not agree

---

[1] See, e.g., *Daily News*, January 5, 1920. *The Times*, February 22, 1923, in a telegram from Delhi, states: "The Criminal Law

with each other's opinions, though both were nation-
alists.   There is no doubt one nation which really
is as superior as each nation thinks itself; it is, of
course, that nation (whichever it may be) to which
my reader belongs.   But all other nations are plainly
in error in adopting the nationalist creed: they ought
to admit the superiority of my reader's nation, and
submit meekly to its demands.   But, alas! their
claim to superiority is just as stubborn as though it
were well founded, just as self-assured as in case of
our own *really* superior nation.

The smallness of the difference between imperialism and oppressed nationalism is seen when an oppressed nation is liberated.   We may take Poland
as a recent and glaring example.   For a century and
a half the Russians oppressed the Poles, and the
Poles professed to desire nothing but freedom.   The
friends of freedom everywhere befriended them and
regarded them as a gallant nation incapable of inflicting upon others such tyranny as they were suffering.   Yet in the very moment of acquiring their national independence they embarked upon a war of
conquest against Russia with a view to inflicting upon
as many Russians as possible the pains and tortures
which Poland had formerly suffered at the hands
of the czar.   There is nothing peculiar or exceptional

Amendment Bill has been passed by the Legislative Assembly,
with a trifling alteration, giving the right of appeal in whipping
cases."   I have in my possession photographs showing Indians
being beaten into unconsciousness because we dislike their politics.

in this behavior; it is the natural behavior of any country afflicted with virulent nationalism.

It is not merely artificial frontiers or the blunders of diplomatists that make the evil of nationalism; it is not merely the fact that some nations are oppressors while others are oppressed. This fact is, of course, a very grave evil, but it is the inevitable outcome of nationalist feeling in a world where a complete equilibrium of national forces is impossible to maintain. So long as the majority of civilized mankind continue to feel that their only social obligation is to their own country, and that for its advancement they are justified in inflicting any degree of damage upon people of other countries, so long no diplomatic arrangements or political reform can produce a tolerable world.

The principle of self-determination, although the weaker nations appeal to it in their struggle with the great powers, is not itself nationalistic; it is rather an endeavor to cope with nationalism from the standpoint of an internationalist. The true nationalist wants self-determination only for his own country, though the need of allies may compel him to an appearance of justice toward other national claims. It is obvious that, while national feeling remains as hot as it is at present, self-determination, if it could be realized and enforced against the stronger nations, would be the best possible arrangement of national boundaries. But it is scarcely conceivable that it should be realized or maintained while national feeling remains what it is. At each frontier opposing armed forces will stand glaring at each other; trade will be made difficult and, when it occurs, will be used to stir up national economic hatred; at the slightest provocation wars will break out in which the victors will throw the principle of self-determination to the winds. It is not by a formula, however admirable, that the evils of nationalism can be cured. Nor can they be cured by adopting passionately the cause of the nations now oppressed, since to-morrow they will become oppressors if our championship is successful. The only cure for the evils of nationalism is the diminution of nationalism, the diversion of men's energies and sentiments from the barren business of national rivalry. I have no doubt that it is at present the most important task which civilization has to face, more important even than the introduction of a better economic system.

I have considered in this chapter what I believe to be the two main forces by which the modern world is being shaped. I have considered each in isolation, without regard to their interrelations. But these interrelations are very important and very interesting. Industrialism has in various ways contributed to the growth of nationalism, while it has for the first time in history produced the technical possibility of a super-national government for the whole world. Socialism professes to be at once international and the champion of oppressed nations, while capitalism favors nationalism as a method of distracting the working-man from socialistic ideas: so long as he can be kept hating foreigners, he will be less vigorous in hating capitalists. All these factors are important in considering the conflict which is threatening to destroy our civilization.

Meanwhile there are old forces from the past, decaying but still strong—such forces as handicrafts and peasant agriculture, religion and literary habits of thought. As the rival protagonists of modern ideas weaken each other by internecine combat, the old forces grow relatively stronger, and it is quite conceivable that they will be in the end the sole victors.

MORAL STANDARDS AND SOCIAL
WELL-BEING [1]

I

To any one who reflects upon industrialism it is clear that it requires, for its successful practice, somewhat different virtues from those that were required in a pre-industrial community. But there is, to my mind, widespread misapprehension as to the nature of those virtues, owing to the fact that moralists confine their survey to a short period of time and are more interested in the success of the individual than in that of the race. There is also, in all conventional moralists, a gross ignorance of psychology, making them unable to realize that certain virtues imply certain correlated vices, so that in recommending a virtue the consideration which ought to weigh is: does this virtue, with its correlative vice, outweigh the opposite virtue with its correlative vice? The fact that a virtue is good in itself is not enough; it is necessary to take account of the vices that it entails and the virtues that it excludes.

I shall define as virtues those mental and physi-

[1] From *The Prospects of Industrial Civilization*, written in collaboration with Dora Russell.

cal habits which tend to produce a good community, and as vices those that tend to produce a bad one. Different people have different conceptions of what makes a community good or bad, and it is difficult to find arguments by which to establish the preferability of one's own conception. I cannot hope, therefore, to appeal to those whose tastes are very different from my own, but I hope and believe that there is nothing very singular in my own tastes. For my part, I should judge a community to be in a good state if I found a great deal of instinctive happiness, a prevalence of feelings of friendship and affection rather than hatred and envy, a capacity for creating and enjoying beauty, and the intellectual curiosity which leads to the advancement and diffusion of knowledge. I should judge a community to be in a bad state if I found much unhappiness from thwarted instinct, much hatred and envy, little sense of beauty, and little intellectual curiosity. As between these different elements of excellence or the reverse, I do not pretend to judge. Suppose, for the sake of argument, that intellectual curiosity and artistic capacity were found to be in some degree incompatible, I should find it difficult to say which ought to be preferred. But I should certainly think better of a community which contained something of both than of one which contained more of the one and none of the other. I do not, however, believe that there is any incompatibility among the four ingredients I have mentioned as constituting a good community; namely, happiness, friendship, enjoyment of beauty, and love of knowledge.

It is to be observed that we do not define as a virtue merely what leads to these good things for its possessor, but what leads to them for the community to which he belongs. For different purposes, the community that has to be considered is different. In the case of acts which have little effect outside the family, the family will be the community concerned. In the official actions of a mayor, the community concerned will be the municipality; in internal politics it will be the nation, and in foreign politics the world. Theoretically, it is always the whole world that is concerned, but practically the effects outside some limited circle are often negligible.

However moralists may recommend altruism, all the moral exhortations that have had widespread effects have appealed to purely selfish desires. Buddhism urged virtue on the ground that it led to Nirvana; Christianity, on the ground that it led to heaven. In each of these great religions, virtue was that line of conduct which would be pursued by a prudent egoist. Neither of these, however, has much influence on the practical morality of our own time. For energetic people, the moral code of our time is that of "success"—the code which my generation learnt in childhood from Smiles's *Self-help*, and which modern young men learn from efficiency experts. In this code, "success" is defined as the acquisition of a large income. According to this code, it is wicked for a young man to be late at the office, even if what has delayed him is fetching the doctor for a sudden illness of his child; but it is not wicked to oust a competitor by well-timed talebearing. Competition, hard work, and rigid self-control are demanded by this code; its rewards are dyspepsia and unutterable boredom, in all who have not a quite exceptional physique. By comparison with its votaries, St. Simeon Stylites was a voluptuary; nevertheless, they, like him, are pure egoists.

In sociology, we are concerned with men in the mass, not with rare and exceptional individuals. It is possible for a few saints to live a life which is in part unselfish, but it does not appear to be possible for the vast majority of mankind. The study of psychology, and more particularly of psychoanalysis, has torn aside the cloaks that our egoism wears, and has shown that when we think we are being unselfish this is hardly ever in fact the case. It would therefore be useless to preach a morality which required unselfishness on the part of any large number of men. I do not think myself that there is any need to do so. Our natural impulses, properly directed and trained, are, I believe, capable of producing a good community, provided praise and blame are wisely apportioned.

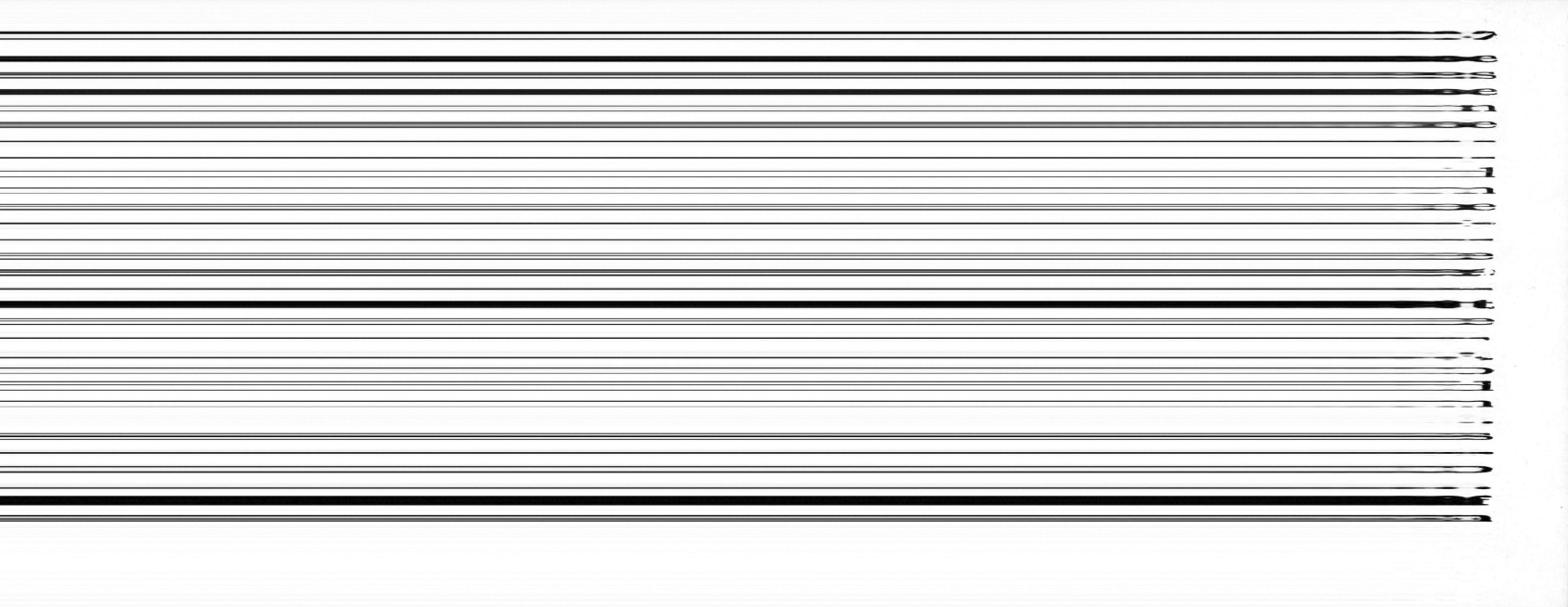

and from co

a habit wh

and a vice

munity. I

one import

moralists,

were the

different;

actions are

these is vi

(except on

of those in

above all,

outside ma

degenerate

ments, but

insanity—t

fetched an

encing the

influencing

classes of

of their c

perstitious

theme to

fore assum

be judged

of that ki

moral cod

viously in

It is through the operation of praise and blame that the positive morality of a community becomes socially effective. We all like praise and dislike blame; moreover, rewards and punishments often accompany them. "Positive morality"—i.e., the habit of attaching praise to certain types of behavior and blame to certain other types—has enormous influence on conduct. In Somaliland, and formerly among the aborigines of Formosa, a man was not thought sufficiently manly to deserve a wife until he had killed some one; in fact, he was expected to bring the head of his victim to the wedding ceremony. The result was that even the mildest and gentlest of men, in obedience to the moral sense of the community, felt obliged to practice homicide. This custom is rapidly dying out among savages, but among the white races the same feeling persists as regards military service in wartime. Thus in spite of the egoism of human nature, the positive morality of neighbors forces men into conduct quite different from that which they would pursue if positive morality were different; they even often sacrifice their lives for fear of being blamed. Positive morality is therefore a very tremendous power. I believe that at present it is quite unadapted to industrialism, and that it will have to be radically changed if industrialism is to survive.

There is one point in which the definition of virtue and vice given above departs from tradition and from common practice. We defined a virtue as a habit which tends to produce a good community, and a vice as one which tends to produce a bad community. In thus judging by results, we agreed in one important respect with the utilitarian school of moralists, among whom Bentham and the two Mills were the most eminent. The traditional view is different; it holds that certain specified classes of actions are vicious, and that abstinence from all these is virtue. It is wicked to murder or steal (except on a large scale); it is wicked to speak ill of those in power, from the Deity to the policeman; above all, it is wicked to have sexual intercourse outside marriage. These prohibitions may, in our degenerate age, be defended by utilitarian arguments, but in some cases—e.g., refusal of divorce for insanity—the utilitarian arguments are very far-fetched and are obviously not what is really influencing the minds of those who use them. What is influencing their minds is the view that certain classes of acts are "wicked," quite independently of their consequences. I regard this view as superstitious, but it would take us too far from our theme to argue the question here. I shall therefore assume, without more ado, that actions are to be judged by the results to be expected from actions of that kind, and not by some supposed *a priori* moral code. I do not mean—what would be obviously impracticable—that we should habitually

calculate the effects of our actions. What I mean is that, in deciding what sort of moral instruction should be given to the young, or what sort of actions should be punished by the criminal law, we should do our best to consider what sort of actions will promote or hinder the general well-being. It might almost seem as if this were a platitude. Yet a tremendous change would be effected if this platitude were acted upon. Our education, our criminal law, and our standards of praise and blame would become completely different from what they are at present. How they would be altered I shall now try to show.

Let us consider one by one the four kinds of excellence which we mentioned, beginning with instinctive happiness.

2

Instinctive Happiness. I mean by this sort of thing that is diminished by ill health and destroyed by a bad liver, the kind of delight in life which one finds always more strongly developed in the young of any mammalian species than in the old. I doubt whether there is anything else that makes as much difference to the value of life from the point of view of the person who has to live it. Those who have instinctive delight in life are happy except when they have positive causes of unhappiness; those who do not have it are unhappy except when

they have positive causes of happiness. Moreover, outward causes of happiness have more effect upon those who delight in life, while those who do not are more affected by outward causes of unhappiness. Of all personal goods, delight in life is therefore the greatest; and it is a condition for many others. I do not deny that it can be too dearly purchased if it is obtained at the cost of injustice and stupidity. In the advanced industrial nations, apart from the agricultural population, I can think of only one small class that lives so as to preserve it; namely, the male portion of the British upper class. The public schools develop a boy's physique at the expense of his intelligence and sympathy; in this way, by the help of a good income, he often succeeds in preserving instinctive happiness. But the system is essentially aristocratic, so that it cannot be regarded as in any degree a contribution to the solution of our problem. Our problem is to preserve instinctive happiness for the many, not only for a privileged few.

The causes of instinctive happiness could best be set forth by a medical man, but without medical knowledge observation makes it easy to see broadly what they are. Physical health and vigor come first, but are obviously not alone sufficient. It is necessary to have scope for instinctive desires, and also for instinctive needs which often exist without corresponding explicit desires. Very few adults,

whether men or women, can preserve instinctive happiness in a state of celibacy; this applies even to those women who have no conscious desire for sexual satisfaction. On this point, the evidence of psycho-analysis may be taken as conclusive. Many women and some men need also to have children sooner or later. To most men, some kind of progressive career is important; both to men and women, a certain amount of occupation imposed by necessity, not chosen for its pleasurable quality, is necessary for the avoidance of boredom. But too much work and too little leisure are more destructive of instinctive happiness than too little work and too much leisure. Another essential is the right amount of human companionship, neither too much nor too little; but as to what is the right amount, people vary greatly. Our instinctive nature seems to be fairly adapted to the hunting stage, as may be seen from the passion of rich men for shooting big game, killing birds, and careering after foxes. In the hunting stage, men had periods of violent exertion alternating with complete quiescence, while women had activities which were more continuous but less strenuous and less exciting. This probably accounts for the fact that men are more prone to gambling than women. One result of adaptation to the hunting stage is that most people like loud noise at times of excitement, alternating with silence at other times. In modern industrial life the noise is continuous, and this certainly has a debilitating nervous effect. I believe that almost every one has a need (though often not a desire) for the sights and smells of the country. The delight of slum children on a country holiday is of a kind that points to the satisfaction of an instinctive need which urban life cannot supply. In recovering from a dangerous illness, the pleasure of being still alive consists mainly in joy in sunshine and the smell of rain and other such sensations familiar to primitive man.

The difference between needs and desires is important in the consideration of instinctive happiness. Our desires are mainly for things which primitive man did not get without difficulty: food and drink (especially the latter), leadership of the tribe, improvements in the methods of hunting and fighting. But we have many needs which are not associated with desires, because under primitive conditions these needs were always satisfied. Such are the needs of country sensations, of occasional silence and occasional solitude, of alternations of excitement and quiescence. To some extent, sex and maternity in women come under this head, because in a primitive community men see to the satisfaction of these feminine needs without any necessity for female coöperation. *Per contra,* there are desires which do not correspond to instinctive needs. The most important of these are the desires for drugs, including alcohol and tobacco. The fact

that these desires are so readily stimulated by habit
is an example of natural maladjustment from a Dar-
winian point of view. They differ from instinctive
needs in two ways. First, from the point of view
of survival, their satisfaction is not biologically useful; drugs do not help a man either to survive himself or to have a numerous progeny. Secondly, from
the psychological point of view, the craving that
they satisfy depends upon the habit of taking them,
not upon a preëxistent need. The instinctive dissatisfaction which leads a man to take to drink is
usually something wholly unconnected with alcohol,
such as business worries or disappointment in love.
Drugs are a substitute for the thing instinctively
needed, but an unsatisfactory substitute, because
they never bring full instinctive satisfaction. [1]

With the advance of what is called civilization,
our social and material environment has changed
faster than our instincts, so that there has been an
increasing discrepancy between the acts to which
we are impelled by instinct and those to which we
are constrained by prudence. Up to a point, this
is quite unavoidable. Murder, robbery, and rape
are actions which may be prompted by instinct, but
an orderly society must repress them. Work, especially when many are employed in one undertaking,
requires regularity, which is utterly contrary to our

---

[1] I do not wish this to be regarded as an argument for prohibition, to which on the whole I am opposed.

untrained nature. And although a man who followed his impulses in a state of nature would (at least in a cold climate) do a good deal of work in the course of an average day, yet it is very rare indeed that a man has any spontaneous impulse to the work which he has to do in a modern industrial community. He works for the sake of the pay, not because he likes the work. There are of course exceptions: artists, inventors, men of learning, healthy mothers who have few children and strong maternal instincts, people in positions of authority, a small percentage of sailors and peasants. But the exceptions are not sufficiently numerous to be an important section of the whole. The irksomeness of work has no doubt always existed since men took to agriculture; it is mentioned in Genesis as a curse, and heaven has always been imagined as a place where no one does any work. But industrial methods have certainly made work more remote from instinct, and have destroyed the joy in craftsmanship which gave handicraftsmen something of the satisfaction of the artist. I do not think that, if industrial methods survive, we can hope to make the bulk of necessary work pleasant. The best we can hope is to diminish its amount, but there is no doubt that its amount could be diminished very greatly. It is chiefly in this direction that we must look for a lessening of the instinctive dissatisfaction involved in work.

A "return to nature," such as Rousseau's disciples dreamt of, is not possible without a complete break-up of civilization. Regimentation, especially, is of the very essence of industrialism, which would necessarily perish without it. If this is an evil and unavoidable, our aim must be to have as little of it as is possible. This aim will be realized by making the hours of industrial labor as short as is compatible with the production of necessaries, and leaving the remaining hours of the day entirely untrammeled. Four hours' boredom a day is a thing which most people could endure without damage; and this is probably about what would be required.

In many other respects, the restraints upon instinct which now exist could be greatly diminished. Production at present has two correlative defects, that it is competitive, and that it is thought important to produce as much as possible. A great deal less work is required now to produce a given amount of goods than was required before the industrial revolution, and yet people live at higher pressure than they did then. This is chiefly due to competition. An immense amount of labor is wasted in getting orders and securing markets. At times when there is a great deal of unemployment, those who are not unemployed are overworked, because otherwise employers could not make a profit. The competitive management of industry for profit is the source of the trouble. For the same reason there is a desire to maximize production because, with industrial methods, the production of immense quantities of a commodity is more capable of yielding a profit than the production of moderate quantities. [1] The whole urgency of the modern business world is toward speeding up, greater efficiency, more intense international competition, when it ought to be toward more ease, less hurry, and combination to produce goods for use rather than profit. Competition, since the industrial revolution, is an anachronism, leading inevitably to all the evils of the modern world.

The sense of strain, which is characteristic of all grades in an industrial community from the highest to the lowest, is due to instinctive maladjustment. Every kind of failure to satisfy deep instinctive needs produces strain, but the manifestations are somewhat different according to the instinct which is thwarted. The chief needs thwarted by industrialism, as at present conducted, are: the need of spontaneous and variable activities, the need of occasional quiet and solitude, and the need of contact with the earth. This applies to the working classes, but in the middle classes the thwarting of instinct is much more serious. A man who has any ambition cannot marry young, must be very careful how he has children, must if possible marry a girl whose

[1] Cf. R. Austin Freeman, *Social Decay and Regeneration,* especially pp. 105-127.

father will help him professionally rather than a girl he likes, and when married must avoid infidelity, except so furtively as not to be found out. Our society is so imbued with the belief that happiness consists in financial success that men do not realize how much they are losing, and how much richer their lives might be if they cared less for money. But the results of their instinctive dissatisfaction are all the worse for being unconscious. Middle-class men, when they are no longer quite young, are generally filled with envy: envy of their more successful colleagues, envy of the young, and (strange as it may seem) envy of working-men. The result of the first kind of envy is to make them hostile to all intellectual or artistic eminence until it is so well established that they dare not challenge it; of the second, to make them rejoice in war because it gives them a chance to thwart the young who have to do the fighting; of the third, to make them politically opposed to everything calculated to benefit wage-earners, such as education, sanitation, maintenance during unemployment, knowledge of birth-control (which the middle class practice as a matter of course), housing reform, and so on. They believe that their opposition to these measures is based on economy and a desire to keep down the taxes, but in this they deceive themselves, because they do not object to the spending of vastly greater sums on armaments and wars. The same man, often, will object to the education rate on the ground that the poor have larger families than the well-to-do, and to birth-control on the ground that it is immoral and unnatural except for those whose income is fairly comfortable. Men are strangely unconscious of their passions, and the envy which dominates most middle-aged professional men is a thing of which they know nothing, though the methods of psycho-analysis reveal it unerringly.

The failure of instinctive satisfaction in the wage-earning classes is less profound than in the professional classes, because, whatever Marxians may say, they have more freedom in the really important matters, such as marriage. Of course this greater freedom is being rapidly diminished by improvement in police methods, and by the continual tightening up of the "moral" standard through the activities of thwarted middle-class busybodies. This has gone so far that at present in English law the penalty for deserting a vindictive wife, if you are a wage-earner, is imprisonment for life.[1]   In spite

---

[1] This fact is not generally known. The mechanism is as follows: The court makes an order for maintenance, the wife makes a scandal where the man is employed, he is dismissed, cannot pay the maintenance, and is imprisoned for contempt of court. He is legally liable for maintenance even while in prison; therefore on the very day he comes out his wife can have him put back for not paying maintenance during the period of his first imprisonment. And so it goes on until he dies or she is glutted with vengeance. This is not a fancy picture, as any one who knows prisoners can testify.

of this tendency, wage-earners, as yet, in good times, suffer less instinctive repression than professionals, because they are less dominated by respectability and snobbery. Nevertheless, the failure to satisfy instinctive needs is serious, particularly as regards spontaneity. The effect shows itself in love of excitement, thoughtless sentimentalism, and (in the more intelligent) hatred of richer people or of foreign nations.

It is evident that the first steps toward a cure for these evils are being taken by the trade unions, in those parts of their policy which are most criticized, such as restriction of output, refusal to believe that the only necessity is more production, shortening of hours, and so on. It is only by these methods that industrialism can be humanized and can realize the possibilities of good which are latent in it. It could be used to lighten physical labor, and to set men free for more agreeable activities. Hitherto, the competitive system has prevented its being so used. It should have made life more leisurely, but it has made it more hustling. Increase of leisure, diminution of hustle, are the ends to be sought, not mere quantitative increase of production. The trade unions have clearly perceived this, and have persisted in spite of lectures from every kind of middle- and upper-class pundit. This is one reason why there is more hope from self-government in industry than from State socialism. The Bolsheviks, when they had established State socialism, ranged themselves on the side of the worst capitalists on all the matters we have been considering. It is obvious that this must always be the case when conditions of work are determined bureaucratically by officials, instead of by the workers themselves.

3

Friendly Feeling. It is impossible to find any single phrase to describe adequately the whole of what I wish to include under this head. I can, I think, best explain by avoiding hackneyed words which *seem* to convey the correct meaning but in fact fail to do so. An average human being is indifferent to the good or evil fortune of most other human beings, but has an emotional interest in a certain number of his fellow-creatures. This interest may involve pleasure in their good fortune and pain in their evil fortune, or it may involve pain in their good fortune and pleasure in their evil fortune, or it may involve one of these attitudes in certain respects and the other in certain other respects. I shall call these three attitudes friendly, hostile, and mixed, respectively. Broadly speaking, the second of the four goods which we wished to see realized in a community is the friendly attitude combined with as little as possible of the hostile attitude. But this is only a rough preliminary characterization of what I mean.

Biologically speaking, the purpose of life is to leave a large number of descendants. Our instincts, in the main, are such as would be likely to achieve this result in a rather uncivilized community. Biological success in such a community is achieved partly by coöperation, partly by competition. The former is promoted by friendly feeling, the latter by hostile feeling. Thus, on the whole, we feel friendly toward those with whom it would be biologically advantageous to coöperate if we lived in uncivilized conditions, and hostile toward those with whom, in like conditions, it would pay us to compete. In all *genuine* friendship and hostility there is an instinctive basis connected with biological egoism (which includes the survival of descendants). Some religious teachers and moralists preach friendly feeling as a duty, but this only leads to hypocrisy. A great deal of morality is a cloak for hostility posing as "true kindness," and enabling the virtuous to think that in persecuting others out of their "vices" they are conferring a benefit. When I speak of friendly feeling I do not mean the sort that can be produced by preaching; I mean the sort which is instinctive and spontaneous. There are two methods of increasing the amount of this kind of feeling. One is physiological, by regulating the action of the glands and the liver; every one knows that regular exercise makes one think better of other people. The other is economic and political, by producing a community in which the interests of different people harmonize as much as possible and as obviously as possible. Moral and religious teaching is supposed to be a third method, but this view seems to rest on a faulty psychology.

The stock instance of the friendly attitude is the feeling of a maternal mother for a young child. As the most obvious example of the unfriendly attitude we may take jealousy. Sex-love is, of course, a good example of instinctive coöperation, since no one can have descendants without another person's help. But in practice it is so hedged about by jealousy that, as a rule, it affords a less adequate example of friendly feeling than maternal affection. Paternal affection involves, as a rule, a mixed attitude. There is usually some genuine affection, but also much love of power, and much desire that children should reflect credit on their parents. A man will be pleased if his boy wins a prize at school, but displeased if he inherits money from his grandfather, so as to become independent of the paternal authority as soon as he is twenty-one. There is sometimes a melancholy satisfaction when one's boy dies for his country, of a sort not calculated to increase filial affection in those young men who witness it.

> *Snug at the club two fathers sat,*
> *Cross, goggle-eyed, and full of chat.*

One of them said: "My eldest lad
Writes cheery letters from Bagdad.
But Arthur's getting all the fun
At Arras with his nine-inch gun."

"Yes," wheezed the other, "that's the luck!
My boy's quite broken-hearted, stuck
In England training all this year.
Still, if there's truth in what we hear,
The Huns intend to ask for more
Before they bolt across the Rhine."
I watched them toddle through the door—
These impotent old friends of mine.[1]

Of course war affords the supreme example of
instinctive coöperation and hostility. In war, the
instinctive prime mover is hostility; the friendly
feeling toward our own side is derivative from hatred
of the enemy. If we hear that some compatriot
with whom we are unacquainted has been captured
by the enemy and brutally ill used, we shall be full
of sympathy, whereas if his brother dies a lingering
death from cancer we shall take it as a mere statis-
tical fact. If we hear that the enemy underfeed
their prisoners, we shall feel genuine indignation,
even if we are ourselves large employers paying
wages which compel underfeeding. The formula
is: sympathy with compatriots in all that they suf-

[1] "Fathers," by Siegfried Sassoon. (*Counter-Attack*, p. 24.)

fer through the common enemy, but indifference to all that they suffer from other causes. This shows that, as we asserted, the friendly feelings arising during war are derivative from the hostile ones, and could not exist in the same form or with the same widespread intensity if hatred did not exist to stimulate them. Those who see in national coöperation during war an instinctive mechanism which could be applied to international coöperation during peace have failed to understand the nature of the mechanism which war brings into play, or the fact that without enmity there is no stimulus to set it in motion.

There is, it is true, in addition to sex and parenthood, a form of instinctive coöperation which involves no enemy, and looks at first sight very hopeful as a social incentive. I mean that kind of coöperation in work which, so far as human beings are concerned, one finds most developed among uncivilized peoples, and which is carried to its highest perfection by ants and bees. Rivers, in his book on *Instinct and the Unconscious* (pp. 94 ff.), describes how the Melanesians carry out collective work apparently without any need of previous arrangements, by the help of the gregarious instinct. I do not believe, however, that much use can be made of this mechanism by civilized communities. The instinct involved appears to be very much weakened by civilization, and is probably incompatible with

even the average degree of intellectual development
that exists where school education is common.
Moreover, even when it exists most strongly, it is
not such as to make complicated large organizations
possible. It seems also that with the progress of
intelligence the individual grows more self-con-
tained, less receptive to immediate impressions
from other personalities, which survive chiefly in
fragmentary and sporadic forms such as hypnotism.
The primitive instinct for collective work is certainly
one to be borne in mind, but I do not think it has
any very important contribution to make to the
solution of industrial problems.

In order to stimulate friendly feeling and diminish hostile feeling, the things that seem most
important are: physical well-being, instinctive satisfaction, and absence of obvious conflict between
the interests of different individuals or groups. On
the first two heads we have already said enough in
considering instinctive happiness. The last head,
however, raises some interesting points. Our present society, under the influence of liberal ideals, has
become one which, while it retains immense social
inequalities, leaves it open to any man to rise or
sink in the social scale. This has resulted from
combining capitalism with a measure of "equality
of opportunity." In medieval society the inequalities were as great as they are now, but they were
stereotyped, and accepted by almost everybody as

ordained by God. They did not therefore cause much envy, or much conflict between different classes. In the society that socialists aim at, there will not be inequality in material goods, and therefore economic competition and economic envy will be non-existent. But at present we have the evils of the medieval system without its advantages: we have retained the injustices, while destroying the conception of life which made men tolerate them. It is evident that, if the prevalence of competition and envy is to be overcome, an economically stereotyped society is essential. It is also evident that, in the absence of the medieval belief that hereditary social grades are of divine ordinance, the only stereotyped society in which people can acquiesce is one which secures economic justice in an obvious form; that is to say, economic equality for all who are willing to work. Until that is secured, our economic system will continue to grind out hatred and ill will. What is called "equality of opportunity" is of course not real equality, even of opportunity, so long as we retain inheritance of private property and better education for the children of the well-to-do. Inequality must breed strife unless it is supported by a philosophy or religion which even the unfortunate accept. At present, no such doctrine is conceivable. Therefore equality in material goods is an essential condition for the prevalence of friendly feelings between different classes, and even between the more fortunate and the less fortunate members of the same class, or between rivals who hope in time to outdistance each other. A society will not produce much in the way of mental goods unless it is materially stereotyped. I believe that this applies to all kinds of mental goods, but for the present it is only friendliness that concerns us.

In preaching the advantages of a materially stereotyped society, I am conscious of running counter to the real religion of our age—the religion of material progress. We think that it would be a great misfortune if the rate at which new mechanical inventions are made were to slacken, or if people were to grow lazy and easy-going. For my part, since I came to know China, I have come to regard "progress" and "efficiency" as the great misfortunes of the Western world. I do not think it is worth while to preach difficult virtues or extremes of self-denial, because the response is not likely to be great. But I have hopes of laziness as a gospel. I think that if our education were strenuously directed to that end, by men with all the fierce energy produced by our present creed and way of life, it might be possible to induce people to be lazy. I do not mean that no one should work at all, but that few people should work more than is necessary for getting a living. At present, the leisure hours of a man's life are on the whole innocent, but his working hours, those for which he is paid (especially if he is highly paid), are as a rule harmful. If we were all lazy, and only worked under the spur of hunger, our whole society would be much happier. Think of a man like the late Lord Northcliffe, working like a galley-slave to produce bloodshed and misery on a scale hitherto unknown in human history. How admirable it would have been if he could have been persuaded to lie in the sun, or play bridge, or study chess-problems, or even take to drink. But, alas, such men have no vices.

4

Enjoyment of Beauty. On this subject it is not necessary to say much, as the defects of industrial civilization in this respect are generally recognized. It may, I think, be taken as agreed that industrialism, as it exists now, destroys beauty, creates ugliness, and tends to destroy artistic capacity. None of these are essential characteristics of industrialism. They spring from two sources: first, that industrialism is new and revolutionary; secondly, that it is competitive and commercial. The result of the first is that people do not aim at permanence in industrial products, and are loath to lavish much care on something that may be superseded by to-morrow. The result of the second is that manufacturers value their wares, not for their intrinsic excellence, but for the profit to be made out of them, which is, roughly, the excess of their apparent value above what they are really worth, so that every defect not evident at first sight is advantageous to the producer. It is obvious that both these causes of ugliness might be expected to be absent from an industrialism which was stereotyped and socialistic, since it would be neither revolutionary nor worked for profit. It therefore remains only to consider the third point, namely, artistic capacity.

It would seem, from the history of art, that nine-tenths of artistic capacity, at least, depends upon tradition, and one-tenth, at most, upon individual merit. All the great flowering periods of art have come at the end of a slowly maturing tradition. There has, of course, been no time for industrialism to generate a tradition, and perhaps, if the absence of tradition were the only thing at fault, we could wait calmly for the operation of time. But I fear that the other element, individual artistic merit, without which no good tradition can be created, can hardly exist in an atmosphere of industrialized commercialism. Commerce which is not industrial is often extraordinarily favorable to art. Athens, Venice, Florence, are noteworthy examples. But commerce which is industrial seems to have quite different artistic results. This comes probably from the utilitarian attitude which it generates. An artist is by temperament a person who sees things as they are in themselves, not in those rough convenient categories which serve for the business of life. To the ordinary man, grass is always green, but to the artist it is all sorts of different colors according to circumstances. This sort of thing, in anybody who is not already a famous artist, strikes the practical business man as a waste of time; it interferes with standardizing and cataloguing. The result is that, although eminent artists are fêted and paid highly, the artistic attitude of mind is not tolerated in the young. A modern industrial community, when it wants an artist, has to import him from abroad; it then pays him such vast sums that his head is turned and he begins to like money better than art. When the whole world has adopted commercial industrialism, the artistic habit of mind will everywhere be stamped out in youth by people who cannot see any value in it unless its possessor is already labeled as a celebrity. This points to the same requirements as we found before: a society which is stable as regards the material side of life and the methods of production, where industrialism has ceased to be competitive and is used to make life more leisurely instead of more strenuous. And the first step toward this end is the general diffusion of a less energetic conception of the good life.

Knowledge. The strongest case for commercial industrialism can be made out under the head of scientific knowledge. Since the industrial revolution there has been an enormous increase both in the general level of education and in the number of men devoted to learning and research. The importance of science for industrial progress is very evident, and all industrial states encourage scientific research. But even in this sphere the utilitarian habit of mind inseparable from our present system has deleterious effects, which are only beginning to be evident. Unless some people love knowledge for its own sake, quite independently of its possible uses, the new discoveries will only concern the working out of ideas inherited from disinterested investigators. Mendelism is now studied by hosts of agriculturists and stock-breeders, but Mendel was a monk who spent his leisure enjoying his peas-blossoms. A million years of practical agriculturists would never have discovered Mendelism. Wireless is of great practical importance: it facilitates slaughter in war, the dissemination of journalistic falsehood in time of peace, and the broadcasting of trivialities to relieve the tedium of evening hours not devoted to success. But the men who made it possible—Faraday, Maxwell, and Hertz—were none of them the least interested in furthering this remarkable enrichment of human life; they were men solely interested in trying to understand physical processes, and it can hardly be said that the existence of industrialism helped them even indirectly. The modern study of the structure of the atom may have a profound effect upon industrial processes, but those who are engaged upon it are very little interested in this possible future effect of their work. It seems likely that the utilitarianism of commercial industry must ultimately kill the pure desire for knowledge, just as it kills the analogous artistic impulse. In America, where the more utilitarian aspects of science are keenly appreciated, no great advance in pure theory has been made. None of the fundamental discoveries upon which practical applications depend have been made in America. It seems probable that, as the point of view appropriate to commercial industry spreads, utilitarianism will make such fundamental discoveries more and more rare, until at last those who love knowledge for its own sake come to be classified in youth as "morons" and kept in institutions for harmless lunatics.

This, however, is not one of the main points I wish to make. There are, in fact, two such points: first, that pure science is infinitely more valuable than its applications; secondly, that its applications, so far, have been in the main immeasurably harmful, and will only cease to be so when men have a less strenuous outlook on life.

To take the second point first: Science, hitherto, has been used for three purposes: to increase the total production of commodities; to make wars more destructive; and to substitute trivial amusements for those that had some artistic or hygienic value.

Increase in total production, though it had its importance a hundred years ago, has now become far less important than increase of leisure and the wise direction of production. On this point it is not necessary to enlarge further. The increasing destructiveness of wars also needs no comment. As for trivial amusements: think of the substitution of the cinema for the theater; think of the difference between the gramophone and the really beautiful songs of Russian peasants; think of the difference between watching a great football match and playing in a small one. Owing to our belief that *work* is what matters, we have become unable to make our amusements anything but trivial. This is part of the price we had to pay for puritanism; it is no accident that the only great industrial countries are Protestant. People whose outlook on life is more leisurely have a higher standard for their amusements: they like good plays, good music, and so on, not merely something that enables them to pass the time vacuously. So far, however, science has only intruded into the world of amusement in ways that have made it more trivial and less artistic. Nor can this be prevented so long as men think that only work is important

As for the greater value of pure rather than applied science, that is a matter which goes deeper, but which it is difficult to argue. Applied science, while men retain their present ideals, has the sort of effects we have been considering, which I for my part find it very difficult to admire. Pure science—the understanding of natural processes, and the discovery of how the universe is constructed—seems to me the most godlike thing that men do. When I am tempted (as I often am) to wish the human race wiped out by some passing comet, I think of scientific knowledge and of art; these two things seem to make our existence not wholly futile. But the *uses* of science, even at the best, are on a lower plane. A philosophy which values them more than science itself is gross and cannot in the long run be otherwise than destructive of science.

On all our heads, therefore, we are led to the conclusion that our social system, our prevailing habits of mind, and our so-called moral ideals are destructive of what is excellent. If excellence is to survive, we must become more leisurely, more just, less utilitarian, and less "progressive."

DECIDING FORCES IN POLITICS [1]

The larger events in the political life of the world
are determined by the interaction of material conditions and human passions. The operation of the
passions on the material conditions is modified by
alien intelligence guided by alien passions. So far,
such modification has been wholly unscientific, but
it may in time become as precise as engineering.

The classification of the passions which is most
convenient in political theory is somewhat different
from that which would be adopted in psychology.

We may begin with desires for the necessaries of
life: food, drink, sex, and (in cold climates) clothing
and housing. When these are threatened, there is no
limit to the activity and violence that men will dis-
play.

Planted upon these primitive desires are a number
of secondary desires. Love of property, of which
the fundamental political importance is obvious, may
be derived historically and psychologically from the
hoarding instinct. Love of the good opinion of
others (which we may call vanity) is a desire which
man shares with many animals; it is perhaps de-

[1] From *Bolshevism in Practice and Theory.*

√ivable from courtship, but has great survival value, among gregarious animals, in regard to others besides possible mates. Rivalry and love of power are perhaps developments of jealousy; they are akin, but not identical.

These four passions—acquisitiveness, vanity, rivalry, and love of power—are, after the basic instincts, the prime movers of almost all that happens in politics. Their operation is intensified and regularized by herd-instinct. But herd-instinct, by its very nature, cannot be a prime mover, since it merely causes the herd to act in unison, without determining what the united action is to be. Among men, as among gregarious animals, the united action, in any given circumstances, is determined partly by the common passions of the herd, partly by the imitation of leaders. The art of politics consists in causing the latter to prevail over the former.

Of the four passions we have enumerated, only one, namely, acquisitiveness, is concerned at all directly with men's relations to their material conditions. The other three—vanity, rivalry, and love of power—are concerned with social relations. I think this is the source of what is erroneous in the Marxian interpretation of history, which tacitly assumes that acquisitiveness is the source of all political actions. It is clear that many men willingly forgo wealth for the sake of power and glory, and that nations habitually sacrifice riches to rivalry with other nations. The desire for some form of superiority is common to almost all energetic men. No social system which attempts to thwart it can be stable, since the lazy majority will never be a match for the energetic minority.

What is called "virtue" is an offshoot of vanity: it is the habit of acting in a manner which others praise.

The operation of material conditions may be illustrated by the statement (Myer's *Dawn of History*) that four of the greatest movements of conquest have been due to drought in Arabia, causing the nomads of that country to migrate into regions already inhabited. The last of these four movements was the rise of Islam. In these four cases, the primal need of food and drink was enough to set events in motion; but as this need could only be satisfied by conquest, the four secondary passions must have very soon come into play. In the conquests of modern industrialism, the secondary passions have been almost wholly dominant, since those who directed them had no need to fear hunger or thirst. It is the potency of vanity and love of power that gives hope for the industrial future of Soviet Russia, since it enables the communist State to enlist in its service men whose abilities might give them vast wealth in a capitalistic society.

Intelligence modifies profoundly the operation of material conditions. When America was first discovered, men only desired gold and silver; consequently the portions first settled were not those that are now most profitable. The Bessemer process created the German iron and steel industry; inventions requiring oil have created a demand for that commodity which is one of the chief influences in international politics.

The intelligence which has this profound effect on politics is not political, but scientific and technical: it is the kind of intelligence which discovers how to make nature minister to human passions. Tungsten had no value until it was found to be useful in the manufacture of shells and electric light, but now people will, if necessary, kill each other in order to acquire tungsten. Scentific intelligence is the cause of this change.

The progress or retrogression of the world depends, broadly speaking, upon the balance between acquisitiveness and rivalry. The former makes for progress, the latter for retrogression. When intelligence provides improved methods of production, these may be employed to increase the general share of goods, or to set apart more of the labor power of the community for the business of killing its rivals. Until 1914, acquisitiveness had prevailed, on the whole, since the fall of Napoleon; the past six years have seen a prevalence of the instinct of rivalry. Scientific intelligence makes it possible to indulge this instinct more fully than is possible for

primitive peoples, since it sets free more men from
the labor of producing necessaries. It is possible
that scientific intelligence may, in time, reach the
point when it will enable rivalry to exterminate the
human race. This is the most hopeful method of
bringing about an end of war.

For those who do not like this method, there is
another, the study of scientific psychology and
physiology. The physiological causes of emotions
have begun to be known through the studies of such
men as Caunon (*Bodily Changes in Pain, Hunger,
Fear and Rage*). In time, it may become possible,
by physiological means, to alter the whole emotional
nature of a population. It will then depend upon
the passions of the rulers how this power is used.
Success will come to the State which discovers how
to promote pugnacity to the extent required for external war, but not to the extent which would lead
to domestic dissensions. There is no method by
which it can be insured that rulers shall desire the
good of mankind, and therefore there is no reason
to suppose that the power to modify men's emotional nature would cause progress.

If men desired to diminish rivalry, there is an
obvious method. Habits of power intensify the
passion of rivalry; therefore, a State in which power
is concentrated will, other things being equal, be
more bellicose than one in which power is diffused.
For those who dislike wars, this is an additional

argument against all forms of dictatorship. But dislike of war is far less common than we used to suppose; and those who like war can use the same argument to support dictatorship.

TOUCH AND SIGHT: THE EARTH AND THE HEAVENS [1]

Everybody knows that Einstein has done something astonishing, but very few people know exactly what it is that he has done. It is generally recognized that he has revolutionized our conception of the physical world, but his new conceptions are wrapped up in mathematical technicalities. It is true that there are innumerable popular accounts of the theory of relativity, but they generally cease to be intelligible just at the point where they begin to say something important. The authors are hardly to blame for this. Many of the new ideas can be expressed in non-mathematical language, but they are none the less difficult on that account. What is demanded is a change in our imaginative picture of the world—a picture which has been handed down from remote, perhaps pre-human, ancestors, and has been learned by each one of us in early childhood. A change in our imagination is always difficult, especially when we are no longer young. The same sort of change was demanded by Copernicus, when he taught that the earth is not stationary and the heavens do not re-

[1] From *The A B C of Relativity.*

301

volve about it once a day. To us now there is no difficulty in this idea, because we learned it before our mental habits had become fixed. Einstein's ideas, similarly, will seem easy to a generation which has grown up with them; but for our generation a certain effort of imaginative reconstruction is unavoidable.

In exploring the surface of the earth, we make use of all our senses, more particularly of the senses of touch and sight. In measuring lengths, parts of the human body are employed in pre-scientific ages: a "foot," a "cubit," a "span," are defined in this way. For longer distances, we think of the time it takes to walk from one place to another. We gradually learn to judge distances roughly by the eye, but we rely upon touch for accuracy. Moreover it is touch that gives us our sense of "reality." Some things cannot be touched: rainbows, reflections in looking-glasses, and so on. These things puzzle children, whose metaphysical speculations are arrested by the information that what is in the looking-glass is not "real." Macbeth's dagger was unreal because it was not "sensible to feeling as to sight." Not only our geometry and physics, but our whole conception of what exists outside us, is based upon the sense of touch. We carry this even into our metaphors: a good speech is "solid," a bad speech is "gas," because we feel that a gas is not quite "real."

In studying the heavens, we are debarred from all senses except sight. We cannot touch the sun, or travel to it; we cannot walk round the moon, or apply a foot rule to the Pleiades. Nevertheless, astronomers have unhesitatingly applied the geometry and physics which they found serviceable on the surface of the earth, and which they had based upon touch and travel. In doing so, they brought down trouble on their heads, which it has been left for Einstein to clear up. It has turned out that much of what we learned from the sense of touch was unscientific prejudice, which must be rejected if we are to have a true picture of the world.

An illustration may help us to understand how much is impossible to the astronomer as compared to the man who is interested in things on the surface of the earth. Let us suppose that a drug is administered to you which makes you temporarily unconscious, and that when you wake you have lost your memory but not your reasoning powers. Let us suppose further that while you were unconscious you were carried into a balloon, which, when you come to, is sailing with the wind in a dark night— the night of the fifth of November if you are in England, or of the fourth of July if you are in America. You can see fireworks which are being sent off from the ground, from trains, and from aeroplanes traveling in all directions, but you cannot see the ground or the trains or the aeroplanes because of the darkness. What sort of picture of the world will you form? You will think that nothing is permanent: there are only brief flashes of light, which, during their short existence, travel through the void in the most various and bizarre curves. You cannot touch these flashes of light, you can only see them. Obviously your geometry and your physics and your metaphysics will be quite different from those of ordinary mortals. If an ordinary mortal is with you in the balloon, you will find his speech unintelligible. But if Einstein is with you, you will understand him more easily than the ordinary mortal would, because you will be free from a host of preconceptions which prevent most people from understanding him.

The theory of relativity depends, to a considerable extent, upon getting rid of notions which are useful in ordinary life but not to our drugged balloonist. Circumstances on the surface of the earth, for various more or less accidental reasons, suggest conceptions which turn out to be inaccurate although they have come to seem like necessities of thought. The most important of these circumstances is that most objects on the earth's surface are fairly persistent and nearly stationary from a terrestrial point of view. If this were not the case, the idea of going a journey would not seem so definite as it does. If you want to travel from King's Cross to Edinburgh, you know that you will find

King's Cross where it always has been, that the railway line will take the course that it did when you
last made the journey, and that Waverley Station
in Edinburgh will not have walked up to the Castle.
You therefore say and think that you have traveled
to Edinburgh, not that Edinburgh has traveled to
you, though the latter statement would be just as
accurate. The success of this common-sense point
of view depends upon a number of things which are
really of the nature of luck. Suppose all the houses
in London were perpetually moving about, like a
swarm of bees; suppose railways moved and changed
their shapes like avalanches; and finally suppose
that material objects were perpetually being formed
and dissolved like clouds. There is nothing impossible in these suppositions: something like them
must have been verified when the earth was hotter
than it is now. But obviously what we call a
journey to Edinburgh would have no meaning in
such a world. You would begin, no doubt, by asking the taxi-driver: "Where is King's Cross this
morning?" At the station you would have to ask
a similar question about Edinburgh, but the book-
ing-office clerk would reply: "What part of Edinburgh do you mean, Sir? Prince's Street has gone
to Glasgow, the Castle has moved up into the High-
lands, and Waverley Station is under water in the
middle of the Firth of Forth." And on the journey
the stations would not be staying quiet, but some

would be traveling north, some south, some east or west, perhaps much faster than the train. Under these conditions you could not say where you were at any moment. Indeed the whole notion that one is always in some definite "place" is due to the fortunate immovability of most of the large objects on the earth's surface. The idea of "place" is only a rough practical approximation: there is nothing logically necessary about it, and it cannot be made precise.

If we were not much larger than an electron, we should not have this impression of stability, which is only due to the grossness of our senses. King's Cross, which to us looks solid, would be too vast to be conceived except by a few eccentric mathematicians. The bits of it that we could see would consist of little tiny points of matter, never coming into contact with each other, but perpetually whizzing round each other in an inconceivably rapid ballet-dance. The world of our experience would be quite as mad as the one in which the different parts of Edinburgh go for walks in different directions. If—to take the opposite extreme—you were as large as the sun and lived as long, with a corresponding slowness of perception, you would again find a higgledy-piggledy universe without permanence—stars and planets would come and go like morning mists, and nothing would remain in a fixed position relatively to anything else. The notion of comparative stability which forms part of our ordinary outlook is thus due to the fact that we are about the size we are, and live on a planet of which the surface is no longer very hot. If this were not the case, we should not find pre-relativity physics intellectually satisfying. Indeed, we should never have invented such theories. We should have had to arrive at relativity physics at one bound, or remain ignorant of scientific laws. It is fortunate for us that we were not faced with this alternative, since it is almost inconceivable that one man could have done the work of Euclid, Galileo, Newton, and Einstein. Yet without such an incredible genius physics could hardly have been discovered in a world where the universal flux was obvious to non-scientific observation.

In astronomy, although the sun, moon, and stars continue to exist year after year, yet in other respects the world we have to deal with is very different from that of everyday life. As already observed, we depend exclusively on sight: the heavenly bodies cannot be touched, heard, smelt or tasted. Everything in the heavens is moving relatively to everything else. The earth is going round the sun, the sun is moving, very much faster than an express train, towards a point in the constellation "Hercules," the "fixed" stars are scurrying hither and thither like a lot of frightened hens. There are no well-marked places in the sky, like King's Cross and

Edinburgh. When you travel from place to place on the earth, you say the train moves and not the stations, because the stations preserve their topographical relations to each other and the surrounding country. But in astronomy it is arbitrary which you call the train and which the station: the question is to be decided purely by convenience and as a matter of convention.

In this respect, it is interesting to contrast Einstein and Copernicus. Before Copernicus, people thought that the earth stood still and the heavens revolved about it once a day. Copernicus taught that "really" the earth rotates once a day, and the daily revolution of sun and stars is only "apparent." Galileo and Newton endorsed this view, and many things were thought to prove it—for example, the flattening of the earth at the poles, and the fact that bodies are heavier there than at the equator. But in the modern theory the question between Copernicus and his predecessors is merely one of convenience; all motion is relative, and there is no difference between the two statements: "the earth rotates once a day" and "the heavens revolve about the earth once a day." The two mean exactly the same thing, just as it means the same thing if I say that a certain length is six feet or two yards. Astronomy is easier if we take the sun as fixed than if we take the earth, just as accounts are easier in a decimal coinage. But to say more for Copernicus is to assume absolute motion, which is a fiction. All motion is relative, and it is a mere convention to take one body as at rest. All such conventions are equally legitimate, though not all are equally convenient.

There is another matter of great importance, in which astronomy differs from terrestrial physics because of its exclusive dependence upon sight. Both popular thought and old-fashioned physics used the notion of "force," which seemed intelligible because it was associated with familiar sensations. When we are walking, we have sensations connected with our muscles which we do not have when we are sitting still. In the days before mechanical traction, although people could travel by sitting in their carriages, they could see the horses exerting themselves and evidently putting out "force" in the same way as human beings do. Everybody knew from experience what it is to push or pull, or to be pushed or pulled. These very familiar facts made "force" seem a natural basis for dynamics. But Newton's law of gravitation introduced a difficulty. The force between two billiard balls appeared intelligible, because we know what it feels like to bump into another person; but the force between the earth and the sun, which are ninety-three million miles apart, was mysterious. Newton himself regarded this "action at a distance" as impossible, and believed that there was some hitherto undiscovered mecha-

nism by which the sun's influence was transmitted to
the planets. However, no such mechanism was discovered, and gravitation remained a puzzle. The
fact is that the whole conception of "force" is a
mistake. The sun does not exert any force on the
planets; in Einstein's law of gravitation, the planet
only pays attention to what it finds in its own neigh-
borhood. For the present we are concerned with
the necessity of abandoning the notion of "force,"
which was due to misleading conceptions derived
from the sense of touch.

As physics has advanced, it has appeared more
and more that sight is less misleading than touch as
a source of fundamental notions about matter. The
apparent simplicity in the collision of billiard balls
is quite illusory. As a matter of fact, the two billiard balls never touch at all; what really happens
is inconceivably complicated, but is more analogous
to what happens when a comet penetrates the solar
system and goes away again than to what common
sense supposes to happen.

Most of what we have said hitherto was already
recognized by physicists before Einstein invented
the theory of relativity. "Force" was known to be
merely a mathematical fiction, and it was generally
held that motion is a merely relative phenomenon—
that is to say, when two bodies are changing their
relative position, we cannot say that one is moving
while the other is at rest, since the occurrence is

merely a change in the relation to each other. But a great labor was required in order to bring the actual procedure of physics into harmony with these new convictions. Newton believed in force and in absolute space and time; he embodied these beliefs in his technical methods, and his methods remained those of later physicists. Einstein invented a new technique, free from Newton's assumptions. But in order to do so he had to change fundamentally the old ideas of space and time, which had been unchallenged from time immemorial. This is what makes both the difficulty and the interest of his theory.

CURRENT TENDENCIES[1]

Philosophy, from the earliest times, has made greater claims, and achieved fewer results, than any other branch of learning. Ever since Thales said that all is water, philosophers have been ready with glib assertions about the sum-total of things; and equally glib denials have come from other philosophers ever since Thales was contradicted by Anaximander. I believe that the time has now arrived when this unsatisfactory state of things can be brought to an end. I shall try, chiefly by taking certain special problems as examples, to indicate wherein the claims of philosophers have been excessive, and why their achievements have not been greater. The problems and the method of philosophy have, I believe, been misconceived by all schools, many of its traditional problems being insoluble with our means of knowledge, while other more neglected but not less important problems can, by a more patient and more adequate method, be solved with all the precision and certainty to which the most advanced sciences have attained.

Among present-day philosophies, we may distinguish three principal types, often combined in vary-

[1] From *Our Knowledge of the External World.*

ing proportions by a single philosopher, but in essence and tendency distinct. The first of these, which I shall call the classical tradition, descends in the main from Kant and Hegel; it represents the attempt to adapt to present needs the methods and results of the great constructive philosophers from Plato downwards. The second type, which may be called evolutionism, derived its predominance from Darwin, and must be reckoned as having had Herbert Spencer for its first philosophical representative; but in recent times it has become, chiefly through William James and M. Bergson, far bolder and far more searching in its innovations than it was in the hands of Herbert Spencer. The third type, which may be called "logical atomism" for want of a better name, has gradually crept into philosophy through the critical scrutiny of mathematics. This type of philosophy, which is the one that I wish to advocate, has not as yet many whole-hearted adherents, but the "new realism" which owes its inception to Harvard is very largely impregnated with its spirit. It represents, I believe, the same kind of advance as was introduced into physics by Galileo: the substitution of piecemeal, detailed, and verifiable results for large untested generalities recommended only by a certain appeal to imagination. But before we can understand the changes advocated by this new philosophy, we must briefly examine and criticize the other two types with which it has to contend.

I. THE CLASSICAL TRADITION

Twenty years ago, the classical tradition, having vanquished the opposing tradition of the English empiricists, held almost unquestioned sway in all Anglo-Saxon universities. At the present day, though it is losing ground, many of the most prominent teachers still adhere to it. In academic France, in spite of M. Bergson, it is far stronger than all its opponents combined; and in Germany it has many vigorous advocates. Nevertheless, it represents on the whole a decaying force, and it has failed to adapt itself to the temper of the age. Its advocates are, in the main, those whose extra-philosophical knowledge is literary, rather than those who have felt the inspiration of science. There are, apart from reasoned arguments, certain general intellectual forces against it—the same general forces which are breaking down the other great syntheses of the past, and making our age one of bewildered groping where our ancestors walked in the clear daylight of unquestioning certainty.

The original impulse out of which the classical tradition developed was the naïve faith of the Greek philosophers in the omnipotence of reasoning. The discovery of geometry had intoxicated them, and its *a priori* deductive method appeared capable of universal application. They would prove, for instance, that all reality is one, that there is no such thing as change, that the world of sense is a world of mere illusion; and the strangeness of their results gave them no qualms because they believed in the correctness of their reasoning. Thus it came to be thought that by mere thinking the most surprising and important truths concerning the whole of reality could be established with a certainty which no contrary observations could shake. As the vital impulse of the early philosophers died away, its place was taken by authority and tradition and reinforced, in the Middle Ages and almost to our own day, by systematic theology. Modern philosophy, from Descartes onwards, though not bound by authority like that of the Middle Ages, still accepted more or less uncritically the Aristotelian logic. Moreover, it still believed, except in Great Britain, that *a priori* reasoning could reveal otherwise undiscoverable secrets about the universe, and could prove reality to be quite different from what, to direct observation, it appears to be. It is this belief, rather than any particular tenets resulting from it, that I regard as the distinguishing characteristic of the classical tradition, and as hitherto the main obstacle to a scientific attitude in philosophy.

The nature of the philosophy embodied in the classical tradition may be made clearer by taking a particular exponent as an illustration. For this purpose, let us consider for a moment the doctrines of Mr. Bradley, who is probably the most distinguished living representative of this school. Mr. Bradley's *Appearance and Reality* is a book consisting of two parts, the first called *Appearance,* the second *Reality.* The first part examines and condemns almost all that makes up our everyday world: things and qualities, relations, space and time, change, causation, activity, the self. All these, though in some sense facts which qualify reality, are not real as they appear. What is real is one single, indivisible timeless whole, called the Absolute, which is in some sense spiritual, but does not consist of souls, or of thought and will as we know them. And all this is established by abstract logical reasoning professing to find self-contradictions in the categories condemned as mere appearance, and to leave no tenable alternative to the kind of Absolute which is finally affirmed to be real.

One brief example may suffice to illustrate Mr. Bradley's method. The world appears to be full of many things with various relations to each other— right and left, before and after, father and son, and so on. But relations, according to Mr. Bradley, are found on examination to be self-contradictory and therefore impossible. He first argues that, if there are relations, there must be qualities between which they hold. This part of his argument need not detain us. He then proceeds:

"But how the relation can stand to the qualities is, on the other side, unintelligible. If it is nothing to the qualities, then they are not related at all; and, if so, as we saw, they have ceased to be qualities, and their relation is a nonentity. But if it is to be something to them, then clearly we shall require a *new* connecting relation. For the relation hardly can be the mere adjective of one or both of its terms; or, at least, as such it seems indefensible. And, being something itself, if it does not itself bear a relation to the terms, in what intelligible way will it succeed in being anything to them? But here again we are hurried off into the eddy of a hopeless process, since we are forced to go on finding new relations without end. The links are united by a link, and this bond of union is a link which also has two ends; and these require each a fresh link to connect them with the old. The problem is to find how the relation can stand to its qualities, and this problem is insoluble." [1]

I do not propose to examine this argument in detail, or to show the exact points where, in my opinion, it is fallacious. I have quoted it only as an example of method. Most people will admit, I think, that it is calculated to produce bewilderment rather than conviction, because there is more likelihood of error in a very subtle, abstract, and difficult argument than in so patent a fact as the interrelated·

[1] *Appearance and Reality*, pp. 32-33.

ness of the things in the world. To the early Greeks, to whom geometry was practically the only known science, it was possible to follow reasoning with assent even when it led to the strangest conclusions. But to us, with our methods of experiment and observation, our knowledge of the long history of *a priori* errors refuted by empirical science, it has become natural to suspect a fallacy in any deduction of which the conclusion appears to contradict patent facts. It is easy to carry such suspicion too far, and it is very desirable, if possible, actually to discover the exact nature of the error when it exists. But there is no doubt that what we may call the empirical outlook has become part of most educated people's habit of mind; and it is this, rather than any definite argument, that has diminished the hold of the classical tradition upon students of philosophy and the instructed public generally.

The function of logic in philosophy, as I shall try to show at a later stage, is all-important; but I do not think its function is that which it has in the classical tradition. In that tradition, logic becomes constructive through negation. Where a number of alternatives seem, at first sight, to be equally possible, logic is made to condemn all of them except one, and that one is then pronounced to be realized in the actual world. Thus the world is constructed by means of logic, with little or no appeal to concrete experience. The true function of logic is, in

my opinion, exactly the opposite of this. As applied
to matters of experience, it is analytic rather than
constructive; taken *a priori,* it shows the possibility
of hitherto unsuspected alternatives more often than
the impossibility of alternatives which seemed *prima
facie* possible. Thus, while it liberates imagination
as to what the world *may* be, it refuses to legislate
as to what the world *is.* This change, which has
been brought about by an internal revolution in
logic, has swept away the ambitious constructions
of traditional metaphysics, even for those whose
faith in logic is greatest; while to the many who regard logic as a chimera the paradoxical systems to
which it has given rise do not seem worthy even of
refutation. Thus on all sides these systems have
ceased to attract, and even the philosophical world
tends more and more to pass them by.

One or two of the favorite doctrines of the school
we are considering may be mentioned to illustrate
the nature of its claims. The universe, it tells us,
is an "organic unity," like an animal or a perfect
work of art. By this it means, roughly speaking,
that all the different parts fit together and coöperate,
and are what they are because of their place in the
whole. This belief is sometimes advanced dogmatically, while at other times it is defended by certain logical arguments. If it is true, every part of
the universe is a microcosm, a miniature reflection
of the whole. If we knew ourselves thoroughly, ac-

cording to this doctrine, we should know everything. Common sense would naturally object that there are people—say in China—with whom our relations are so indirect and trivial that we cannot infer anything important as to them from any fact about ourselves. If there are living beings in Mars or in more distant parts of the universe, the same argument becomes even stronger. But further, perhaps the whole contents of the space and time in which we live form only one of many universes, each seeming to itself complete. And thus the conception of the necessary unity of all that is resolves itself into the poverty of imagination, and a freer logic emancipates us from the strait-waistcoated benevolent institution which idealism palms off as the totality of being.

Another very important doctrine held by most, though not all, of the school we are examining is the doctrine that all reality is what is called "mental" or "spiritual," or that, at any rate, all reality is dependent for its existence upon what is mental. This view is often particularized into the form which states that the relation of knower and known is fundamental, and that nothing can exist unless it either knows or is known. Here again the same legislative function is ascribed to *a priori* argumentation: it is thought that there are contradictions in an unknown reality. Again, if I am not mistaken, the argument is fallacious, and a better logic will show that no limits can be set to the extent and nature of the unknown. And when I speak of the unknown, I do not mean merely what we personally do not know, but what is not known to any mind. Here as elsewhere, while the older logic shut out possibilities and imprisoned imagination within the walls of the familiar, the newer logic shows rather what may happen, and refuses to decide as to what *must* happen.

The classical tradition in philosophy is the last surviving child of two very diverse parents: the Greek belief in reason, and the medieval belief in the tidiness of the universe. To the schoolmen, who lived amid wars, massacres, and pestilences, nothing appeared so delightful as safety and order. In their idealizing dreams, it was safety and order that they sought: the universe of Thomas Aquinas or Dante is as small and neat as a Dutch interior. To us, to whom safety has become monotony, to whom the primeval savageries of nature are so re, mote as to become a mere pleasing condiment to our ordered routine, the world of dreams is very differ, ent from what it was amid the wars of Guelf and Ghibelline. Hence William James's protest against what he calls the "block universe" of the classical tradition; hence Nietzsche's worship of force; hence the verbal bloodthirstiness of many quiet literary men. The barbaric substratum of human nature, unsatisfied in action, finds an outlet in imagination. In philosophy, as elsewhere, this tendency is visible;

and it is this, rather than formal argument, that has thrust aside the classical tradition for a philosophy which fancies itself more virile and more vital.

II. EVOLUTIONISM

Evolutionism, in one form or another, is the prevailing creed of our time. It dominates our politics, our literature, and not least our philosophy. Nietzsche, pragmatism, Bergson, are phases in its philosophic development, and their popularity far beyond the circles of professional philosophers shows its consonance with the spirit of the age. It believes itself firmly based on science, a liberator of hopes, an inspirer of an invigorating faith in human power, a sure antidote to the ratiocinative authority of the Greeks and the dogmatic authority of medieval systems. Against so fashionable and so agreeable a creed it may seem useless to raise a protest; and with much of its spirit every modern man must be in sympathy. But I think that, in the intoxication of a quick success, much that is important and vital to a true understanding of the universe has been forgotten. Something of Hellenism must be combined with the new spirit before it can emerge from the ardor of youth into the wisdom of manhood. And it is time to remember that biology is neither the only science, nor yet the model to which all other sciences must adapt themselves.

Evolutionism, as I shall try to show, is not a truly scientific philosophy, either in its method or in the problems which it considers. The true scientific philosophy is something more arduous and more aloof, appealing to less mundane hopes, and requiring a severer discipline for its successful practice.

Darwin's *Origin of Species* persuaded the world that the difference between different species of animals and plants is not the fixed immutable difference that it appears to be. The doctrine of natural kinds, which had rendered classification easy and definite, which was enshrined in the Aristotelian tradition, and protected by its supposed necessity for orthodox dogma, was suddenly swept away forever out of the biological world. The difference between man and the lower animals, which to our human conceit appears enormous, was shown to be a gradual achievement, involving intermediate beings who could not with certainty be placed either within or without the human family. The sun and planets had already been shown by Laplace to be very probably derived from a primitive more or less undifferentiated nebula. Thus the old fixed landmarks became wavering and indistinct, and all sharp outlines were blurred. Things and species lost their boundaries, and none could say where they began or where they ended.

But if human conceit was staggered for a moment by its kinship with the ape, it soon found a way to reassert itself, and that way is the "philosophy" of evolution. A process which led from the amœba to man appeared to the philosophers to be obviously a progress—though whether the amœba would agree with this opinion is not known. Hence the cycle of changes which science had shown to be the probable history of the past was welcomed as revealing a law of development towards good in the universe—an evolution or unfolding of an ideal slowly embodying itself in the actual. But such a view, though it might satisfy Spencer and those whom we may call Hegelian evolutionists, could not be accepted as adequate by the more whole-hearted votaries of change. An ideal to which the world continuously approaches is, to these minds, too dead and static to be inspiring. Not only the aspirations, but the ideal too, must change and develop with the course of evolution; there must be no fixed goal, but a continual fashioning of fresh needs by the impulse which is life and which alone gives unity to the process.

Ever since the seventeenth century, those whom William James described as the "tender-minded" have been engaged in a desperate struggle with the mechanical view of the course of nature which physical science seems to impose. A great part of the attractiveness of the classical tradition was due to the partial escape from mechanism which it provided. But now, with the influence of biology, the "tender-minded" believe that a more radical escape is possible, sweeping aside not merely the laws of physics, but the whole apparently immutable apparatus of logic, with its fixed concepts, its general principles, and its reasonings which seem able to compel even the most unwilling assent. The older kind of teleology, therefore, which regarded the End as a fixed goal, already partially visible, towards which we were gradually approaching, is rejected by M. Bergson as not allowing enough for the absolute dominion of change. After explaining why he does not accept mechanism, he proceeds: [1]

"But radical finalism is quite as unacceptable, and for the same reason. The doctrine of teleology, in its extreme form, as we find it in Leibniz for example, implies that things and beings merely realize a program previously arranged. But if there is nothing unforeseen, no invention or creation in the universe, time is useless again. As in the mechanistic hypothesis, here again it is supposed that *all is given*. Finalism thus understood is only inverted mechanism. It springs from the same postulate, with this sole difference, that in the movement of our finite intellects along successive things, whose successiveness is reduced to a mere appearance, it holds in front of us the light with which it claims to guide us, instead of putting it behind. It substitutes the attraction of the future for the impulsion of the past. But succession remains none

[1] *Creative Evolution,* English translation. p. 41.

the less a mere appearance, as indeed does movement itself. In the doctrine of Leibniz, time is reduced to a confused perception, relative to the
human standpoint, a perception which would vanish,
like a rising mist, for a mind seated at the center
of things.

"Yet finalism is not, like mechanism, a doctrine
with fixed rigid outlines. It admits of as many in-
flections as we like. The mechanistic philosophy is
to be taken or left: it must be left if the least grain
of dust, by straying from the path foreseen by
mechanics, should show the slightest trace of spontaneity. The doctrine of final causes, on the contrary, will never be definitively refuted. If one
form of it be put aside, it will take another. Its
principle, which is essentially psychological, is very
flexible. It is so extensible, and thereby so comprehensive, that one accepts something of it as soon as
one rejects pure mechanism. The theory we shall
put forward in this book will therefore necessarily
partake of finalism to a certain extent."

M. Bergson's form of finalism depends upon his
conception of life. Life, in his philosophy, is a
continuous stream, in which all divisions are artificial
and unreal. Separate things, beginnings and endings, are mere convenient fictions: there is only
smooth, unbroken transition. The beliefs of to-day
may count as true to-day, if they carry us along the
stream; but to-morrow they will be false, and must

be replaced by new beliefs to meet the new situation. All our thinking consists of convenient fictions, imaginary congealings of the stream: reality flows on in spite of all our fictions, and though it can be lived, it cannot be conceived in thought. Somehow, without explicit statement, the assurance is slipped in that the future, though we cannot foresee it, will be better than the past or the present: the reader is like the child who expects a sweet because it has been told to open its mouth and shut its eyes. Logic, mathematics, physics disappear in this philosophy, because they are too "static"; what is real is an impulse and movement towards a goal which, like the rainbow, recedes as we advance, and makes every place different when we reach it from what it appeared to be at a distance.

Now I do not propose at present to enter upon a technical examination of this philosophy. At present I wish to make only two criticisms of it— first, that its truth does not follow from what science has rendered probable concerning the facts of evolution, and secondly, that the motives and interests which inspire it are so exclusively practical, and the problems with which it deals are so special, that it can hardly be regarded as really touching any of the questions that to my mind constitute genuine philosophy.

(1) What biology has rendered probable is that the diverse species arose by adaptation from a less

differentiated ancestry. This fact is in itself exceedingly interesting, but it is not the kind of
fact from which philosophical consequences follow.
Philosophy is general, and takes an impartial interest in all that exists. The changes suffered by
minute portions of matter on the earth's surface are
very important to us as active sentient beings; but to
us as philosophers they have no greater interest than
other changes in portions of matter elsewhere. And
if the changes on the earth's surface during the last
few millions of years appear to our present ethical
notions to be in the nature of a progress, that gives
no ground for believing that progress is a general
law of the universe. Except under the influence of
desire, no one would admit for a moment so crude
a generalization from such a tiny selection of facts.
What does result, not specially from biology, but
from all the sciences which deal with what exists, is
that we cannot understand the world unless we can
understand change and continuity. This is even
more evident in physics than it is in biology. But
the analysis of change and continuity is not a problem upon which either physics or biology throws
any light: it is a problem of a new kind belonging
to a different kind of study. The question whether
evolutionism offers a true or a false answer to this
problem is not, therefore, a question to be solved by
appeals to particular facts, such as biology and
physics reveal. In assuming dogmatically a certain

answer to this question, evolutionism ceases to be scientific, yet it is only in touching on this question that evolutionism reaches the subject-matter of philosophy. Evolutionism thus consists of two parts: one not philosophical, but only a hasty generalization of the kind which the special sciences might hereafter confirm or confute; the other not scientific, but a mere unsupported dogma, belonging to philosophy by its subject-matter, but in no way deducible from the facts upon which evolution relies.

(2) The predominant interest of evolutionism is in the question of human destiny, or at least of the destiny of Life. It is more interested in morality and happiness than in knowledge for its own sake. It must be admitted that the same may be said of many other philosophies, and that a desire for the kind of knowledge which philosophy really can give is very rare. But if philosophy is to become scientific—and it is our object to discover how this can be achieved—it is necessary first and foremost that philosophers should acquire the disinterested intellectual curiosity which characterizes the genuine man of science. Knowledge concerning the future —which is the kind of knowledge that must be sought if we are to know about human destiny—is possible within certain narrow limits. It is impossible to say how much the limits may be enlarged with the progress of science. But what is evident

is that any proposition about the future belongs by its subject-matter to some particular science, and is to be ascertained, if at all, by the methods of that science.   Philosophy is not a short cut to the same kind of results as those of the other sciences: if it is to be a genuine study, it must have a province of its own, and aim at results which the other sciences can neither prove nor disprove.

The consideration that philosophy, if there is such a study, must consist of propositions which could not occur in the other sciences, is one which has very far-reaching consequences.   All the questions which have what is called a human interest—such, for example, as the question of a future life—belong, at least in theory, to special sciences, and are capable, at least in theory, of being decided by empirical evidence.   Philosophers have too often, in the past, permitted themselves to pronounce on empirical questions, and found themselves, as a result, in disastrous conflict with well-attested facts.   We must, therefore, renounce the hope that philosophy can promise satisfaction to our mundane desires. What it can do, when it is purified from all practical taint, is to help us to understand the general aspects of the world and the logical analysis of familiar but complex things.   Through this achievement, by the suggestion of fruitful hypotheses, it may be indirectly useful in other sciences, notably mathematics, physics, and psychology.   But a genuinely scientific philosophy cannot hope to appeal to any except those who have the wish to understand, to escape from intellectual bewilderment. It offers, in its own domain, the kind of satisfaction which the other sciences offer. But it does not offer, or attempt to offer, a solution of the problem of human destiny, or of the destiny of the universe.

Evolutionism, if what has been said is true, is to be regarded as a hasty generalization from certain rather special facts, accompanied by a dogmatic rejection of all attempts at analysis, and inspired by interests which are practical rather than theoretical. In spite, therefore, of its appeal to detailed results in various sciences, it cannot be regarded as any more genuinely scientific than the classical tradition which it has replaced. How philosophy is to be rendered scientific, and what is the true subject-matter of philosophy, I shall try to show first by examples of certain achieved results, and then more generally. We will begin with the problem of the physical conceptions of space and time and matter, which, as we have seen, are challenged by the contentions of the evolutionists. That these conceptions stand in need of reconstruction will be admitted, and is indeed increasingly urged by physicists themselves. It will also be admitted that the reconstruction must take more account of change and the universal flux than is done in the older mechanics with its fundamental conception of an indestructible matter. But I do not think the reconstruction required is on Bergsonian lines, nor do I think that his rejection of logic can be anything but harmful. I shall not, however, adopt the method of explicit controversy, but rather the method of independent inquiry, starting from what, in a pre-philosophic stage, appear to be facts, and keeping always as close to these initial data as the requirements of consistency will permit.

Although explicit controversy is almost always fruitless in philosophy, owing to the fact that no two philosophers ever understand one another, yet it seems necessary to say something at the outset in justification of the scientific as against the mystical attitude. Metaphysics, from the first, has been developed by the union or the conflict of these two attitudes. Among the earliest Greek philosophers, the Ionians were more scientific and the Sicilians more mystical.[1] But among the latter, Pythagoras, for example, was in himself a curious mixture of the two tendencies: the scientific attitude led him to his proposition on right-angled triangles, while his mystic insight showed him that it is wicked to eat beans. Naturally enough, his followers divided into two sects, the lovers of right-angled triangles and the abhorrers of beans; but the former sect died out, leaving, however, a haunting flavor of mysticism over much Greek mathematical speculation, and in par-

---

[1] Cf. Burnet, *Early Greek Philosophy*, pp. 85 ff.

ticular over Plato's views on mathematics. Plato, of course, embodies both the scientific and the mystical attitudes in a higher form than his predecessors, but the mystical attitude is distinctly the stronger of the two, and secures ultimate victory whenever the conflict is sharp. Plato, moreover, adopted from the Eleatics the device of using logic to defeat common sense, and thus to leave the field clear for mysticism—a device still employed in our own day by the adherents of the classical tradition.

The logic used in defense of mysticism seems to me faulty as logic, and in a later lecture I shall criticize it on this ground. But the more thorough-going mystics do not employ logic, which they despise: they appeal instead directly to the immediate deliverance of their insight. Now, although fully developed mysticism is rare in the West, some tincture of it colors the thoughts of many people, particularly as regards matters on which they have strong convictions not based on evidence. In all who seek passionately for the fugitive and difficult goods, the conviction is almost irresistible that there is in the world something deeper, more significant, than the multiplicity of little facts chronicled and classified by science. Behind the veil of these mundane things, they feel, something quite different obscurely shimmers, shining forth clearly in the great moments of illumination, which alone give anything worthy to be called real knowledge of truth. To seek such moments, therefore, is to them the way of wisdom, rather than, like the man of science, to observe coolly, to analyze without emotion, and to accept without question the equal reality of the trivial and the important.

Of the reality or unreality of the mystic's world I know nothing. I have no wish to deny it, nor even to declare that the insight which reveals it is not a genuine insight. What I do wish to maintain —and it is here that the scientific attitude becomes imperative—is that insight, untested and unsupported, is an insufficient guarantee of truth, in spite of the fact that much of the most important truth is first suggested by its means. It is common to speak of an opposition between instinct and reason; in the eighteenth century, the opposition was drawn in favor of reason, but under the influence of Rousseau and the romantic movement instinct was given the preference, first by those who rebelled against artificial forms of government and thought, and then, as the purely rationalistic defense of traditional theology became increasingly difficult, by all who felt in science a menace to creeds which they associated with a spiritual outlook on life and the world. Bergson, under the name of "intuition," has raised instinct to the position of sole arbiter of metaphysical truth. But in fact the opposition of instinct and reason is mainly illusory. Instinct, intuition or insight is what first leads to the beliefs which subsequent reason confirms or confutes; but the confirmation, where it is possible, consists, in the last analysis, of agreement with other beliefs no less instinctive. Reason is a harmonizing, controlling force rather than a creative one. Even in the most purely logical realms, it is insight that first arrives at what is new.[1]

Where instinct and reason do sometimes conflict is in regard to single beliefs, held instinctively, and held with such determination that no degree of inconsistency with other beliefs leads to their abandonment. Instinct, like all human faculties, is liable to error. Those in whom reason is weak are often unwilling to admit this as regards themselves, though all admit it in regard to others. Where instinct is least liable to error is in practical matters as to which right judgment is a help to survival; friendship and hostility in others, for instance, are often felt with extraordinary discrimination through very careful disguises. But even in such matters a wrong impression may be given by reserve or flattery; and in matters less directly practical, such as philosophy deals with, very strong instinctive beliefs may be wholly mistaken, as we may come to know through their perceived inconsistency with other equally strong beliefs. It is such considerations that necessitate the harmonizing mediation of

[1] This section dealing with reason and intuition has been printed in a course of Lowell lectures but forms part of *Current Tendencies* as it was originally written.

reason, which tests our beliefs by their mutual compatibility, and examines, in doubtful cases, the possible sources of error on the one side and on the other.   In this there is no opposition to instinct as a whole, but only to blind reliance upon some one interesting aspect of instinct to the exclusion of other more commonplace but not less trustworthy aspects.   It is such onesidedness, not instinct itself, that reason aims at correcting.

These more or less trite maxims may be illustrated by application to Bergson's advocacy of "intuition" as against "intellect."   There are, he says, "two profoundly different ways of knowing a thing.   The first implies that we move round the object; the second that we enter into it.   The first depends on the point of view at which we are placed and on the symbols by which we express ourselves. The second neither depends on a point of view nor relies on any symbol.   The first kind of knowledge may be said to stop at the *relative;* the second, in those cases where it is possible, to attain the *absolute.*" [1]   The second of these, which is intuition, is, he says, "the kind of intellectual *sympathy* by which one places oneself within an object in order to coincide with what is unique in it and therefore inexpressible" (p. 6).   In illustration, he mentions self-knowledge: "there is one reality, at least, which we all seize from within, by intuition and not by

[1] *Introduction to Metaphysics,* p. 1.

simple analysis. It is our own personality in its flowing through time—our self which endures" (p. 8). The rest of Bergson's philosophy consists in reporting, through the imperfect medium of words, the knowledge gained by intuition, and the consequent complete condemnation of all the pretended knowledge derived from science and common sense.

This procedure, since it takes sides in a conflict of instinctive beliefs, stands in need of justification by proving the greater trustworthiness of the beliefs on one side than of those on the other. Bergson attempts this justification in two ways—first, by explaining that intellect is a purely practical faculty designed to secure biological success; secondly, by mentioning remarkable feats of instinct in animals, and by pointing out characteristics of the world which, though intuition can apprehend them, are baffling to intellect as he interprets it.

Of Bergson's theory that intellect is a purely practical faculty developed in the struggle for survival, and not a source of true beliefs, we may say, first, that it is only through intellect that we know of the struggle for survival and of the biological ancestry of man: if the intellect is misleading, the whole of this merely inferred history is presumably untrue. If, on the other hand, we agree with M. Bergson in thinking that evolution took place as Darwin believed, then it is not only intellect, but all our faculties, that have been developed under

the stress of practical utility. Intuition is seen at
its best where it is directly useful—for example, in
regard to other people's characters and dispositions.
Bergson apparently holds that capacity for this kind
of knowledge is less explicable by the struggle for
existence than, for example, capacity for pure mathematics. Yet the savage deceived by false friendship
is likely to pay for his mistake with his life; whereas
even in the most civilized societies men are not put
to death for mathematical incompetence. All the
most striking of his instances of intuition in animals
have a very direct survival value. The fact is, of
course, that both intuition and intellect have been
developed because they are useful, and that, speaking broadly, they are useful when they give truth
and become harmful when they give falsehood. Intellect, in civilized man, like artistic capacity, has
occasionally been developed beyond the point where
it is useful to the individual; intuition, on the other
hand, seems on the whole to diminish as civilization
increases. Speaking broadly, it is greater in children
than in adults, in the uneducated than in the educated. Probably in dogs it exceeds anything to be
found in human beings. But those who find in these
facts a recommendation of intuition ought to return
to running wild in the woods, dyeing themselves with
woad and living on hips and haws.

Let us next examine whether intuition possesses
any such infallibility as Bergson claims for it. The

best instance of it, according to him, is our acquaintance with ourselves; yet self-knowledge is proverbially rare and difficult. Most men, for example, have in their nature meannesses, vanities, and envies of which they are quite unconscious, though even their best friends can perceive them without any difficulty. It is true that intuition has a convincingness which is lacking to intellect: while it is present, it is almost impossible to doubt its truth. But if it should appear, on examination, to be at least as fallible as intellect, its greater subjective certainty becomes a demerit, making it only the more irresistibly deceptive. Apart from self-knowledge, one of the most notable examples of intuition is the knowledge people believe themselves to possess of those with whom they are in love: the wall between different personalities seems to become transparent, and people think they see into another soul as into their own. Yet deception in such cases is constantly practiced with success; and even where there is no intentional deception, experience gradually proves, as a rule, that the supposed insight was illusory, and that the slower, more groping methods of the intellect are in the long run more reliable.

Bergson maintains that intellect can only deal with things in so far as they resemble what has been experienced in the past, while intuition has the power of apprehending the uniqueness and novelty that always belong to each fresh moment. That there is something unique and new at every moment, is certainly true; it is also true that this cannot be fully expressed by means of intellectual concepts. Only direct acquaintance can give knowledge of what is unique and new. But direct acquaintance of this kind is given fully in sensation, and does not require, so far as I can see, any special faculty of intuition for its apprehension. It is neither intellect nor intuition, but sensation, that supplies new data; but when the data are new in any remarkable manner, intellect is much more capable of dealing with them than intuition would be. The hen with a brood of ducklings no doubt has intuitions which seem to place her inside them, and not merely to know them analytically; but when the ducklings take to the water, the whole apparent intuition is seen to be illusory, and the hen is left helpless on the shore. Intuition, in fact, is an aspect and development of instinct, and, like all instinct, is admirable in those customary surroundings which have molded the habits of the animal in question, but totally incompetent as soon as the surroundings are changed in a way which demands some non-habitual mode of action.

The theoretical understanding of the world, which is the aim of philosophy, is not a matter of great practical importance to animals, or to savages, or even to most civilized men. It is hardly to be supposed, therefore, that the rapid, rough and ready methods of instinct or intuition will find in this field a favorable ground for their application. It is the older kinds of activity, which bring out our kinship with remote generations of animal and semi-human ancestors, that show intuition at its best. In such matters as self-preservation and love, intuition will act sometimes (though not always) with a swiftness and precision which are astonishing to the critical intellect. But philosophy is not one of the pursuits which illustrate our affinity with the past: it is a highly refined, highly civilized pursuit, demanding, for its success, a certain liberation from the life of instinct, and even, at times, a certain aloofness from all mundane hopes and fears. It is not in philosophy. therefore, that we can hope to see intuition at its best. On the contrary, since the true objects of philosophy, and the habits of thought demanded for their apprehension, are strange, unusual, and remote, it is here, more almost than anywhere else, that intellect proves superior to intuition, and that quick unanalyzed convictions are least deserving of uncritical acceptance.

Before embarking upon the somewhat difficult and abstract discussions which lie before us, it will be well to take a survey of the hopes we may retain and the hopes we must abandon. The hope of satisfaction to our more human desires—the hope of demonstrating that the world has this or that desirable ethical characteristic—is not one which, so far as I can see, philosophy can do anything whatever to satisfy. The difference between a good world and a bad one is a difference in the particular characteristics of the particular things that exist in these worlds: it is not a sufficiently abstract difference to come within the province of philosophy. Love and hate, for example, are ethical opposites, but to philosophy they are closely analogous attitudes towards objects. The general form and structure of those attitudes towards objects which constitute mental phenomena is a problem for philosophy; but the difference between love and hate is not a difference of form or structure, and therefore belongs rather to the special science of psychology than to philosophy. Thus the ethical interests which have often inspired philosophers must remain in the background: some kind of ethical interest may inspire the whole study, but none must obtrude in the detail or be expected in the special results which are sought.

If this view seems at first sight disappointing, we may remind ourselves that a similar change has been found necessary in all the other sciences. The physicist or chemist is not now required to prove the ethical importance of his ions or atoms; the biologist is not expected to prove the utility of the plants or animals which he dissects. In pre-scientific ages this was not the case. Astronomy, for example, was studied because men believed in astrology: it was thought that the movements of the planets had the most direct and important bearing upon the lives of human beings. Presumably, when this belief decayed and the disinterested study of astronomy began, many who had found astrology absorbingly interesting decided that astronomy had too little human interest to be worthy of study. Physics, as it appears in Plato's *Timæus* for example, is full of ethical notions: it is an essential part of its purpose to show that the earth is worthy of admiration. The modern physicist, on the contrary, though he has no wish to deny that the earth is admirable, is not concerned, as physicist, with its ethical attributes: he is merely concerned to find out facts, not to consider whether they are good or bad. In psychology, the scientific attitude is even more recent and more difficult than in the physical sciences: it is natural to consider that human nature is either good or bad, and to suppose that the difference between good and bad, so all-important in practice, must be important in theory also. It is only during the last century that an ethically neutral science of psychology has grown up; and here too ethical neutrality has been essential to scientific success.

In philosophy, hitherto, ethical neutrality has been seldom sought and hardly ever achieved. Men have remembered their wishes, and have judged philosophies in relation to their wishes. Driven from the particular sciences, the belief that the notions of good and evil must afford a key to the understanding of the world has sought a refuge in philosophy. But even from this last refuge, if philosophy is not to remain a set of pleasing dreams, this belief must be driven forth. It is a commonplace that happiness is not best achieved by those who seek it directly; and it would seem that the same is true of the good. In thought, at any rate, those who forget good and evil and seek only to know the facts are more likely to achieve good than those who view the world through the distorting medium of their own desires.

The immense extension of our knowledge of facts in recent times has had, as it had in the Renaissance, two effects upon the general intellectual outlook. On the one hand, it has made men distrustful of the truth of wide, ambitious systems: theories come and go swiftly, each serving, for a moment, to classify known facts and promote the search for new ones, but each in turn proving inadequate to deal with the new facts when they have been found. Even those who invent the theories do not, in science, regard them as anything but a temporary makeshift. The ideal of an all-embracing synthesis, such as the Middle Ages believed themselves to have attained, recedes further and further beyond the limits of what seems feasible. In such a world, as in the world of Montaigne, nothing seems worth while except the discovery of more and more facts, each in turn the deathblow to some cherished theory; the ordering intellect grows weary, and becomes slovenly through despair.

On the other hand, the new facts have brought new powers; man's physical control over natural forces has been increasing with unexampled rapidity, and promises to increase in the future beyond all easily assignable limits. Thus alongside of despair as regards ultimate theory there is an immense optimism as regards practice: what man can *do* seems almost boundless. The old fixed limits of human power, such as death, or the dependence of the race on an equilibrium of cosmic forces, are forgotten, and no hard facts are allowed to break in upon the dream of omnipotence. No philosophy is tolerated which sets bounds to man's capacity of gratifying his wishes; and thus the very despair of theory is invoked to silence every whisper of doubt as regards the possibilities of practical achievement.

In the welcoming of new fact, and in the suspicion of dogmatism, as regards the universe at large, the modern spirit should, I think, be accepted as wholly an advance. But both in its practical pretensions and in its theoretical despair it seems to me to go too far. Most of what is greatest in man is called forth in response to the thwarting of his hopes by immutable natural obstacles; by the pretense of omnipotence, he becomes trivial and a little absurd. And on the theoretical side, ultimate metaphysical truth, though less all-embracing and harder of attainment than it appeared to some philosophers in the past, can, I believe, be discovered by those who are willing to combine the hopefulness, patience, and open-mindedness of science with something of the Greek feeling for beauty in the abstract world of logic and for the ultimate intrinsic value in the contemplation of truth.

The philosophy, therefore, which is to be genuinely inspired by the scientific spirit, must deal with somewhat dry and abstract matters, and must not hope to find an answer to the practical problems of life. To those who wish to understand much of what has in the past been most difficult and obscure in the constitution of the universe, it has great rewards to offer—triumphs as noteworthy as those of Newton and Darwin, and as important in the long run, for the molding of our mental habits. And it brings with it—as a new and powerful method of investigation always does—a sense of power and a hope of progress more reliable and better grounded than any that rests on hasty and fallacious generalization as to the nature of the universe at large. Many hopes which inspired philosophers in the past it cannot claim to fulfil; but other hopes, more purely intellectual, it can satisfy more fully than former ages could have deemed possible for human minds.

WORDS AND MEANING[1]

The problem with which we shall be concerned in this paper is the problem of determining what is the relation called "meaning." The word "Napoleon," we say, "means" a certain person. In saying this, we are asserting a relation between the word "Napoleon" and the person so designated. It is this relation that we must now investigate.

Let us first consider what sort of object a word is when considered simply as a physical thing, apart from its meaning. To begin with, there are many instances of a word, namely, all the different occasions when it is employed. Thus a word is not something unique and particular, but a set of occurrences. If we confine ourselves to spoken words, a word has two aspects, according as we regard it from the point of view of the speaker or from that of the hearer. From the point of view of the speaker, a single instance of the use of a word consists of a certain set of movements in the throat and mouth, combined with breath. From the point of view of the hearer, a single instance of the use of a word consists of a certain series of sounds, each being approximately represented by a single letter

[1] From *The Analysis of Mind.*

in writing, though in practice a letter may represent several sounds, or several letters may represent one sound. The connection between the spoken word and the word as it reaches the hearer is casual. Let us confine ourselves to the spoken word, which is the more important for the analysis of what is called "thought." Then we may say that a single instance of the spoken word consists of a series of movements, and the word consists of a whole set of such series, each member of the set being very similar to each other member. That is to say, any two instances of the word "Napoleon" are very similar, and each instance consists of a series of movements in the mouth.

A single word, accordingly, is by no means simple: it is a class of similar series of movements (confining ourselves still to the spoken word). The degree of similarity required cannot be precisely defined: a man may pronounce the word "Napoleon" so badly that it can hardly be determined whether he has really pronounced it or not. The instances of a word shade off into other movements by imperceptible degrees. And exactly analogous observations apply to words heard or written or read. But in what has been said so far we have not even broached the question of the *definition* of a word, since "meaning" is clearly what distinguishes a word from other sets of similar movements, and "meaning" remains to be defined.

It is natural to think of the meaning of a word as something conventional. This, however, is only true with great limitations. A new word can be added to an existing language by a mere convention, as is done, for instance, with new scientific terms. But the basis of a language is not conventional, either from the point of view of the individual or from that of the community. A child learning to speak is learning habits and associations which are just as much determined by the environment as the habit of expecting dogs to bark and cocks to crow. The community that speaks a language has learnt it, and modified it by processes almost all of which are not deliberate, but the results of causes operating according to more or less ascertainable laws. If we trace any Indo-European language back far enough, we arrive hypothetically (at any rate according to some authorities) at the stage when language consisted only of the roots out of which subsequent words have grown. How these roots acquired their meanings is not known, but a conventional origin is clearly just as mythical as the social contract by which Hobbes and Rousseau supposed civil government to have been established. We can hardly suppose a parliament of hitherto speechless elders meeting together and agreeing to call a cow a cow and a wolf a wolf. The association of words with their meanings must have grown up by some natural process, though at present the nature of the process is unknown.

Spoken and written words are, of course, not the only way of conveying meaning. A large part of one of Wundt's two vast volumes on language in his *Völker-psychologie* is concerned with gesture-language. Ants appear to be able to communicate a certain amount of information by means of their antennæ. Probably writing itself, which we now regard as merely a way of representing speech, was originally an independent language, as it has remained to this day in China. Writing seems to have consisted originally of pictures, which gradually became conventionalized, coming in time to represent syllables, and finally letters on the telephone principle of "T for Tommy." But it would seem that writing nowhere began as an attempt to represent speech: it began as a direct pictorial representation of what was to be expressed. The essence of language lies, not in the use of this or that special means of communication, but in the employment of fixed associations (however these may have originated) in order that something now sensible—a spoken word, a picture, a gesture, or what not—may call up the "idea" of something else. Whenever this is done, what is now sensible may be called a "sign" or "symbol," and that of which it is intended to call up the "idea" may be called its "meaning." This is a rough outline of what constitutes "meaning." But we must fill in the outline in various ways. And, since we are concerned with what is called "thought," we must pay more attention than we otherwise should do to the private as opposed to the social use of language. Language profoundly affects our thoughts, and it is this aspect of language that is of most importance to us in our present inquiry. We are almost more concerned with the internal speech that is never uttered than we are with the things said out loud to other people.

When we ask what constitutes meaning, we are not asking what is the meaning of this or that particular word. The word "Napoleon" means a certain individual; but we are asking, not who is the individual meant, but what is the relation of the word to the individual which makes the one mean the other. But just as it is useful to realize the nature of a word as part of the physical world, so it is useful to realize the sort of thing that a word may mean. When we are clear both as to what a word is in its physical aspect, and as to what sort of thing it can mean, we are in a better position to discover the relation of the two which *is* meaning.

The things that words mean differ more than words do. There are different sorts of words, distinguished by the grammarians; and there are logical distinctions, which are connected to some extent, though not so closely as was formerly supposed, with the grammatical distinctions of parts of speech. It is easy, however, to be misled by grammar, particularly if all the languages we know belong to one family. In some languages, according to some authorities, the distinction of parts of speech does not exist; in many languages it is widely different from that to which we are accustomed in the Indo-European languages. These facts have to be borne in mind if we are to avoid giving metaphysical importance to mere accidents of our own speech.

In considering what words mean, it is natural to start with proper names, and we will again take "Napoleon" as our instance. We commonly imagine, when we use a proper name, that we mean one definite entity, the particular individual who was called "Napoleon." But what we know as a person is not simple. There *may* be a single simple ego which was Napoleon, and remained strictly identical from his birth to his death. There is no way of proving that this cannot be the case, but there is also not the slightest reason to suppose that it is the case. Napoleon as he was empirically known consisted of a series of gradually changing appearances: first a squalling baby, then a boy, then a slim and beautiful youth, then a fat and slothful person very magnificently dressed. This series of appearances, and various occurrences having certain kinds of causal connections with them, constitute Napoleon as empirically known, and therefore are Napoleon in so far as he forms part of the experienced world.

Napoleon is a complicated series of occurrences, bound together by causal laws, not, like instances of a word, by similarities. For although a person changes gradually, and presents similar appearances on two nearly contemporaneous occasions, it is not these similarities that constitute the person, as appears from the *Comedy of Errors* for example.

Thus in the case of a proper name, while the word is a set of similar series of movements, what it means is a series of occurrences bound together by causal laws of that special kind that makes the occurrences taken together constitute what we call one person, or one animal or thing, in case the name applies to an animal or thing instead of to a person. Neither the word nor what it names is one of the ultimate indivisible constituents of the world. In language there is no direct way of designating one of the ultimate brief existents that go to make up the collections we call things or persons. If we want to speak of such existents—which hardly happens except in philosophy—we have to do it by means of some elaborate phrase, such as "the visual sensation which occupied the center of my field of vision at noon on January 1, 1919." Such ultimate simples I call "particulars." Particulars *might* have proper names, and no doubt would have if language had been invented by scientifically trained observers for purposes of philosophy and logic. But as language was invented for practical ends, particulars have remained one and all without a name.

We are not, in practice, much concerned with the actual particulars that come into our experience in sensation; we are concerned rather with whole systems to which the particulars belong and of which they are signs. What we see makes us say "Hullo, there's Jones," and the fact that what we see is a sign of Jones (which is the case because it is one of the particulars that make up Jones) is more interesting to us than the actual particular itself. Hence we give the name "Jones" to the whole set of particulars, but do not trouble to give separate names to the separate particulars that make up the set.

Passing on from proper names, we come next to general names, such as "man," "cat," "triangle." A word such as "man" means a whole class of such collections of particulars as have proper names. The several members of the class are assembled together in virtue of some similarity or common property. All men resemble each other in certain important respects; hence we want a word which shall be equally applicable to all of them. We only give proper names to the individuals of a species when they differ *inter se* in practically important respects. In other cases we do not do this. A poker, for instance, is just a poker; we do not call one "John" and another "Peter."

There is a large class of words, such as "eating," "walking," "speaking," which mean a set of similar occurrences. Two instances of walking have the same name because they resemble each other, whereas two instances of Jones have the same name because they are causally connected. In practice, however, it is difficult to make any precise distinction between a word such as "walking" and a general name such as "man." One instance of walking cannot be concentrated into an instant: it is a process in time, in which there is a causal connection between the earlier and later parts, as between the earlier and later parts of Jones. Thus an instance of walking differs from an instance of man solely by the fact that it has a shorter life. There is a notion that an instance of walking, as compared with Jones, is unsubstantial, but this seems to be a mistake. We think that Jones walks, and that there could not be any walking unless there were somebody like Jones to perform the walking. But it is equally true that there could be no Jones unless there were something like walking for him to do. The notion that actions are performed by an agent is liable to the same kind of criticism as the notion that thinking needs a subject or ego. To say that it is Jones who is walking is merely to say that the walking in question is part of the whole series of occurrences which is Jones. There is no *logical* impossibility in walking occurring as an isolated phenomenon, not forming part of any such series as we call a "person."

We may therefore class with "eating," "walking," "speaking" words such as "rain," "sunrise," "lightning," which do not denote what would commonly be called actions. These words illustrate, incidentally, how little we can trust to the grammatical distinction of parts of speech, since the substantive "rain" and the verb "to rain" denote precisely the same class of meteorological occurrences. The distinction between the class of objects denoted by such a word and the class of objects denoted by a general name such as "man," "vegetable," or "planet," is that the sort of object which is an instance of (say) "lightning" is much simpler than (say) an individual man. (I am speaking of lightning as a sensible phenomenon, not as it is described in physics.) The distinction is one of degree, not of kind. But there is, from the point of view of ordinary thought, a great difference between a process which, like a flash of lightning, can be wholly comprised within one specious present and a process which, like the life of a man, has to be pieced together by observation and memory and the apprehension of causal connections. We may say broadly, therefore, that a word of the kind we have been discussing denotes a set of similar occurrences, each (as a rule) much more brief and less complex than a person or thing. Words themselves, as we have seen, are sets of similar occurrences of this kind. Thus there is more logical affinity between a word and what it means in the case of words of our present sort than in any other case.

There is no very great difference between such words as we have just been considering and words denoting qualities, such as "white" or "round." The chief difference is that words of this latter sort do not denote processes, however brief, but static features of the world. Snow falls, and is white; the falling is a process, the whiteness is not. Whether there is a universal, called "whiteness," or whether white things are to be defined as those having a certain kind of similarity to a standard thing, say freshly fallen snow, is a question which need not concern us, and which I believe to be strictly insoluble. For our purposes, we may take the word "white" as denoting a certain set of similar particulars or collections of particulars, the similarity being in respect of a static quality, not of a process.

From the logical point of view, a very important class of words are those that express relations, such as "in," "above," "before," "greater," and so on. The meaning of one of these words differs very fundamentally from the meaning of one of any of our previous classes, being more abstract and logically simpler than any of them. If our business were logic, we should have to spend much time on these words. But as it is psychology that concerns us, we will merely note their special character and pass on, since the logical classification of words is not our main business.

We will consider next the question, what is implied by saying that a person "understands" a word, in the sense in which one understands a word in one's own language, but not in a language of which one is ignorant. We may say that a person understands a word when (*a*) suitable circumstances make him use it, (*b*) the hearing of it causes suitable behavior in him. We may call these two active and passive understanding respectively. Dogs often have passive understanding of some words, but not active understanding, since they cannot use words.

It is not necessary, in order that a man should "understand" a word, that he should "know what it means," in the sense of being able to say "this word means so-and-so." Understanding words does not consist in knowing their dictionary definitions, or in being able to specify the objects to which they are appropriate. Such understanding as this may belong to lexicographers and students, but not to ordinary mortals in ordinary life. Understanding language is more like understanding cricket: [1] it is a matter of habits, acquired in oneself and rightly presumed in others. To say that a word has a

---

[1] This point of view, extended to the analysis of "thought" is urged with great force by J. B. Watson, both in his *Behavior*, and in *Psychology from the Standpoint of a Behaviorist* (Lippincott, 1919), Chap. IX.

meaning is not to say that those who use the word correctly have ever thought out what the meaning is: the use of the word comes first, and the meaning is to be distilled out of it by observation and analysis. Moreover, the meaning of a word is not absolutely definite: there is always a greater or less degree of vagueness. The meaning is an area, like a target: it may have a bull's-eye, but the outlying parts of the target are still more or less within the meaning, in a gradually diminishing degree as we travel further from the bull's-eye. As language grows more precise, there is less and less of the target outside the bull's-eye, and the bull's-eye itself grows smaller and smaller; but the bull's-eye never shrinks to a point, and there is always a doubtful region, however small, surrounding it. [1]

A word is used "correctly" when the average hearer will be affected by it in the way intended. This is a psychological, not a literary, definition of 'correctness.' The literary definition would substitute, for the average hearer, a person of high education living a long time ago; the purpose of this

---

[1] On the understanding of words, a very admirable little book is Ribot's *Evolution of General Ideas,* Open Court Co., 1899. Ribot says (p. 131): "We learn to understand a concept as we learn to walk, dance, fence or play a musical instrument: it is a habit, i.e. an organized memory. General terms cover an organized, latent knowledge which is the hidden capital without which we should be in a state of bankruptcy, manipulating false money or paper of no value. General ideas are habits in the intellectual order."

definition is to make it difficult to speak or write correctly.

The relation of a word to its meaning is of the nature of a causal law governing our use of the word and our actions when we hear it used. There is no more reason why a person who uses a word correctly should be able to tell what it means than there is why a planet which is moving correctly should know Kepler's laws.

To illustrate what is meant by "understanding" words and sentences, let us take instances of various situations.

Suppose you are walking in London with an absent-minded friend, and while crossing a street you say, "Look out, there's a motor coming." He will glance round and jump aside without the need of any "mental" intermediary. There need be no "ideas," but only a stiffening of the muscles, followed quickly by action. He "understands" the words, because he does the right thing. Such "understanding" may be taken to belong to the nerves and brain, being habits which they have acquired while the language was being learnt. Thus understanding in this sense may be reduced to mere physiological causal laws.

If you say the same thing to a Frenchman with a slight knowledge of English he will go through some inner speech which may be represented by "Que dit-il? Ah, oui, une automobile!" After this, the rest follows as with the Englishman. Watson would contend that the inner speech must be incipiently pronounced; we should argue that it *might* be merely imaged. But this point is not important in the present connection.

If you say the same thing to a child who does not yet know the word "motor," but does know the other words you are using, you produce a feeling of anxiety and doubt: you will have to point and say, "There, that's a motor." After that the child will roughly understand the word "motor," though he may include trains and steam-rollers. If this is the first time the child has heard the word "motor," he may for a long time continue to recall this scene when he hears the word.

So far, we have found four ways of understanding words:

(1) On suitable occasions you use the word properly.

(2) When you hear it you act appropriately.

(3) You associate the word with another word (say in a different language) which has the appropriate effect on behavior.

(4) When the word is being first learnt, you may associate it with an object, which is what it "means," or a representative of various objects that it "means."

In the fourth case, the word acquires, through association, some of the same causal efficacy as the object. The word "motor" can make you leap aside, just as the motor can, but it cannot break your bones. The effects which a word can share with its object are those which proceed according to laws other than the general laws of physics, i.e. those which, according to our terminology, involve vital movements as opposed to merely mechanical movements. The effects of a word that we understand are always mnemic phenomena in the sense explained, [1] in so far as they are identical with, or similar to, the effects which the object itself might have.

So far, all the uses of words that we have considered can be accounted for on the lines of behaviorism.

But so far we have only considered what may be called the "demonstrative" use of language, to point out some feature in the present environment. This is only one of the ways in which language may be used. There are also its narrative and imaginative uses, as in history and novels. Let us take as an instance the telling of some remembered event.

We spoke a moment ago of a child who hears the word "motor" for the first time when crossing a street along which a motor-car is approaching. On a later occasion, we will suppose, the child remem-

[1] See Chap. IV, *The Analysis of Mind.*

bers the incident and relates it to some one else.
In this case, both the active and passive understanding of words is different from what it is when
words are used demonstratively. The child is not
seeing a motor, but only remembering one; the
hearer does not look round in expectation of seeing
a motor coming, but "understands" that a motor
came at some earlier time. The whole of this occurrence is much more difficult to account for on
behaviorist lines. It is clear that, in so far as the
child is genuinely remembering, he has a picture of
the past occurrence, and his words are chosen so as
to describe the picture; and in so far as the hearer
is genuinely apprehending what is said, the hearer is
acquiring a picture more or less like that of the
child. It is true that this process may be telescoped
through the operation of the word-habit. The child
may not genuinely remember the incident, but only
have the habit of the appropriate words, as in the
case of a poem which we know by heart, though
we cannot remember learning it. And the hearer
also may only pay attention to the words, and not
call up any corresponding picture. But it is, nevertheless, the possibility of a memory-image in the
child and an imagination-image in the hearer that
makes the essence of the narrative "meaning" of the
words. In so far as this is absent, the words are
mere counters, capable of meaning, but not at the
moment possessing it.

Yet this might perhaps be regarded as something of an over-statement. The words alone, without the use of images, may cause appropriate emotions and appropriate behavior. The words have been used in an environment which produced certain emotions; by a telescoped process, the words alone are now capable of producing similar emotions. On these lines it might be sought to show that images are unnecessary. I do not believe, however, that we could account on these lines for the entirely different response produced by a narrative and by a description of present facts. Images, as contrasted with sensations, are the response expected during a narrative; it is understood that present action is not called for. Thus it seems that we must maintain our distinction: words used demonstratively describe and are intended to lead to sensations, while the same words used in narrative describe and are only intended to lead to images.

We have thus, in addition to our four previous ways in which words can mean, two new ways, namely the way of memory and the way of imagination. That is to say:

(5) Words may be used to describe or recall a memory-image: to describe it when it already exists, or to recall it when the words exist as a habit and are known to be descriptive of some past experience.

(6) Words may be used to describe or create an

to the bodily muscles. . . . The object meets the child's vision. He runs to it and tries to reach it and says 'box.' . . . Finally the word is uttered without the movement of going towards the box being executed. . . . Habits are formed of going to the box when the arms are full of toys. The child has been taught to deposit them there. When his arms are laden with toys and no box is there, the word-habit arises and he calls 'box'; it is handed to him, and he opens it and deposits the toys therein. This roughly marks what we would call the genesis of a true language-habit." [1]

We need not linger over what is said in the above passage as to the use of the word "box" in the presence of the box. But as to its use in the absence of the box, there is only one brief sentence, namely: "When his arms are laden with toys and no box is there, the word-habit arises and he calls 'box.'" This is inadequate as it stands, since the habit has been to use the word when the box is present, and we have to explain its extension to cases in which the box is absent.

Having admitted images, we may say that the word "box," in the absence of the box, is caused by an image of the box. This may or may not be true—in fact, it is true in some cases but not in others. Even, however, if it were true in all cases,

---

[1] Just the same account of language is given by Professor Watson.

it would only slightly shift our problem: we should now have to ask what causes an image of the box to arise. We might be inclined to say that desire for the box is the cause. But when this view is investigated, it is found that it compels us to suppose that the box can be desired without the child's having either an image of the box or the word "box." This will require a theory of desire which may be, and I think is, in the main true, but which removes desire from among things that actually occur, and makes it merely a convenient fiction, like force in mechanics.[1] With such a view, desire is no longer a true cause, but merely a short way of describing certain processes.

In order to explain the occurrence of either the word or the image in the absence of the box, we have to assume that there is something, either in the environment or in our own sensations, which has frequently occurred at about the same time as the word "box." One of the laws which distinguish psychology (or nerve-physiology?) from physics is the law that, when two things have frequently existed in close temporal contiguity, either comes in time to cause the other.[2] This is the basis both of habit and of association. Thus, in our case, the arms

[1] See Chap. III, *The Analysis of Mind*.

[2] For a more exact statement of this law, with the limitations suggested by experiment, see A. Wohlgemuth, "On Memory and the Direction of Associations," *British Journal of Psychology*, vol. v, part iv (March, 1913).

full of toys have frequently been followed quickly by the box, and the box in turn by the word "box." The box itself is subject to physical laws, and does not tend to be caused by the arms full of toys, however often it may in the past have followed them— always provided that, in the case in question, its physical position is such that voluntary movements cannot lead to it. But the word "box" and the image of the box are subject to the law of habit; hence it is possible for either to be caused by the arms full of toys. And we may lay it down generally that, whenever we use a word, either aloud or in inner speech, there is some sensation or image (either of which may be itself a word) which has frequently occurred at about the same time as the word, and now, through habit, causes the word. It follows that the law of habit is adequate to account for the use of words in the absence of their objects; moreover, it would be adequate even without introducing images. Although, therefore, images seem undeniable, we cannot derive an additional argument in their favor from the use of words, which could, theoretically, be explained without introducing images.

When we understand a word, there is a reciprocal association between it and the images of what it "means." Images may cause us to use words which mean them, and these words, heard or read, may in turn cause the appropriate images. Thus speech

is a means of producing in our hearers the images
which are in us. Also, by a telescoped process,
words come in time to produce directly the effects
which would have been produced by the images
with which they were associated. The general law
of telescoped processes is that, if A causes B and B
causes C, it will happen in time that A will cause C
directly, without the intermediary of B. This is a
characteristic of psychological and neural causation.
In virtue of this law, the effects of images upon our
actions come to be produced by words, even when
the words do not call up appropriate images. The
more familiar we are with words, the more our
"thinking" goes on in words instead of images. We
may, for example, be able to describe a person's appearance correctly without having at any time had
any image of him, provided, when we saw him, we
thought of words which fitted him; the words alone
may remain with us as a habit, and enable us to
speak as if we could recall a visual image of the man.
In this and the other ways the understanding of a
word often comes to be quite free from imagery;
but in first learning the use of language it would
seem that imagery always plays a very important
part.

Images as well as words may be said to have
"meaning"; indeed, the meaning of images seems
more primitive than the meaning of words. What
we call (say) an image of St. Paul's may be said to

"mean" St. Paul's. But it is not at all easy to say exactly what constitutes the meaning of an image. A memory-image of a particular occurrence, when accompanied by a memory-belief, may be said to mean the occurrence of which it is an image. But most actual images do not have this degree of definiteness. If we call up an image of a dog, we are very likely to have a vague image, which is not representative of some one special dog, but of dogs in general. When we call up an image of a friend's face, we are not likely to reproduce the expression he had on some one particular occasion, but rather a compromise expression derived from many occasions. And there is hardly any limit to the vagueness of which images are capable. In such cases, the meaning of the images, if defined by relation to the prototype, is vague: there is not one definite prototype, but a number, none of which is copied exactly. [1]

There is, however, another way of approaching the meaning of images, namely, through their causal efficacy. What is called an image "of" some definite object, say St. Paul's, has some of the effects which the object would have. This applies especially to the effects that depend upon association. The emotional effects, also, are often similar; images may stimulate desire almost as strongly as do the objects

---

[1] Cf. Semon, *Mnemische Empfindungen,* chap. xvi, especially pp. 301-308.

they represent.   And conversely desire may cause images: [1] a hungry man will have images of food, and so on.   In all these ways the causal laws concerning images are connected with the causal laws concerning the objects which the images "mean." An image may thus come to fulfil the function of a general idea.   The vague image of a dog, which we spoke of a moment ago, will have effects which are only connected with dogs in general, not the more special effects which would be produced by some dogs but not by others.   Berkeley and Hume, in their attack on general ideas, do not allow for the vagueness of images: they assume that every image has the definiteness that a physical object would have.   This is not the case, and a vague image may well have a meaning which is general.

In order to define the "meaning" of an image, we have to take account both of its resemblance to one or more prototypes, and of its causal efficacy.   If there were such a thing as a pure imagination-image, without any prototype whatever, it would be destitute of meaning.   But according to Hume's principle, the simple elements in an image, at least, are derived from prototypes—except possibly in very rare exceptional cases.   Often, in such instances as our image of a friend's face or of a nondescript

---

[1] This phrase is in need of interpretation, as appears from the analysis of desire.   But the reader can easily supply the interpretation for himself.

dog, an image is not derived from one prototype, but
from many; when this happens, the image is vague,
and blurs the features in which the various prototypes differ. To arrive at the meaning of the image
in such a case, we observe that there are certain respects, notably associations, in which the effects of
images resemble those of their prototypes. If we
find, in a given case, that our vague image, say, of
a nondescript dog, has those associative effects
which all dogs would have, but not those belonging
to any special dog or kind of dog, we may say that
our image means "dog" in general. If it has all the
associations appropriate to spaniels but no others,
we shall say it means "spaniel"; while if it has all
the associations appropriate to one particular dog,
it will mean that dog, however vague it may be as
a picture. The meaning of an image, according to
this analysis, is constituted by a combination of
likeness and associations. It is not a sharp or definite conception, and in many cases it will be impossible to decide with any certainty what an image
means. I think this lies in the nature of things, and
not in defective analysis.

We may give somewhat more precision to the
above account of the meaning of images, and extend
it to meaning in general. We find sometimes that, *in
mnemic causation,* an image or word, as stimulus,
has the same effect (or very nearly the same effect)
as would belong to some object, say, a certain dog.

In that case we say that the image or word means
that object.   In other cases the mnemic effects are
not all those of one object, but only those shared
by objects of a certain kind, e.g. by all dogs.   In
this case the meaning of the image or word is
general: it means the whole kind.   Generality and
particularity are a matter of degree.   If two particulars differ sufficiently little, their mnemic effects will
be the same; therefore no image or word can mean
the one as opposed to the other; this sets a bound
to the particularity of meaning.   On the other hand,
the mnemic effects of a number of sufficiently dis-
similar objects will have nothing discoverable in
common; hence a word which aims at complete
generality, such as "entity" for example, will have
to be devoid of mnemic effects, and therefore of
meaning.   In practice, this is not the case: such
words have *verbal* associations, the learning of
which constitutes the study of metaphysics.

The meaning of a word, unlike that of an image,
is wholly constituted by mnemic causal laws, and
not in any degree by likeness (except in exceptional
cases).   The word "dog" bears no resemblance to
a dog, but its effects, like those of an image of a
dog, resemble the effects of an actual dog in certain
respects.   It is much easier to say definitely what a
word means than what an image means, since words,
however they originated, have been framed in later
times for the purpose of having meaning, and men

have been engaged for ages in giving increased precision to the meanings of words. But although it is easier to say what a word means than what an image means, the relation which constitutes meaning is much the same in both cases. A word, like an image, has the same associations as its meaning has. In addition to other associations, it is associated with images of its meaning, so that the word tends to call up the image and the image tends to call up the word. But this association is not essential to the intelligent use of words. If a word has the right associations with other objects, we shall be able to use it correctly, and understand its use by others, even if it evokes no image. The theoretical understanding of words involves only the power of associating them correctly with other words; the practical understanding involves associations with other bodily movements.

The use of words is, of course, primarily social, for the purpose of suggesting to others ideas which we entertain or at least wish them to entertain. But the aspect of words that specially concerns us is their power of promoting our own thought. Almost all higher intellectual activity is a matter of words, to the nearly total exclusion of everything else. The advantages of words for purposes of thought are so great that I should never end if I were to enumerate them. But a few of them deserve to be mentioned.

In the first place, there is no difficulty in producing a word, whereas an image cannot always be brought into existence at will, and when it comes it often contains much irrelevant detail. In the second place, much of our thinking is concerned with abstract matters which do not readily lend themselves to imagery, and are apt to be falsely conceived if we insist upon finding images that may be supposed to represent them. The word is always concrete and sensible, however abstract its meaning may be, and thus by the help of words we are able to dwell on abstractions in a way which would otherwise be impossible. In the third place, two instances of the same word are so similar that neither has associations not capable of being shared by the other. Two instances of the word "dog" are much more alike than (say) a pug and a great Dane; hence the word "dog" makes it much easier to think about dogs in general. When a number of objects have a common property which is important but not obvious, the invention of a name for the common property helps us to remember it and to think of the whole set of objects that possess it. But it is unnecessary to prolong the catalogue of the uses of language in thought.

At the same time, it is possible to conduct rudimentary thought by means of images, and it is important, sometimes, to check purely verbal thought by reference to what it means. In philosophy especially the tyranny of traditional words is dangerous, and we have to be on our guard against assuming that grammar is the key to metaphysics, or that the structure of a sentence corresponds at all accurately with the structure of the fact that it asserts. Sayce maintained that all European philosophy since Aristotle has been dominated by the fact that philosophers spoke Indo-European languages, and therefore supposed the world, like the sentences they were used to, necessarily divisible into subjects and predicates. When we come to the consideration of truth and falsehood, we shall see how necessary it is to avoid assuming too close a parallelism between facts and the sentences which assert them. Against such errors, the only safeguard is to be able, once in a way, to discard words for a moment and contemplate facts more directly through images. Most serious advances in philosophic thought result from some such comparatively direct contemplation of facts. But the outcome has to be expressed in words if it is to be communicable. Those who have a relatively direct vision of facts are often incapable of translating their vision into words, while those who possess the words have usually lost the vision. It is partly for this reason that the highest philosophical capacity is so rare; it requires a combination of vision with abstract words which is hard to achieve, and too quickly lost in the few who have for a moment achieved it.

DEFINITION OF NUMBER [1]

The question "What is a number?" is one which has been often asked, but has only been correctly answered in our own time. The answer was given by Frege in 1884, in his *Grundlagen der Arithmetik*.[2] Although this book is quite short, not difficult, and of the very highest importance, it attracted almost no attention, and the definition of number which it contains remained practically unknown until it was rediscovered by the present author in 1901.

In seeking a definition of number, the first thing to be clear about is what we may call the grammar of our inquiry. Many philosophers, when attempting to define number, are really setting to work to define plurality, which is quite a different thing. *Number* is what is characteristic of numbers, as *man* is what is characteristic of men. A plurality is not an instance of number, but of some particular number. A trio of men, for example, is an instance of the number 3, and the number 3 is an instance of number; but the trio is not an instance of number.

---

[1] From *Introduction to Mathematical Philosophy*.
[2] The same answer is given more fully and with more development in his *Grundgesetze der Arithmetik,* vol. 1, 1893.

This point may seem elementary and scarcely worth mentioning; yet it has proved too subtle for the philosophers, with few exceptions.

A particular number is not identical with any collection of terms having that number: the number 3 is not identical with the trio consisting of Brown, Jones, and Robinson. The number 3 is something which all trios have in common, and which distinguishes them from other collections. A number is something that characterizes certain collections, namely, those that have that number.

Instead of speaking of a "collection," we shall as a rule speak of a "class," or sometimes a "set." Other words used in mathematics for the same thing are "aggregate" and "manifold." We shall have much to say later on about classes. For the present, we will say as little as possible. But there are some remarks that must be made immediately.

A class or collection may be defined in two ways that at first sight seem quite distinct. We may enumerate its members, as when we say, "The collection I mean is Brown, Jones, and Robinson." Or we may mention a defining property, as when we speak of "mankind" or "the inhabitants of London." The definition which enumerates is called a definition by "extension," and the one which mentions a defining property is called a definition by "intension." Of these two kinds of definition, the one by intension is logically more fundamental.

This is shown by two considerations: (1) that the extensional definition can always be reduced to an intensional one; (2) that the intensional one often cannot even theoretically be reduced to the extensional one. Each of these points needs a word of explanation.

(1) Brown, Jones, and Robinson all of them possess a certain property which is possessed by nothing else in the whole universe, namely the property of being either Brown or Jones or Robinson. This property can be used to give a definition by intension of the class consisting of Brown and Jones and Robinson. Consider such a formula as "x is Brown or x is Jones or x is Robinson." This formula will be true for just three x's, namely, Brown and Jones and Robinson. In this respect it resembles a cubic equation with its three roots. It may be taken as assigning a property common to the members of the class consisting of these three men, and peculiar to them. A similar treatment can obviously be applied to any other class given in extension.

(2) It is obvious that in practice we can often know a great deal about a class without being able to enumerate its members. No one man could actually enumerate all men, or even all the inhabitants of London, yet a great deal is known about each of these classes. This is enough to show that definition by extension is not *necessary* to knowledge

about a class. But when we come to consider infinite classes, we find that enumeration is not even theoretically possible for beings who only live for a finite time. We cannot enumerate all the natural numbers: they are 0, 1, 2, 3, *and so on.* At some point we must content ourselves with "and so on." We cannot enumerate all fractions or all irrational numbers, or all of any other infinite collections. Thus our knowledge in regard to all such collections can only be derived from a definition by intension.

These remarks are relevant, when we are seeking the definition of number, in three different ways. In the first place, numbers themselves form an infinite collection, and cannot therefore be defined by enumeration. In the second place, the collections having a given number of terms themselves presumably form an infinite collection: it is to be presumed, for example, that there are an infinite collection of trios in the world, for if this were not the case the total number of things in the world would be finite, which, though possible, seems unlikely. In the third place, we wish to define "number" in such a way that infinite numbers may be possible; thus we must be able to speak of the number of terms in an infinite collection, and such a collection must be defined by intension, i.e. by a property common to all its members and peculiar to them.

For many purposes, a class and a defining characteristic of it are practically interchangeable. The vital difference between the two consists in the fact that there is only one class having a given set of members, whereas there are always many different characteristics by which a given class may be defined. Men may be defined as featherless bipeds, or as rational animals, or (more correctly) by the traits by which Swift delineates the Yahoos. It is this fact that a defining characteristic is never unique which makes classes useful; otherwise we could be content with the properties common and peculiar to their members.[1] Any one of these properties can be used in place of the class whenever uniqueness is not important.

Returning now to the definition of number, it is clear that number is a way of bringing together certain collections, namely, those that have a given number of terms. We can suppose all couples in one bundle, all trios in another, and so on. In this way we obtain various bundles of collections, each bundle consisting of all the collections that have a certain number of terms. Each bundle is a class whose members are collections, i.e., classes; thus each is a class of classes. The bundle consisting of all couples, for example, is a class of classes: each couple is a class with two members, and the whole

[1] This is explained in other chapters of *Introduction to Mathematical Philosophy,* classes may be regarded as logical fictions, manufactured out of defining characteristics. But for the present it will simplify our exposition to treat classes as if they were real.

bundle of couples is a class with an infinite number of members, each of which is a class of two members.

How shall we decide whether two collections are to belong to the same bundle? The answer that suggests itself is: "Find out how many members each has, and put them in the same bundle if they have the same number of members." But this presupposes that we have defined numbers, and that we know how to discover how many terms a collection has. We are so used to the operation of counting that such a presupposition might easily pass unnoticed. In fact, however, counting, though familiar, is logically a very complex operation; moreover it is only available, as a means of discovering how many terms a collection has, when the collection is finite. Our definition of number must not assume in advance that all numbers are finite; and we cannot in any case, without a vicious circle, use counting to define numbers, because numbers are used in counting. We need, therefore, some other method of deciding when two collections have the same number of terms.

In actual fact, it is simpler logically to find out whether two collections have the same number of terms than it is to define what that number is. An illustration will make this clear. If there were no polygamy or polyandry anywhere in the world, it is clear that the number of husbands living at any moment would be exactly the same as the number of wives. We do not need a census to assure us of this, nor do we need to know what is the actual number of husbands and of wives. We know the number must be the same in both collections, because each husband has one wife and each wife has one husband. The relation of husband and wife is what is called "one-one."

A relation is said to be "one-one" when, if x has the relation in question to y, no other term x' has the same relation to y, and x does not have the same relation to any term y' other than y. When only the first of these two conditions is fulfilled, the relation is called "one-many"; when only the second is fulfilled, it is called "many-one." It should be observed that the number 1 is not used in these definitions.

In Christian countries, the relation of husband to wife is one-one; in Mohammedan countries it is one-many; in Tibet it is many-one. The relation of father to son is one-many; that of son to father is many-one, but that of eldest son to father is one-one. If n is any number, the relation of n to $n+1$ is one-one; so is the relation of n to $2n$ or to $3n$. When we are considering only positive numbers, the relation of n to n^2 is one-one; but when negative numbers are admitted, it becomes two-one, since n and $-n$ have the same square. These instances should suffice to make clear the notions of one-one, one-many, and many-one relations, which play a great part in the principles of mathematics, not only in relation to the definition of numbers, but in many other connections.

Two classes are said to be "similar" when there is a one-one relation which correlates the terms of the one class each with one term of the other class, in the same manner in which the relation of marriage correlates husbands with wives. A few preliminary definitions will help us to state this definition more precisely. The class of those terms that have a given relation to something or other is called the *domain* of that relation: thus fathers are the domain of the relation of father to child, husbands are the domain of the relation of husband to wife, wives are the domain of the relation of wife to husband, and husbands and wives together are the domain of the relation of marriage. The relation of wife to husband is called the *converse* of the relation of husband to wife. Similarly *less* is the converse of *greater, later* is the converse of *earlier,* and so on. Generally, the converse of a given relation is that relation which holds between y and x whenever the given relation holds between x and y. The *converse domain* of a relation is the domain of its converse: thus the class of wives is the converse domain of the relation of husband to wife. We may now state our definition of similarity as follows:—

One class is said to be "similar" to another when there is a one-one relation of which the one class is the domain, while the other is the converse domain.

It is easy to prove (1) that every class is similar to itself, (2) that if a class α is similar to β, then β is similar to α, (3) that if α is similar to β and β to γ, then α is similar to γ. A relation is said to be *reflexive* when it possesses the first of these properties, *symmetrical* when it possesses the second, and *transitive* when it possesses the third. It is obvious that a relation which is symmetrical and transitive must be reflexive throughout its domain. Relations which possess these properties are an important kind, and it is worth while to note that similarity is one of this kind of relations.

It is obvious to common sense that two finite classes have the same number of terms if they are similar, but not otherwise. The act of counting consists in establishing a one-one correlation between the set of objects counted and the natural numbers (excluding 0) that are used up in the process. Accordingly common sense concludes that there are as many objects in the set to be counted as there are numbers up to the last number used in the counting. And we also know that, so long as we confine ourselves to finite numbers, there are just n numbers from 1 up to n. Hence it follows that the last number used in counting a collection is the number of terms in the collection, provided the collection is finite. But this result, besides being only applicable to finite collections, depends upon and assumes the fact that two classes which are similar have the same number of terms; for what we do when we count (say) 10 objects is to show that the set of these objects is similar to the set of numbers 1 to 10. The notion of similarity is logically presupposed in the operation of counting, and is logically simpler though less familiar. In counting, it is necessary to take the objects counted in a certain order, as first, second, third, etc., but order is not of the essence of number: it is an irrelevant addition, an unnecessary complication from the logical point of view. The notion of similarity does not demand an order: for example, we saw that the number of husbands is the same as the number of wives, without having to establish an order of precedence among them. The notion of similarity also does not require that the classes which are similar should be finite. Take, for example, the natural numbers (excluding 0) on the one hand, and the fractions which have 1 for their numerator on the other hand: it is obvious that we can correlate 2 with ½, 3 with ⅓, and so on, thus proving that the two classes are similar.

We may thus use the notion of "similarity" to decide when two collections are to belong to the same bundle, in the sense in which we were asking this question earlier in this chapter. We want to make one bundle containing the class that has no members: this will be for the number 0. Then we want a bundle of all the classes that have one member: this will be for the number 1. Then, for the number 2, we want a bundle consisting of all couples; then one of all trios; and so on. Given any collection, we can define the bundle it is to belong to as being the class of all those collections that are "similar" to it. It is very easy to see that if (for example) a collection has three members, the class of all those collections that are similar to it will be the class of trios. And whatever number of terms a collection may have, those collections that are "similar" to it will have the same number of terms. We may take this as a *definition* of "having the same number of terms." It is obvious that it gives results conformable to usage so long as we confine ourselves to finite collections.

So far we have not suggested anything in the slightest degree paradoxical. But when we come to the actual definition of numbers we cannot avoid what must at first sight seem a paradox, though this impression will soon wear off. We naturally think that the class of couples (for example) is something different from the number 2. But there is no doubt about the class of couples: it is indubitable and not difficult to define, whereas the number 2, in any other sense, is a metaphysical entity about which we can never feel sure that it exists or that we have tracked it down. It is therefore more prudent to content ourselves with the class of couples, which we are sure of, than to hunt for a problematical number 2 which must always remain elusive. Accordingly we set up the following definition:—

The number of a class is the class of all those classes that are similar to it.

Thus the number of a couple will be the class of all couples. In fact, the class of all couples will *be* the number 2, according to our definition. At the expense of a little oddity, this definition secures definiteness and indubitableness; and it is not difficult to prove that numbers so defined have all the properties that we expect numbers to have.

We may now go on to define numbers in general as any one of the bundles into which similarity collects classes. A number will be a set of classes such as that any two are similar to each other, and none outside the set are similar to any inside the set. In other words, a number (in general) is any collection which is the number of one of its members; or, more simply still:

A number is anything which is the number of some class.

Such a definition has a verbal appearance of being circular, but in fact it is not. We define "the number of a given class" without using the notion of number in general; therefore we may define number in general in terms of "the number of a given class" without committing any logical error.

Definitions of this sort are in fact very common·

The class of fathers, for example, would have to be defined by first defining what it is to be the father of somebody; then the class of fathers will be all those who are somebody's father. Similarly if we want to define square numbers (say), we must first define what we mean by saying that one number is the square of another, and then define square numbers as those that are the squares of other numbers. This kind of procedure is very common, and it is important to realize that it is legitimate and even often necessary.

We have now given a definition of numbers which will serve for finite collections. It remains to be seen how it will serve for infinite collections. But first we must decide what we mean by "finite" and "infinite," and this cannot be done within the limits of the present chapter.

THE END

MODERN LIBRARY GIANTS

A series of sturdily bound and handsomely printed, full-sized library editions of books formerly available only in expensive sets. These volumes contain from 600 to 1,400 pages each.

THE MODERN LIBRARY GIANTS REPRESENT A
SELECTION OF THE WORLD'S GREATEST BOOKS

G68	**Paine, Tom:** *Selected Work*
G86	**Pasternak, Boris:** *Doctor Zhivago*
G5	**Plutarch:** *Lives* (The Dryden Translation)
G40	**Poe, Edgar Allan:** *Complete Tales and Poems*
G29	**Prescott, William H.:** *The Conquest of Mexico* and *The Conquest of Peru*
G62	**Pushkin:** *Poems, Prose and Plays*
G65	**Rabelais:** *Complete Works*
G12	**Scott, Sir Walter:** *The Most Popular Novels* (Quentin Durward, Ivanhoe & Kenilworth)
G4	**Shelley & Keats:** *Complete Poems*
G32	**Smith, Adam:** *The Wealth of Nations*
G61	**Spaeth, Sigmund:** *A Guide to Great Orchestral Music*
G92	**Spengler, Oswald:** *The Decline of the West* (one volume)
G91	**Spenser, Edmund:** *Selected Poetry*
G75	**Stevenson, Robert Louis:** *Selected Writings*
G53	**Sue, Eugene:** *The Wandering Jew*
G42	**Tennyson:** *The Poems and Plays*
G23	**Tolstoy, Leo:** *Anna Karenina*—tr. revised
G1	**Tolstoy, Leo:** *War and Peace*
G49	**Twain, Mark:** *Tom Sawyer* and *Huckleberry Finn*
G50	**Whitman, Walt:** *Leaves of Grass*
G83	**Wilson, Edmund:** *The Shock of Recognition*

MISCELLANEOUS

G77	*An Anthology of Famous American Stories*
G54	*An Anthology of Famous British Stories*
G67	*Anthology of Famous English and American Poetry*
G81	*An Encyclopedia of Modern American Humor*
G47	*The English Philosophers from Bacon to Mill*
G16	*The European Philosophers from Descartes to Nietzsche*
G31	*Famous Science-Fiction Stories*
G85	*Great Ages and Ideas of the Jewish People*
G89	*Great Classical Myths*
G72	*Great Tales of Terror and the Supernatural*
G9	*Great Voices of the Reformation*
G87	*Medieval Epics*
G48	*The Metropolitan Opera Guide*
G46	*A New Anthology of Modern Poetry*
G69	*One Hundred and One Years' Entertainment*
G93	*Parodies: An Anthology from Chaucer to Beerbohm and After*
G90	*Philosophies of Art and Beauty: Readings in Aesthetics from Plato to Heidegger*
G21	*Sixteen Famous American Plays*
G63	*Sixteen Famous British Plays*
G71	*Sixteen Famous European Plays*
G45	*Stoic and Epicurean Philosophers*
G22	*Thirty Famous One-Act Plays*
G66	*Three Famous Murder Novels, Before the Fact,* **Francis Iles,** *Trent's Last Case,* E. C. **Bentley,** *The House of the Arrow,* A. E. W. **Mason**
G10	*Twelve Famous Plays of the Restoration and Eighteenth Century* (1660–1820): Dryden, Congreve, Wycherley, Gay, etc.
G56	*The Wisdom of Catholicism*
G59	*The Wisdom of China and India*
G79	*The Wisdom of Israel*

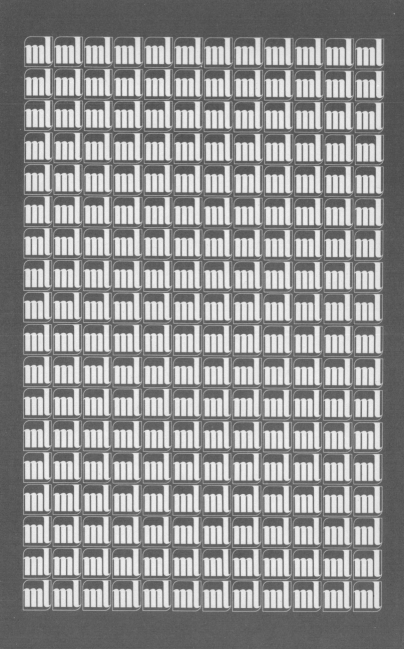